Charlotte Mary Yonge

Landmarks Of History. Ancient History

From The Earliest Times To The Mahometan Conquest. Twelfth Edition

Charlotte Mary Yonge

Landmarks Of History. Ancient History
From The Earliest Times To The Mahometan Conquest. Twelfth Edition

ISBN/EAN: 9783337112646

Printed in Europe, USA, Canada, Australia, Japan

Cover: Foto ©ninafisch / pixelio.de

More available books at **www.hansebooks.com**

LANDMARKS OF HISTORY.

ANCIENT HISTORY:

FROM THE EARLIEST TIMES TO THE MAHOMETAN CONQUEST.

BY THE AUTHOR OF "KINGS OF ENGLAND," &c.

TWELFTH EDITION.

LONDON:
J. AND C. MOZLEY, 6, PATERNOSTER ROW
MASTERS AND SON, 78, NEW BOND STREET.
1866.

PREFACE.

The design of the following sketches is to bring into connection the events most necessary to be remembered in Ancient History, and to convey a general idea of the characteristics and course of the "changing empires" of classical times, with an especial view to the better understanding of Scripture History and the growth of the Church. In so small a space it has been impossible to give much detail; and where anecdotes have been introduced, they are either such as must necessarily be known, or such as may lead to the better comprehension of the characters and ways of thinking of the great men of old. There are many more complete histories of Greece and Rome written for children, but it is hoped that these Landmarks may be found to supply the connection between the different branches of Ancient History, including that of the Jews; as well as to furnish a class-book for parochial schools where no more than a general idea of universal history is wanted.

If the present volume be found to answer its purpose, it is intended to follow it up with Landmarks of Mediæval History, beginning from the reign of Charlemagne, and reaching to the Reformation; and Landmarks of Modern History, extending from the Reformation to the present time.

July 14*th*, 1852.

P.S. TO THE SIXTH EDITION.

THE introduction to the present edition was added at the request of the Calcutta University, by whose kind permission it has been republished here, for the use of the more advanced readers. Young children would probably find it too difficult

August 5*th*, 1862.

INTRODUCTION.

PART I. THE ANTEDILUVIANS.

THE universe was made by Almighty God, who placed the sun amid the stars, with the planets circling round him in their courses. Our earth is the third planet in distance from the sun, and though small among the other spheres, and as nothing amid the multitudes in infinite space, yet the great Creator has watched over it, and directed all its changes.

By these changes, it was gradually fitted to be the abode of the present race of animals, and of man, the master of them all, like them in having a body of flesh, but made in the image of God, since he possesses an immortal soul.

One man and one woman were first created to be the parents of the human kind; and as long as they were obedient, they lived in a state of perfect happiness, of which the world has never lost the memory, but has kept up a dim recollection of glad times of perfect peace and favour with God.

An evil spirit, taking the form of a serpent, led first the woman, and she led her husband, to disobedience, and thus they forfeited the peculiar favour and protection they had hitherto enjoyed. Food no longer grew for them without toil; their bodies required garments; the woman became inferior to the man; and they were no longer guarded from the tempter, who would lead them into crimes, then wreak upon them the punishment they justly deserved, in death, pain, and sorrow; and to all these troubles, not only themselves, but all their offspring, became liable.

Even then the promise was held out, that one sprung of woman should yet, at His own cost, free mankind from the serpent deceiver; and this trust lived on for ages in the world, and was shown in many a story, and many a representation of a mighty One struggling with and trampling down a serpent foe.

They were also still allowed to approach their Maker in prayer; although, to show them that it was only through death that sin could be atoned for, they were required to bring an offering of an animal, innocent in itself, though of course not sufficient in worth to be taken instead of a man, and thus only capable of showing their faith in a coming Deliverer, whose death should bring them near to God.

"In faith," Abel, the second son of our first parents, offered his lamb, and was accepted; but Cain, his elder brother, angered that his less faithful sacrifice was rejected, committed the first act of murder on the earth, and was therefore cast out of his father's home, where the thoughts and ways of the times of innocence were still remembered, and partly practised, by Seth, the third son, and his descendants.

Life was more than ten times longer than at present; and Cain's children multiplying round him in his exile, he built them a city, or collection of solid buildings, instead of merely hiding in caves, or living under trees.

There the days of purity were quickly forgotten: Lamech, fourth in descent from Cain, broke the law pronounced over the first marriage, and took two wives; and he was likewise a murderer, like his great grandfather. The words in which he uttered the bitterness of his heart after the crime, are the first poetical composition known to exist. Some think that the "young man," whom he slew, might have been a human sacrifice, and his song the beginning of a wild ceremony of worship. At any rate, song was soon followed up by music; for his son Jubal invented the harp, made of the tendons of animals strained over a frame, or over a tortoise shell; and the organ, a row of hollow reeds, blown into in succession; and these would have been used both at feasts, and at the dances and other observances of their new rites of worship.

Another son, called Jabal, first invented the tent, that wandering home made of woven goat's hair, so needful to the roving herdsman, who, going from pasture to pasture, leads a fierce and lawless life; and the third brother, Tubal Cain, discovered the use of the harder metals, and first welded brass, and whetted the sharp iron.*

* "He looked, and saw a spacious plain, whereon
Were tents of various hue; by some were herds
Of cattle grazing; others, whence the sound
Of instruments, that made melodious chime,
Was heard of harp or organ; and who moved
Their stops and chords, was seen his volant touch
Instinct through all proportions, low and high,
Fled and pursued transverse the resonant fugue.
In other parts stood one, who, at the forge
Labouring, two massy clods of iron and brass
Had melted; whether found where casual fire
Had wasted woods on mountain or in vale
Down to the veins of earth, thence gliding hot

Wherever very old remains of the human race are found, stone arrow heads and knives mark their first stage, then come remains of brass implements, and lastly of iron ones. And the people armed with iron weapons, soon gain an easy victory over those who can merely defend themselves with clumsy stone and feeble brass, so that violence quickly prevails; and thus old tradition has painted to us the changes of the earlier world, as the age of gold, when all was blessed; the age of silver, fallen, yet still peaceful; the age of brass, a time of deceit and wrong; and the age of iron, the time of war and violence.

The sons of Seth, who had long held aloof from the crimes of the other race, began to be infected, and frightful corruptions prevailed everywhere. Beings of huge size and monstrous wickedness walked the earth; and feasting, rioting, and excess of all kinds, continued unchecked, and fostered by all the arts of life, to which the long term of years and the early vigour of the world gave ample scope. No heed was paid to the warning voice of a solitary son of Seth, who declared that these crimes were bringing down vengeance on them, and proclaimed that a flood of water would sweep away the wicked.

He himself constructed an ark, or huge vessel, capable of containing not only himself and his family, but pairs of all the animals, and sevens of the domestic ones used for food and sacrifice. The ark was built

---

To some cave's mouth; or whether washed by stream
From under ground; the liquid ore he drained
Into fit moulds prepared, from which he wrought
First his own tools, then what might else be wrought,
Fusil, or graven, in metal."—*Milton.*

and provisioned, and Noah himself, his wife, with his three sons and their wives, were safely within it, when the rain descended, sea and rivers rose above their bounds, and the whole inhabited world was submerged for the space of an entire year. It is thought possible that the ground may have been made to sink; so that between the swelling rivers, the rushing storms, and the overflowing sea, the land was for that time entirely covered. All that it contained perished, except what was secured in the ark; and the earth was purified from the dark crimes of its earlier ages. Of this deluge, likewise, every nation has preserved a recollection; and under different forms, the dwellers in the most distant countries tell of the universal destruction, and of the few saved in a floating vessel.

At the year's end, the ark rested on Mount Ararat, in Armenia; and Noah and his family came forth, and received a promise that water should never again destroy the world. The rainbow in the cloud was appointed as the pledge of this promise, and has ever since been regarded as the messenger of mercy.

The Flood is computed to have taken place 1540 years from the time whence the age of the first man is reckoned; but how long ago this may have been, is not known with any certainty.

PART II. THE DISPERSION OF THE NATIONS.

On leaving the Ark, mankind found themselves in Western Asia, the region where the legends of all nations centre as their origin. Noah, and his three sons, Shem, Ham, and Japhet, here at first abode; but Ham, for irreverence to his father, was laid under a prophetic curse, which bore that his children should be servants to their brethren, while though Shem was blessed, yet Japhet should be enlarged, and dwell in the tents of Shem.

At first, however, Ham's family seem to have taken the lead, and leaving their first settlements for the fertile valley of the Euphrates, resolved to build a city and a tower of the bricks of the soft clay, in remembrance perhaps of the cities of the Cainites, and in the hope of defying another flood. This faithless outrage was put a stop to by a sudden confusion of their speech. The one language they had hitherto spoken became changed in their mouths, and they could no longer understand one another. The builders went their several ways, the place was called Babel, or Confusion; and thenceforth began the division of the human race into nations, distinct from one another by character and speech.

The law of division has continued ever since, causing people of the same stock to diverge more and more from one another, and acquire a character of their own. Yet on examination the relationship can be traced; and it is proved both by features and language, that all nations are of one blood, but with three chief divisions; and in accordance with this, the last early legend, common to most countries, is of a defiance of Heaven, a fall; or a tower-building, and a dispersion.

If mankind are classified by their physical conformation, they fall into three chief outlines, the Negro, the Semitic, and the Caucasian.

The Negro races have skulls with receding foreheads, flat noses, thick lips, and woolly hair; their skins are dark, and their frames strong, capable of enduring the great heat of the climates to which they are native. Their character is such that, though able to exert great strength, and subject to bursts of fierce passion, they are easily subdued, and when enslaved remain patiently in bondage, and become faithfully attached to their master. Left to themselves, they make no advances in arts or ideas, and if they devise any form of worship, it is unmeaning and unconnected with memories of the past. They fall a ready prey to more able and skilful nations, and fulfil the fate foretold to their forefather, that they should become servants to their brethren. Yet under cultivation from other nations, they return to higher powers; in the course of generations, their brows rise, and they show themselves capable of improvement.

The Semitic races have high brows, rounded skulls, and fine features, straight dark hair, and beautifully moulded limbs, slender, active, and delicate. They have more activity and endurance than force, and are generally more patient than strong, yet though very brave, not always firm. Their religion is usually a strong belief in the One God, and a horror and dread of image worship; their life is that of shepherd wanderers, free as air; and though, under cultivation, they have very high powers of poetry and imagination, yet in general they remain in the same state of civilization and knowledge from which their forefathers started, without making any advance; and some have even dropped below this point, and become as degraded and more helpless than the negroes.

The Caucasians are the most capable of improvement and of victory. Their forms are less refined, but stronger, than those of the Semitic races; and their minds, though very dull in their rudest state, receive fresh ideas, improve upon them, and constantly make progress, never content with the last step, and always seeking onward. With the attainment of fresh powers, their heads and countenances alter, and tribes whose looks were anciently no more intelligent than those of the negro, and more hideous, have since advanced beyond the prime races of the Semitic family, not so much in beauty as in expression. Left to themselves, they have been prone to find out many inventions in religion, but not unmeaning like those of the negroes, and usually rising out of dimly remembered truth, or allegory made substantial. Their courage and spirit are great, and the conquering nations have always belonged to this stock.

In like manner, the languages of the world are in three chief divisions—Agglutinate, Semitic, Aryan.

The Agglutinate is so called because two words are glued together to express the number, case, or person, of the first, a word being repeated twice for the plural, another added to form a case, and the like. All the words are of one syllable, and there is no grammar; the construction is rude and awkward, and scanty in expression, and those of different nations are so different and various as to show the curse of confusion still on them, though on close examination, similarities are detected, enabling them to be ranged in groups, and shown to be fragments of what was once more complete.

The other two classes of language have apparently originally been Agglutinate, but the words once added to express the relations of the original noun or verb have been as it were welded into them, so that they undergo changes expressing number or case, person or tense, without losing their primary form. These changes are called inflections—they have formed grammar, and give great force and beauty to their speech, enabling it to express the ideas of cultivated people.

So far the two are alike; but whereas the words of the various languages of each branch, and their rules of construction, resemble one another somewhat as the dialects of the provinces of the same country are alike, the two chief branches are entirely distinct. Each is a family of languages, bearing a visible relation to a common stock, but these two parent stocks are so unlike, that only minute analysis has detected traces that they may have had a common parent.

The prevalence of these three classes of language coincides in the main with the three families of the human kind, but not with absolute exactness, for the sons of Ham did not at once lapse into the Agglutinate speech, which the mere savage, of whatever birth, always uses, though with civilization he adopts forms akin to those of the other nations.

Thus after the Dispersion, the descendants of Cush, son of Ham, appear to have remained near Babel, forming in time the great nation called Assyrian, dwelling on the banks of the Euphrates, and speaking a Semitic language, which they retained even after they had been subdued by the Chaldeans, who were of the victorious blood of Japhet, and made the Assyrians a conquering people.

Another family of Hamites, named after Misraim, became dwellers in the valley of the Nile, in the fertile soil of Egypt. Their language was Semitic, but their features in the portraits they have left of themselves, as well as the form of their heads, are of the negro type, though with some Semitic characteristics. Both these nations seem to have preserved some recollection of the tradition of the cherub who had guarded the entrance of Paradise after the Fall of Man, for the remains they have left, of sculptured sphynxes, and winged lions and bulls with human faces, are thought to be in both countries attempts at representing the same symbolic manifestation of Divine Power. They are thought likewise to have preserved the remembrance of the arts practised before the Flood, for they were builders of cities, tillers of the land, and had early become highly civilized.

The same arts were used, and the same class of language spoken, by the sons of Canaan, who spread themselves over the mountain land between the Mediterranean and the Euphrates, and quickly became rich and prosperous, buying and selling between the other two great nations, and rendering themselves the merchants of the old world. They advanced beyond the Egyptians, who only recorded words by symbols, for they invented letters to express sounds; and this invention has under varied forms been adopted by the whole civilized world. But either they had brought with them traditions of the foul worship of the Cainites, or they invented new gods for themselves; for theirs was from the first time we hear of it a cruel and licentious worship, contributing not to raise man by the thought of anything higher and purer than himself, but to degrade him by teaching him to practise vice in honour of his gods. And thus the Canaanite worship became too alluring to their neighbours, and gradually infected other nations.

From other sons of Ham, or Canaan, descend those races that migrated to the southward, and filled Africa, darkening under the tropical sun, and falling into savage life; as the Negro, the Kafir, the Hottentot, and the Bushman, all using Agglutinate dialects, and with either no religion at all, or the basest superstitions. It is possible, a' o, that of the Hamitic race may have been the earliest inhabitants of the great peninsulas to the south of Asia, and from thence proceeded to the Asiatic and Polynesian archipelagos, where the islanders have many of the Negro characteristics.

The chief of the Semitic races continued in Western Asia, around the sources of the great rivers, Tigris and Euphrates, and became in time the race known as Syrians, living to the north-west of Assyria.

From the Syrians were chosen out the Hebrews, in whom the blessing spoken by Noah was realized. Their language is the most perfect of the Semitic tongues, and their forms and features of so superior an order, that they are physically reckoned among the Caucasians. They had a divine revelation, and except when infected by the Canaanites, preserved their allegiance to it.

From them branched out the Arabs, who have ever since inhabited the great peninsula between the Red Sea and Persian Gulf, leading the life of roving shepherds, using a Semitic tongue, adoring one unseen God, and preserving their freedom. Only once in the history of the world, have any section of their race been known to lead a settled life in cities, or to study arts and sciences; but during that time their advances were rapid, and their successes brilliant.

The Idumeans, who dwelt in the rocks north of the Red Sea, were another branch of the same family; and so are the various tribes, who have strayed over the north of Africa, and mixing with the negroes, produced the Berbers, Numidians, and Moors.

It is likely, too, that other Shemites spread over the greater part of Asia; although these have been succeeded by other nations, and have deteriorated so much, that they are difficult to trace to their origin. It is probable, however, that these are the Malays of the eastern peninsula of India, and the islands adjoining, since we find in them the slight lithe frames, and wandering untameable nature, of the Semitic races; and still further degraded are the Australian natives, like them, unreclaimed rovers, and besides, feeble and helpless. The Malayan stock has likewise filled most of the islands of the South Seas. And that the great continent of America has likewise been peopled with sons of Shem, is almost certain. The inhabitants have the slender forms, straight features, and straight hair, agreeing with such a descent; and the great body of them are inveterate wanderers, incapable of being civilized, and perishing under the attempt. They are too, in general, adorers of one great Spirit, without images or temples; and some of their tribes, in North America, had traditions of having been driven to cross the sea to their present abode, after having once lived in a warmer country, where dwelt a creature, evidently a monkey. Traditions of the Fall and the Flood are also found there. Two of their nations alone ever lived a settled life, or advanced in civilization, and these were in the mountains of Mexico and Peru, and, according to their own account, were guided by a teacher from the west, probably one of the third race, of which we are next to speak. All these have, of course, the degenerate monosyllabic varieties of speech.

Both the families mentioned above, seem to have fallen from a higher point; the third has been constantly rising from a lower one. Of one race of the progeny of the third son, which once seems, in a very degraded condition, to have overspread Europe, nothing is left but their flint arrow heads and stone hatchets, buried in the ground; and half burnt wooden houses, sunk in some of the Alpine lakes; except the stunted dwellers in the extreme north, the Samoieds of Asia, Lapps of Europe, and Esquimaux of America, living that kind of savage life which is the effect of intense cold, and speaking a monosyllabic tongue.

South of them, from the Caspian to the Pacific, roamed fierce hordes of horsemen and herdsmen, living on milk and flesh, and speaking a rude monosyllabic tongue. From time to time, they have been seized with a passion for conquest, and have then invaded the lands adjoining. When settled there, they have become mixed into the original nation, giving it life and spirit, and losing the ill formed physiognomy called Mongolian, have advanced to the Caucasian type, so called because its perfection is to be seen in the inhabitants of the Caucasus Mountains. One nation alone of this stock is an exception to this rule. Though early fixed in the great peninsula of China, and civilized to a certain point unknown ages ago, this people has remained at the same point—industrious, but not advancing, and still retaining the same Mongolian features, and Agglutinate speech, expressed by written symbols instead of letters.

The original Mongol or Tartar stock, still remains in

its old quarters; but the chief business of history is with the various swarms that have proceeded from it, on their mission to be enlarged and dwell in the tents of Shem. At some unknown period, the more advanced of this race must once have spoken the parent tongue of that class of language called the Aryan, because all sprung from it contain the root *Ar*, used in some connection with husbandry. All the nations (except the Jews) of Caucasian conformation, speak languages evidently taken from one used before their forefathers parted, and only altered by pronunciation, change of sense, or coining of new words to express new objects, but by the same rules. The simplest words, such as the ten first numbers, the terms for the nearest family relationships, the names of domestic animals, and the more homely verbs, are almost always the same in them, and confirm what the bodily conformation of those who use them had shown, that all are sprung from one source.

Of the races thus derived, the Chaldeans early became the ruling people in Assyria, and adopted the language there, and the worship of the winged bulls. Thenceforth the Assyrian Empire conquered.

The Medes and Persians took possession of the hills of Iran, and in their turn became conquerors. They learnt a Semitic religion, adoring the sun and fire as divine symbols; but the book in which their religion is taught, the Zend, is in a language which plainly connects the present Persian with the ancient Aryan.

The Hindoos occupied the great peninsula of Hindostan, and there produced their sacred books, the Vedas, in the old Sanscrit, of which all their modern dialects are corruptions; and there grew up their religion, at first allegorical, but in process of time the symbols becoming mistaken for realities.

Further north, the Ionian or Javanite (the same word differently pronounced) made his home in the isles and rocks of the Eastern Mediterranean, and was called in after time the Greek. He brought a language nearly related to the Sanscrit, which he learnt to write in Canaanite letters; and a worship of the powers of nature by symbolic rites, which were speedily corrupted by his intercourse with Egypt and Canaan; and in due time he became a great and victorious people.

Westward again, in the long Italian peninsula, another Aryan tongue was used, which was called the Latin: and by-and-by the leading city, Rome, became the ruler of the West. Its religion was of the same type as that of the Greeks.

Meantime, the northern branch had spread; and, probably by the use of brazen weapons, had overthrown the Lapp race, and settled in the midst of Europe, under the title of Kelts; but behind them came an iron weaponed race, of more firm and resolute mould, known as Teutons, or Germans; and in process of time, forced the Kelts into the granite hills, that fence the west coast of Europe from the Atlantic waves; and there they still remain, and still speak their variety of the Aryan tongue.

The Teuton, or German family, (to which the English belong,) Aryan too in speech, were the victors over the great Latin conquerors, and have since peopled Europe, and influenced almost all its languages. Their worship was, likewise, chiefly of the powers of nature, and with allegoric tales attached to it. Behind them are the Slavonic nations, living in eastern Europe, and less removed from the Mongol in face, though in language thorough Aryans.

And lastly the Turk, Mongol in face and in speech, has obtained a footing between the Mediterranean and the Black Seas. Turkey is the only country in Europe that does not use one form or another of the great Indo-European, or Aryan language, that is, as it were, the mark of the race of Japhet. It is also the only European country that has not adopted the true religion, revealed first to the Hebrews, but when perfected by the Divine Deliverer of the earth, destined to spread among all nations.

PART III. SOURCES OF HISTORY.

It is only from the time of the Dispersion at Babel, that history can be said to begin; and it is but a small portion of the world that has in truth a history, for many nations have been so ignorant, and so indifferent to the adventures of their forefathers, as to have preserved no record of them. And even of those who have kept the names of their rulers in remembrance, it is only those who have mingled in the great course of events that took place in the north-east of the great continent, that are concerned in general history. In truth, those nations alone, in ancient times, who came in contact with the Jews, the chosen race, have any clear light thrown upon their doings.

The first history in existence, the only one indeed of the earlier events of the world's history, was revealed to Moses by divine inspiration, about 3,300 years ago; and thenceforward a minute record was kept of the government, the wars, and disasters, of the Hebrews, who have thus the earliest and most certain history in the world.

China and Ceylon both have long chronicles from a very early period, but totally unconnected with those of the rest of the world, and therefore taking no place in the universal history.

Egyptian records go back almost as far as those of the Jews; but they are in a forgotten tongue, and expressed in the hieroglyphics, or symbol writing, either on sheets of the pressed rind of the paper rush, or engraved on the walls of their huge sepulchres and temples. Only recently has a clue to their meaning been discovered, in a stone which bears the same inscription, in Greek letters and in ancient hieroglyphics; but previously all knowledge of Egyptian events was derived from the mention of them by writers of other nations.

So, too, Assyria has been lately found to have a full chronicle traced out in cuneiform or wedge-shaped letters, moulded on clay tablets and cylinders, ranged around the chambers of the ruined palaces, that lie buried deep beneath the desert sand, that has drifted over the deserted cities on the banks of the Euphrates, which hitherto had been only known through the writings of the Jews and Greeks.

Except for these remains, it would seem to be only the Caucasian races that have developed the power of recording their history, so as to become a lesson in God's providential dealings with mankind.

All their memorials, however, begin in clouds of mist, reaching back to the time when writing was unknown, and the traditions of the Patriarchs had begun to be obscured. The Creation, Fall, Promise, Flood, and-

Dispersion, were dimly remembered, and commemorated in songs and poems, that were handed down from father to son, from priest to priest, and gradually interwoven with each nation's own peculiar dreams, traditions, and speculations, thus forming what are called *myths*, from a word meaning a story; and when the knowledge of writing was attained, were collected, and regarded as the foundation of the religion, and account of the origin, of the nation.

Thus the Hindu has the Vedas, so called from *vid*, to know. In times of exceeding antiquity, these were written down in Sanscrit. The earlier ones are hymns in honour of the Supreme Light, gradually passing into symbolic descriptions of the apparent strife between light and darkness, and in the course of a few centuries followed by other poems developing the Brahminical doctrines and legends of the origin of man and animals, and their versions of the primeval traditions.

So again Persia's earlier records are disguised in poetical narratives, excepting for the inscriptions which were made in the rocks in the Assyrian fashion during her time of greatness.

Greece had a mass of poetic myth—some, high legend of almost forgotten revelation; some, personification and deification of the powers of nature; some, philosophical speculation; and some, the praise of great ancestors, from some one of whom every Greek claimed to be sprung.

Less imaginative, the ancient Italians likewise had their hymns, their poems, and their misty accounts of their own origin; but none of these are now extant.

The Kelts had their myths of the Creation and the Flood, and their songs of their brave ancestors; and the Teutonic races sung of great struggles between Summer and Winter, the Frost and the Thunder, and of the great leaders who brought their race from the East, the Land of Summer.

After these myths follows a period when the names of real characters are preserved; but incredible adventures are attributed to them, and nothing becomes clear till the nation is sufficiently advanced to keep its own chronicles, and even then it is only a man's account of his own time, and the transactions in which he has borne a part, that can be fully accepted, since hearsay evidence, however sincerely repeated, needs corroboration.

The earliest of these writers whose works have been preserved is Herodotus, a Greek, who, 2,300 years ago, travelled through the adjacent countries to obtain information, and who related the great struggle that took place in his own time between Persia and Greece. He is called the Father of History, not only from the priority of his work, but from the qualities which have made it not a mere chronicle of facts, but a composition full of power, thought, and spirited simplicity, describing men as well as events. From his time, the stream of contemporary history has been unbroken, being written by the most civilized nation of the time, or sometimes by two or more, so that truth can be established by united testimony.

Before him, where the Scriptures are silent, we have only such intelligence as can be gleaned from fragments of lost books quoted by other authors, and more recently from the already mentioned inscriptions.

Evidence to confirm the assertions of writers is to be sought in such remains as have been left by the persons of whom they speak, and memorials of the events, such as portions of buildings, sculptures, and inscriptions in temples or on monuments, such as are to be found wherever a nation has attained to any degree of art. In many countries, ancient graves contain a whole treasury of weapons, ornaments, and utensils, showing what were the implements of daily life; and others, as in ancient Italy, contain vases painted with scenes representing the subjects of their devotion, or their occupations. Old battle fields are marked by mounds containing bones, and often fragments of armour; and frequently coins are discovered, bearing the stamp either of the effigy of some deity, of the emblem of the city, or of the figure of the sovereign who issued them, with names or other inscriptions that help to confirm the reality of the narratives of historians.

The length of time over which history extends is about 3,800 years. Before that we only know a few scattered facts, but not how long an interval elapsed between them, and though it has been usual to reckon up the ages of the persons in the early genealogies in the Bible, and thus conclude that from the Flood to the beginning of Hebrew history is about five hundred years, yet it is not certain that all the generations may have been given, or that the numbers are perfectly clear, and this chronology is therefore unfixed. As therefore there is no point to start from at the beginning, it is usual to count the dates in Ancient History backwards from the year of the birth of the Deliverer, for whom the old world was under preparation; and the years are therefore numbered as so many B. C.—before Christ

LANDMARKS OF HISTORY.

CHAPTER I.

PART I. THE PATRIARCHS. B.C. 1921–1707.

The Ark rested on Mount Ararat after the Flood; and the children of men spread themselves along the banks of the two great rivers, that rise in the neighbouring hills. There, on the plain beside the Euphrates, they tried to raise a tower whose top should reach to heaven; and there God confounded their speech, and made them speak different languages. After this we know little of them, until, about two thousand years before our Lord was to come into the world, God began to mark out the family from whom He should spring. Some of the sons of Shem were living far north on the course of the Euphrates, preserving some part of the true faith, that had come down to them from Noah.

To one of these men called Hebrews, named Abram, there came, about B.C. 1921, a call from God, to leave his own country and his father's house, and go to a land that should be shown to him. Abram obeyed the call, and was led to the strip of land that lies between the desert and the Mediterranean Sea. There a long line of hills, sloping sharply off on either side, received the clouds from heaven, and shed them down in plentiful streams, of which the Jordan is the largest. This rich and lovely country, Abram was told should belong to his heirs, when as yet no child had been born to him. Moreover, the descendants of Ham's son, Canaan, had filled the country, and called it after his name; setting up little kingdoms in the valleys, and guarding them by cities or forts, built with huge stones upon the tops of the hills.

Abram's nephew, Lot, went to live in the rich but wicked city of Sodom; and there, together with the other inhabitants, was seized, and carried captive by the kings of Shinar and Elam, who came from the east, and conquered the cities of the plain of Jordan.

Abram armed his servants, pursued the kings, defeated them, and brought home the captives and their spoil in safety; yet he would receive nothing for himself, and only asked a blessing from Melchizedec, a mysterious priest and king, who dwelt upon the Hill of Salem.

After this, his name was altered to Abraham, meaning the father of a multitude; and he was told that his son should at length be born. This assurance was given the day before Sodom and the other guilty cities of the Plain perished in one terrible ruin, which has made the place where they stood into a dismal volcanic lake, which is still called the Dead Sea. Lot alone was saved, and was the father of the Moabites and Ammonites, who lived around the Dead Sea.

The child of promise was born, and named Isaac; but Abraham's faith had another sore trial in being commanded to offer him up in sacrifice; but this was meant to prove how far his obedience would go—his hand was stayed, and Isaac was given back to him At last, after a long life of patient faith, Abraham died, and was laid to rest in the Cave of Machpelah, his only possession in the Promised Land.

Other sons besides Isaac had been born to him in his old age, but as they were not heirs of the promise, he sent them away; and Ishmael, the eldest, and son of his Egyptian slave, Hagar, is reckoned as the father of the warlike wandering tribes of Arabs, who have ever since roved about in the wild open countries to the east; living by their families in tents, and pasturing their flocks wherever they find a spring, or a patch of green.

Isaac spent the same patient life of faith as his father, still living in tents, and wandering about the south part of the Promised Land. Of his twin sons, Esau, the elder, heeded not a promise that seemed likely to bring him no profit in his life-time, and went southwards to the hills, called after him Edom or the red, where his descendants, the Idumeans, (of whom Job was probably one,) hewed out for themselves wonderfully sculptured caves in the rocks.

The younger son, Jacob, also called Israel, at first visited Abraham's original home, there married, and then returned with his large family to the land of promise. There the favourite son, Joseph, was treacherously sold by his envious brothers to the Ishmaelites, who carried him into Egypt. Rising from his misfortunes to be the chief counsellor of the king, he sent for his father, and established him, his brethren, and their families, in the richest part of the country.

PART II. EGYPT. B.C. 1707–1491.

Egypt lies on the banks of the Nile. The inhabitants, sons of Misraim, Ham's son, were able and industrious; they cultivated the soil, which was yearly watered and enriched by the swellings of the stream, and raised those wondrous buildings which have been a mystery to all succeeding ages.

The Pyramids, mountains of solid masonry, square, and tapering to a point, still remain, rising from the sandy plain where they were erected as tombs for the kings; and even to the present day, the corpses of their dead are found undecayed, preserved in their embalmed cases, swathed in the fine linen of Egypt, and laid in chambers, which are painted in colours still fresh and clear, with the history of their lives; and where the hieroglyphics—writing, that is to say, in pictures and symbols—engraved on stones and rocks, remain in all their perfection.

The idols of Egypt were of enormous size, with gigantic features, composed to an expression of calm solemnity. A long range of carved figures of stone once sat in array, in chairs, on the Plain of Thebes; and the head of a gigantic statue, which is now in the British Museum, and is called the Young Memnon, may give us an idea how strange and impressive the scene must have been when all were perfect. Near the Great Pyramid there is also a wonderful figure of immense size, now termed the Sphynx, a monster with a human head and the body of a lion, so large, that between his paws there is a temple, where is sculptured a figure of the Sphynx itself receiving the offerings of a King of Egypt.

The Egyptians seem to have believed in two chief powers—Osiris, whom they deemed the source of all good, and the malignant Typhon, the cause of evil; and they imagined that these two, who were equal in strength, were continually at war with each other. All cattle were sacred to Osiris, and in especial a black bull, with certain peculiar marks, called Apis, which was kept at Memphis, the capital city, and worshipped as a representative of the god. Dogs, cats, crocodiles, and the bird called ibis, were likewise worshipped, and are found embalmed in great numbers; and the beetle was held in high honour, being considered as an emblem of immortality.

It was part of the Egyptian religion, like that of the Hindus, that the people were divided into castes—that is to say, each man was obliged to follow his father's profession. The sons of a priest were priests, those of a soldier were soldiers, those of a husbandman were husbandmen; and it was impossible to quit the hereditary calling, be it what it might. The priests possessed much knowledge unknown to the other Egyptians; they practised mysterious arts of enchantment; and their authority was so great, that the kings themselves could do nothing without their consent. At one time the Egyptians suffered much from an invasion of a nation called Hyksos, or Shepherd-kings, but at what period, or who they were, is unknown. There is a long list of kings of Egypt, but no more than their names can be clearly discovered, excepting that Cheops built the Great Pyramid, and that Mœris caused the lake to be made which bears his name, to drain off the water when the overflowings of the Nile were so great as to occasion a flood.

The families of Jacob's twelve sons grew and multiplied in spite of the oppressions of Pharaoh, until the time before appointed by God, when in the year 1491 Moses led them out of Egypt.

The same year, on Mount Sinai, were given those Commandments, which the chosen people bound themselves to keep; they were guarded by every regulation of the Divine Wisdom from mingling with the heathen, and they pledged themselves to keep, from generation to generation, the covenant with their Maker, which marked them as His peculiar people. Then, too, in case they would not keep the covenant, were denounced those curses which the whole course of the world has since been fulfilling.

PART III. THE PHŒNICIANS. B.C. 1451–1096.

SCARCELY was the covenant made before it was broken, and the forty years' wandering in the desert was the first punishment of rebellious Israel. After this, Joshua led them into the Promised Land, where they were enabled to conquer and utterly destroy the Canaanite inhabitants of the cities where they fixed themselves.

Others of these Canaanites were permitted to remain in those parts of the country which the Israelites were not yet numerous enough to occupy, though all intercourse with them was strictly forbidden. The most noted of these tribes were the Philistines in the south, the portion of Judah, and the Zidonians in the north, between the sea and the mountains of Lebanon.

The Zidonians, more usually called Phœnicians, were a very rich and powerful race, and their two great cities, Tyre and Zidon, were the first sea-ports where commerce was practised. The deep purple or scarlet dye obtained from a shell-fish of the Mediterranean, was in high request for colouring royal garments; the wood of the cedars of Lebanon was no less prized for buildings; and the spices and balm of the land of Canaan, were also exchanged with the Egyptians for corn and fine linen. The Phœnicians built ships, which brought gold and silver from Chittim, or Asia Minor, and from Tarshish, believed to be Spain; and the wandering Arabs escorted the caravans of their merchants, who travelled, even to the opposite borders of the desert, in search of the ivory, jewels, and gold of India. Tyre and Zidon were the first and wealthiest of merchant cities.

In these rich cities, a very corrupt and abominable religion was practised, even in these early times, so quickly had the sons of Ham lost all trace of the true faith. The Phœnicians were among the grossest of all idolators, adoring Baal as their chief god, and among others, Moloch, or the planet Saturn, to whom they offered their children, by placing the poor babes between the hands of a brazen statue, over a furnace, into which they were dropped. They also adored Ashtoreth, or Astarte, the moon, or qeeen of heaven, to whom the women offered cakes, together with Tammuz, her lover, whose death they bewailed in the autumn, with their heads shaven, and every token of grief; while in the spring they rejoiced with music and dancing, believing that he had revived and was restored to her.

The memory of the superstitions of Egypt long remained among the Israelites, and was shown in their proneness to worship the golden calf, which reminded them of Apis; and on the other hand the Phœnicians, speaking a language much resembling their own, and possessed of such tempting wealth, continually led them into alliances, which occasioned them to fall into idolatry. During the first four centuries after their entrance into Palestine, the tribes were under the immediate rule of their own elders or magistrates, and no king or chief was owned save the Lord their God, Whose government was constantly made known to them by messages through the priest, by the instant punishment that fell on them when they went after other gods, as well as by the miraculous deliverances effected in His name by His messengers, the Judges.

PART IV. THE KINGDOM OF ISRAEL. B. C. 1096–823.

In 1096 the Israelites demanded a king, like the nations around them; and Saul, of the tribe of Benjamin, was anointed by Samuel. He disobeyed the voice of the Lord, was therefore rejected from being king, and was slain, with his brave and faithful son, in battle with the Philistines upon Mount Gilboa, in 1056.

David, the sweet Psalmist of Israel, was raised to the throne, where, as it was revealed to him, his seed was to endure for ever; though if his children should break the law, their offence should be visited with the rod, and their sin with scourges.

Solomon succeeded him in 1016, and in 1000 completed the glorious Temple of Jerusalem. In this reign were fulfilled the promises of temporal prosperity given to Moses; Solomon held Phœnicia under his power, forced the Syrians of Damascus to pay him tribute, and extended his dominion from the river Euphrates to the torrent of Egypt. His riches exceeded those of any prince who ever existed; his magnificence dazzled all who approached him; and his wisdom, his chosen gift, has ever since been a proverb from east to west; but he allowed himself to be perverted by his numerous wives, erected idol temples at Jerusalem, and at length received the sentence that his kingdom should be divided.

After his death, in 975, Jeroboam and the ten tribes revolted, and founded the idolatrous kingdom of Israel or Samaria. The weakened kingdom of Judah was invaded by Shishak, King of Egypt, supposed by some to be the great conqueror called Sesostris, whose chariot is said to have been drawn by captive kings in golden chains. A chamber in one of the tombs in Egypt has lately been discovered, adorned with paintings representing an Egyptian conqueror triumphing over a nation whose countenances are said to be evidently intended to represent the Jewish features. The history of Sesostris, and the period at which he lived, are, however, too uncertain for this Shishak to be identified with him.

Samaria seems in general to have possessed more temporal power than Judea. Ahab allied himself with the Phœnicians, married Jezebel, a princess of the Zidonians, and practised the same arts of commerce as that nation; but the crimes of his family brought upon them the destruction announced by Elijah the prophet, and all were cut off by Jehu.

His daughter, Athaliah, had married Jehoram, King of Judah, and when her son, Ahaziah, fell with the other descendants of Ahab, she cut off the rest of the seed royal, excepting Joash, in whom the line of David was preserved. In the meantime, the Syrians of the beautiful well-watered city of Damascus, were rising into power, and became dangerous enemies to Judah and Israel, until they fell under the dominion of the first of the four great powers appointed "to lay waste fenced cities into ruinous heaps."

CHAPTER II.

THE ASSYRIAN EMPIRE. B.C. 2300–561.

PART I. NINEVEH. B.C. 2300–606.

THE two great rivers, Euphrates and Tigris, both rising in the mountains of Armenia, at first take a different course, and then gradually approach, and joining their streams, flow together to the Persian Gulf. The tongue of land between them, flat and well-watered, was the seat of the first of the four great empires.

It was at first called the plain of Shinar; and here it was that the Tower of Babel, or Confusion, was raised by the presumptuous sons of men. At Babel, Nimrod, son of Cush and grandson of Ham, commenced his kingdom; and Ashur, his officer, from whom the name of Assyria is derived, founded Nineveh on the banks of the Tigris. It became a city of great size, covering an enormous space, which was inclosed by walls of almost incredible thickness, formed of bricks cemented with the bitumen which abounded in the plain of Shinar, and containing magnificent palaces, the walls covered with paintings and sculptures, and their courts guarded by gigantic figures of majestic winged lions and bulls.

It is remarkable that no less than two whole books of the Old Testament relate to the history of Nineveh; and it would seem that the prophets of the true God were there regarded with respect, at least in the time of Jonah.

Babylon, and the province of Media, further to the east, were subject to Nineveh; and in the year 723, the ten tribes of Israel, having filled up the measure of their crimes, were besieged by King Shalmaneser, and carried away captive by his successor, Sargon, who planted them partly at Nineveh, partly in the cities of the Medes. The next king, Sennacherib, subdued all the neighbouring cities, conquered the lesser towns of the Phœnicians, and set out on his way to conquer Egypt. On the road he sent his messenger, Rabshakeh, to summon Jerusalem to surrender, and boast that the God in whom Hezekiah trusted should not be able to deliver him.

Never was Jerusalem more safe than at that moment; Sennacherib, the instrument of God's wrath, had done His work for the present, and was now to be turned back again. Hearing that the King of Ethiopia intended to come and defend Egypt against him, Sennacherib put off his attack upon Hezekiah, and hurried on to be beforehand with the Ethiopians, but he never came to a battle. His whole host were in one night cut off by a miracle. "Early in the morning, they were all dead corpses."

At Nineveh, Sennacherib was murdered by two of his sons; a third, Esarhaddon, was his successor, in whose reign it was that Tobit lived. At the death of Tobit, he charged his son to remove to Media, since he believed that the prophecies of vengeance against Nineveh would soon be accomplished; and so accordingly they were.

The last king of Nineveh, whom Herodotus calls Sardanapalus, but whose real name seems to have been Saracus, was one of the most luxurious princes in the east, so given up to ease and amusement, that all ordinary diversions had lost their zest, and he offered large rewards to any man who could devise some new pleasure. Instead of attending to the affairs of his empire, he shut himself up in his palace with his numerous wives and female slaves, wore their garments, and like them, spun, wove, and embroidered.

The subject princes of Media and Babylon revolted, and uniting their forces, laid siege to the city of Nineveh in 606; but even their approach failed to rouse him, for he put his faith in what the heathen histories call an ancient oracle, which declared that Nineveh should be safe until the river became its enemy. Very probably this was the prophecy of Nahum, which said, "The gates of the rivers shall be opened, and the palace shall be dissolved."

Secure in this belief, Sardanapalus continued his feasts and revellings until intelligence was brought him that the Tigris had actually overflowed its banks, and broken down a portion of the wall. Then, convinced that his time was come, he resolved that his death should be more noted than his life had been, and setting fire to his palace, he there burnt himself, with all his wives, slaves, and treasures, in one lofty funeral pile

From that time forward we have no mention of this mighty city. Its existence had almost been forgotten, and doubts were entertained whether the mounds of earth which still remain on the banks of the Tigris, did actually mark its site. Of late, however, these hills have been opened, and, buried deep beneath the sands, which the desert winds have for thousands of years been gathering over them, have been found the magnificent remains of Nineveh, the fire-scathed palaces, "the courts of the young and old Lion," the pictured walls, all laid up there for centuries upon centuries, to show us in these latter days how God's words of old have been fulfilled.

PART II. BABYLON. B. C. 747–561.

After the fall of Nineveh, Babylon became the chief city of the Assyrian Empire. The Euphrates flowed through the midst of it; and it seems to have been more like a district inclosed within fortifications, than a single town, for more than half of the space was taken up with fields and gardens, shut in by a wall of such thickness, that three chariots could drive abreast upon the top. It had a hundred brazen doors in the wall, and great folding-gates opening upon the river, which were closed by night and opened by day. Among the most noted of its wonders were the reservoirs and canals, provided for carrying off the floods when the river was swelled by the melting snows on the mountains where it rose. In the middle of the city stood the Temple of Bel, said to be the Tower of Babel, and the magnificent royal palace, with the gardens, where one of the kings, to please his wife, a Median princess, who pined for the mountains of her native land, had caused an artificial hill to be raised, the sides of which were planted with choice trees and shrubs, and laid out in a succession of terraces, known as the hanging gardens of Babylon.

Thus much can we learn respecting the splendour of the city which said within herself, "I am the lady of kingdoms," and which Holy Scripture has marked out as the very type of this world, both in her greatness and her fall.

It is thought that the Chaldeans, who were the possessors of Babylon at the time of the destruction of Nineveh, were not of the ancient Assyrian nation, but one of the wandering tribes of the North, who had conqured the former race, and fixed their abode there, about the year 747. Many stories are told of Ninus, and the conquering queen Semiramis; but we have no certainty respecting any of the Babylonian monarchs, till the time of the Jewish Hezekiah, who received messengers from Merodach Baladan, King of Babylon, after his recovery from his sickness. The Chaldeans were great observers of the stars, and it was probably in consequence of the miracle of the alteration in the course of the sun that their notice was attracted.

The wicked Manasseh, son of Hezekiah, was taken captive in 675, and carried to Babylon; and though on his repentance he was afterwards restored, yet the sentence had gone forth against Judah, which never again recovered the blow it had then received. It is thought to have been during this invasion that Bethulia was delivered from its enemies by Judith's slaughter of Holofernes.

Amon's crimes filled up the measure; and the righteous Josiah lived under the certainty of the judgments in store for his people. He appears to have been tributary to the Chaldeans, perhaps holding under them that part of Samaria where he destroyed Jeroboam's altars. The prophets generally called upon the Jews to submit to the Chaldeans, and resist the Egyptians; and when Pharaoh Necho, King of Egypt, attempted to pass through Judea to invade the Assyrian Empire, he collected his forces, and fought the battle of Megiddo, in which he was slain in 609, the righteous taken away from the evil to come.

His son and successor, Jehoahaz, was dethroned and carried off to Egypt by Pharaoh Necho, who set up Jehoiakim in his stead. On the retreat of Pharaoh, Nebuchadnezzar took Jerusalem and carried away many of the Jews. Again Jehoiakim revolted, and was besieged by the Babylonians; he died in the course of the siege, and his son Jehoiachin was taken captive, with many of his nobles, and carried to Babylon, with great part of the treasures of the temple.

Zedekiah, the last king, trusting to the promised aid of Egypt, in spite of the warnings of Jeremiah, made another revolt, and was besieged at Jerusalem. After twelve months, during which the city suffered the greatest distress from famine, it was taken by Nebuchadnezzar, and Zedekiah himself, after his sons had been slain, and his eyes put out, was carried a prisoner to Babylon in 587.

Nebuchadnezzar next laid siege to Tyre, against which judgment had been denounced by Ezekiel. It was a thirteen years' siege, and the Chaldean troops suffered excessively; but they at length took it, and totally destroyed it. Many of the inhabitants escaped, and founded a new city on a small island near the shore, which soon equalled the former Tyre in wealth and luxury.

He then invaded Egypt, where many of the

rebellious Jews had taken refuge, contrary to the repeated commands given through the prophet Jeremiah. The whole country quickly fell into his hands, and from that time forward Egypt never had a prince of her own.

The prime counsellor at Babylon, during these its most prosperous days, was a Jewish slave of royal blood, Daniel the prophet, to whom was shadowed forth in marvellous visions the future fate of the whole world. In his book we find narrated the history of Nebuchadnezzar's boast, and of its punishment. The king died in 561, the year after he was restored to reason, and his grandson, Belshazzar, was the last king of Babylon.

CHAPTER III.

THE PERSIAN EMPIRE. B.C. 559-521.

PART I. FALL OF CRŒSUS. B. C. 559-546.

THE Medes, after their rebellion against the Ninevites, became a free and powerful nation. Their first king was Deioces; and his family reigned over them for many years. Either in alliance or subject to them, were the Persians, inhabiting the mountains between the Caspian Sea and Persian Gulf, and in these early days very unlike the Medes, who had learnt all the luxuries and refinements of the Assyrians.

The Persians, on the contrary, were a hardy and warlike race, who trained up their sons in simple habits, and taught them patiently to endure the hardships of war; indeed, it was commonly said that their education consisted in learning to draw the bow, to ride, and to speak the truth. Their religion was far less grossly corrupt than that of the neighbouring nations. They adored the rising sun, and the sacred fire, idolatrously indeed, but not as themselves divine, only as the emblems of One, more pure, bright, and consuming. From the name of their priests, the Magi, this religion is called the Magian, and it is to the present day professed by a few scattered tribes in the East. Its great teacher and founder was named Zoroaster.

The first great man of this race was Cyrus, or more properly Kai Khoosroo, so called from a Persian word signifying the sun. He was the son of a Persian prince, and of the daughter of Astyages, king of Media, and was brought up to lead the hardy and active life of his father's people. In early youth he came to Ecbatana, the capital of Media, and obtaining the command both of the Medes and Persians, reduced all the lesser nations of the north and west, until his progress excited the jealousy of Crœsus, King of Lydia.

Lydia, in the peninsula since called Asia Minor or Lesser Asia, was a fertile province, the mountains of which contained several veins of gold, which metal was also often found in the sands of the river Pactolus. Crœsus, the king, was proud of his wealth, and loved to display it; but he was at the same time a gentle and estimable prince, fond of learning. It is said that Æsop, the clever deformed slave, composed for his benefit many of the fables which have since almost passed into proverbs. Another visitor at his court was Solon, one of the seven wise men of Greece, to whom Crœsus showed the whole bright array of his treasures, and asked at the end, "Whom do you think the happiest of men?"

Solon answered by naming a Greek, who had spent a quiet, useful, and peaceable life, and died at last while fighting in the cause of his country.

Crœsus, who had expected to hear himself named, desired to hear whom Solon deemed the next happiest.

He mentioned two youths who had shown such pious affection to their mother, that she prayed that they might receive the best reward that Heaven could bestow upon man. While she was yet praying, they fell asleep, and their sleep was a peaceful death. "These," said Solon, "were the next happiest of men."

"Do you not, then, think me a happy man?" said Crœsus, vexed at seeing how little account the wise man seemed to take of his wealth.

"Alas!" said Solon, "who can be said to have been happy while he still lives?"

Two years after, Crœsus was obliged to own the truth of this reply, when he lost his eldest son by an accident. Soon after, he rashly entered upon the war with the Medes and Persians, who totally defeated him at Thymbra, and besieged him in Sardis, his capital. Cyrus took the city by assault, made Crœsus prisoner, and ordered him to be burnt to death. The pile of wood was raised, and Crœsus was chained to it, when at that very moment calling to mind the saying which had warned him not to trust in present prosperity, he broke out into an exclamation of "O Solon, Solon, Solon!"

Hearing the cry, Cyrus asked its meaning, and desired that the captive should be led to him to explain it. He was so much struck by Solon's lesson, that he not only spared the life of Crœsus, but made him his favoured friend and counsellor ever after, seeing in his misfortunes a warning against putting too much confidence in the power and greatness to which he was at present raised.

PART II. THE FALL OF BABYLON. B.C. 538–529.

CYRUS next turned his arms against the Assyrian Empire, and laid siege to Babylon. Secure in the strength of their walls, and believing that their cornfields would preserve them from famine, the Babylonians scorned his attempts, and in derision of them, gave themselves up to reckless merriment.

The sentence of Heaven had been long since pronounced against them; and Cyrus, who had two hundred years before been called by name to this very work, was instructed in the means of overcoming them. He caused his men to dig trenches, so as to leave the bed of the river dry, but still his approach would have been checked by the gates of brass which guarded the river, had not the citizens, in the carelessness of their riotous festivity, left them unclosed. "I will open the two-leaved gates, and loosen the loins of kings," had been predicted by the mouth of Isaiah.

On the night that the Persians were advancing, Belshazzar was in the height of his revelry, and had caused the sacred vessels of the Jewish Temple to be brought forth to adorn his feast. His mirth was cut short by the sight of the handwriting on the wall, the dreadful import of which was explained to him by Daniel the prophet. A few more hours, and Cyrus had led his conquering army into the heart of Babylon, and Belshazzar was slain. With the capital, the whole Assyrian Empire, including Syria, Phœnicia, and Palestine, fell into his hands, and in 536 he fulfilled the task for which he had been chosen, by restoring the Jews to their own city, and giving the edict for rebuilding the Temple. It is probable that Daniel might have shown him the prophecies of Isaiah, where he is mentioned by name as the shepherd appointed by the Most High. Indeed, it is related of him that he was wont to declare that a king should be the shepherd of his people, a saying not unlikely to have been suggested by the prophecy.

Zerubbabel, the head of the royal family of Judah, and Joshua, the high priest, conducted the Jews on their return, but without the supreme authority, for Judea was from henceforth reckoned only as a province of the Persian Empire.

Cyaxares, the Mede, uncle to Cyrus, remained at Babylon, and governed the adjoining country. He is believed to be the king called in Scripture Darius, who was persuaded by the flattery of his malignant courtiers, to make the decree which occasioned Daniel to be thrown into the den of lions. The word Dara, in the Persian language, signifies a king, and was not a proper name, but was only so used in consequence of a mistake of the Greeks, and the Greek names have for the most part been used by the translators of the Bible.

The rest of the history of Cyrus is very uncertain. It has been written by two Greek authors, Herodotus and Xenophon, the first of whom had no good opportunity of ascertaining the truth, and the second did not intend so much to write a history of what Cyrus actually was, as to describe his idea of what a king ought to be. His account represents Cyrus as living to a good old age, and dying peaceably, while giving wise counsels to his children; whereas Herodotus says that he was killed in battle with Tomyris, queen of the Scythians, by whom his head was cut off and thrown into a bag full of blood, while she bade him satiate himself with that in which he delighted.

The old Persian poems describe their Kai Khoosroo as reigning with great power and prosperity until he reached the age of ninety, when he resolved to resign his crown, and spend his latter years in quiet. He took leave of his friends near a pleasant stream of water, and was never seen again, though his people long after looked forward to his re-appearing in great power and splendour. He was revered by them as a prophet and father, and doubtless his name should be honoured by us, as that of one of the few kings, not of the chosen seed, spoken of with favour in the Scriptures.

PART III.   SUCCESSORS OF CYRUS.   B.C. 529–507.

AFTER the conquest of Assyria, the Persians lost their formerly hardy and simple habits, and learnt to depend upon the luxuries which they had formerly despised. The palaces of the kings were full of riches and splendour, filled with multitudes of slaves, whose office was to administer in every imaginable way to their ease or diversion; and their harems were full of throngs of wives and female slaves, whose faces it was death for any other man to look upon. Their sons were brought up in the midst of idleness and luxury, and became weak, proud, selfish, and violent, so that though the founder of a dynasty might be an able and vigorous man, his children rapidly degenerated.

The king was distinguished from his nobles by his tiara, a sort of high cap, the top of which he wore erect, while all others were forced to wear theirs bent backwards. The empire was divided into provinces, the governors of which were called Satraps, it is thought from a Persian word signifying the umbrella carried over their head, as a sign of rank, as well as a shade from the sun. A tribute was paid to the king, which was stored in the treasuries of Persepolis, Ecbatana, Babylon, and Susa, the expenses of the royal household being defrayed by certain cities, each of which had to provide a different article of food or of dress.

Cambyses, the son of Cyrus, was a cruel and frantic tyrant. He made an expedition into Egypt, and overran Ethiopia, but there was bewildered in the desert, and his army suffered dreadfully from hunger. On his return to Egypt he killed his brother Smerdis, in a mad fit of jealousy, and insisted on marrying his sister Atossa. He also enraged the Egyptians by striking his sword into the thigh of Apis, their sacred bull; and there was universal rejoicing when, shortly after, he wounded himself accidentally with his own sword, and died in consequence of the hurt, in 521.

One of the Magi in Persia pretended to be Smerdis, and reigned for nearly a year, but his deceit was suspected; and as it was known that the Magian had been sentenced to lose his ears, one of the nobles, whose daughter was in the royal harem, sent word to her to find out whether the king had ears. She returned for answer that they had been cut off, and the impostor was therefore slain by her father and six other nobles, and as Atossa was now the only surviving child of Cyrus, they agreed that one of their number should marry her and reign; and that the choice should be decided, as they thought, by the sun. All seven rode out of Susa together just at sunrise, and he whose horse first neighed was to be king. By the contrivance of his groom, it was the horse of Darius, the son of Gushtasp, or, as the Greeks called him, Darius Hystaspes, that thus conferred a crown on his master, who became King of Persia in 520.

He was a wise and able prince, and his empire extended from the banks of the Indus to the shores of the Black Sea; almost all Asia Minor was under his power, and he extended his conquests over the isles of the Ægean Sea, now called the Archipelago. So far did his ambition extend, that he attempted also to subdue Europe, beginning with the Scythians, a wild race, who found pasture for their flocks on the steppes north of the Euxine, (the Black Sea,) lived almost constantly on horseback, excelled in archery, and wandered from place to place with their tents and families. Bent on overcoming these savages, Darius crossed the Hellespont, laid a bridge of boats across the Danube, and entered their country. He found it bare and desolate, without subsistence, and with no enemy to conquer, for the Scythians perpetually fled before him, never offered him battle, and never even let him come in sight of them; but devoured all the scanty pasture, and at last derided him by sending him a present of a mouse, a bird, a frog, and five arrows, meaning that unless he could burrow like a mouse, fly like a bird, or swim like a frog, he could never escape their arrows.

At last he was forced to return, closely pursued by the enemy, and reduced to such distress by famine, that he considered his own preservation to be owing to a faithful camel which followed him closely with its load of provisions; and on his arrival at Susa, he appointed a whole district for the support of the camel, as if it had been a royal prince.

The next enemies whom Darius attacked, require a more detailed notice.

CHAPTER IV.

GREECE. B.C. 1400-499.

PART I. GREEK MYTHOLOGY.

To the westward of the Eastern Empire lies the Mediterranean Sea, scattered with numerous rocky islands, and broken up by peninsulas, themselves deeply indented by lesser seas, bays, and gulfs. These countries, termed in the prophetic writings, the isles of the Gentiles, became the scene of some of the chief events of the history of the world, and not only this, but the source of many of the ideas which have ever since floated down the stream of time, and acted upon the minds of generation after generation.

The peninsula between the Archipelago and Adriatic, together with the lesser peninsula connected with it by the Isthmus of Corinth, was all alike known by the name of Greece, and inhabited by a people speaking the same language, professing the same faith, and considering themselves as in many respects, united. The high mountain ranges, and the deep gulfs which intersected the country, formed, however, so many natural divisions, and almost every vale, inclosed between the mountains and the sea, was a little state, with its own separate government, interests, and passions; and so remarkable were the events that there took place, and so fully have they been recorded, that it is hardly possible to believe that the space was so small where these transactions occurred.

The Greeks were descendants of Japhet, and derived their first knowledge of civilization from Egypt and Phœnicia; so far is tolerably certain, but nothing farther, as their early history is a tissue of fables, some beautiful, others absurd, and several gross; but many of these stories, adorned by the poets, have become so universally known, and have had so much influence on other civilized nations, that it is necessary to say a few words on them.

Perhaps, too, the superstitions of the Greeks were not equally blameable with those of the Eastern nations, who were nearer the source of light, and had frequent intercourse with the people to whom revelation was continued. The Greeks had lost almost all traditional knowledge of God, possessing only the witness left within themselves, in the world of nature, and in the retributive justice which overtakes the evil-doer and his children after him; and earnestly did their poets and philosophers struggle to feel after the truth, and to catch at the least ray of light amid the dark mists of ignorance and idolatry.

According to their mythology, (the stories, that is, of their false religion,) Zeus, now better known by the name of Jupiter, the father of gods and men, dwelt above, in a palace, of which the lofty Mount Olympus, in Thessaly, was the outer court. His weapons were the thunderbolts, which he hurled against his enemies, and his authority governed Heaven and Earth; yet even he was subject to the decrees of Fate, a mysterious power, in which, perhaps, was ignorantly acknowledged the true Almighty will. His brother Neptune ruled the sea, and Pluto dwelt in the dark world beneath, where the wicked were condemned to perpetual punishment, though the brave and good enjoyed no corresponding happiness, but flitted about the groves as melancholy shades, ever regretting the life they had lost. So ran their stories; but the Greek philosophers yearned with longing hearts for some security even in this dreary Elysium.

The haughty Hera, or wife of Zeus, was queen of the skies, and the other divinities were his children. Pallas Athene, the virgin goddess of celestial wisdom, sprang fully armed from his head, to aid in his war with the giants, who strove to scale the heights of Heaven, and with the Gorgon's head sculptured on her shield, turned all to stone who dared to oppose her. Ares, was god of war; Hermes, of eloquence and cunning; and Aphrodite, (probably derived from the Astarte of the Phœnicians,) the goddess of beauty and love, arose from the sea-foam. There were also the twins, Apollo and Artemis. The car of Artemis was the moon, and Apollo ruled the sun, whose flaming chariot daily came forth from the gates, opened by his daughter, the rosy-fingered Eos, traversed the sky, and went to rest in the waves of the ocean. He was also the god of poetry, and the leader of the Muses, nine sisters who dwelt on Mount Parnassus, and inspired all works of imagination.

These were the greater gods, and in addition multitudes of others were adored. Every wood had its spirit, every stream and fountain its protecting nymph, or river-god; and besides these, there were the heroes, who had been raised to the skies for their great deeds upon earth. Dionyses, the Indian conqueror, was god of wine; Hercules (believed to be in part derived from Phœnician legends of the Israelite Samson,) after his twelve labours in ridding the world of monsters, reposed among the gods, wrapped in his lion's skin, and was invoked when strength and endurance were needed; Castor and Pollux, the horseman and wrestler, were raised to the skies, and two bright stars in the constellation of the Twins still bear their names.

PART II. SIEGE OF TROY. B.C. 1183.

The Greek histories all begin with what was called the heroic age, when the heroes before mentioned were still upon earth, and when, according to their legends, the gods visibly interfered in the affairs of men.

The most noted of these half-fabulous tales is the siege of Troy, which Homer's Iliad has made famous throughout the world.

Helen, the beautiful Queen of Sparta, deserted her husband Menelaus, for the sake of Paris, one of the fifty sons of Priam, King of Troy, or Ilium, in Asia Minor, and fled with him to his own city. All the princes of Greece, united under the command of Agamemnon, King of Mycæne, brother of Menelaus, sailed for Troy, and besieged the city. The siege lasted no less than ten years, during which time Troy was valourously defended by Hector, eldest son of Priam; while the chief champion of the Greeks was Achilles, the son of a sea-nymph, brave and gifted beyond all others, but doomed, and well knowing his doom, to die before the war was ended.

In the tenth year of the siege, Hector was slain by Achilles, and soon after Achilles himself fell by a treacherous arrow from the bow of Paris. The wise Ulysses, King of Ithaca, at length devised a stratagem for entering the city. An immense hollow wooden-horse was constructed, and filled with armed men, after which the whole Greek fleet sailed away, leaving this strange monster in front of the deserted camp. A spy who had been left for the purpose, contrived to be made prisoner by the Trojans, and told them that it had been declared by a Greek soothsayer, that though destruction would attend the Greeks if they attempted to carry the horse with them, yet the safety of Troy would be secured by bringing it within their gates.

The deluded Trojans dragged the monster into the city, and that very night the enemy broke forth from their ambush, opened the gates to the rest, who had been lying in wait in the neighbourhood, set fire to the city, killed Priam and all his remaining sons, slaughtered many of the Trojans, and made slaves of the rest, excepting those who escaped with Æneas, a Trojan prince, who will be mentioned hereafter. After this conquest, the Greeks set out on their return, but almost all met with great misfortunes, in consequence, it was said, of their having profaned the temples of the gods at Troy.

Agamemnon was murdered by his wife Clytemnestra, who in her turn was put to death by her son Orestes, and the miseries of this house, derived from the wickedness of their ancestors, Atreus and Thyestes, were almost a proverb. Ulysses wandered for ten years before he arrived at his own island of Ithaca, where he had to fight his way through great dangers before he could regain his crown. His adventures, the story of the "wrath of Achilles," and the fall of Hector, were sung to the Greeks by the blind minstrel Homer, the first of poets. These songs, chanted to the sound of the harp, were handed down by tradition for many years, and at length were, by the Athenian King Pisistratus, collected into two poems, the Iliad, so called from Ilium, or Troy, and the Odyssey, from Odysseus, the Greek name for Ulysses, and have ever since been highly prized for the beautiful poetry in which they abound.

PART III. GREEK MANNERS.

The proper name of ancient Greece was Hellas, and all the Greeks claimed to be the children of the same ancestor, Hellen, from whom were descended the different tribes which bore the names of his sons and grandsons. The chief of these were the Æolians, Dorians, Ionians, and Achaians; there were some others of less note. All spoke the same language, but the dialects differed in some degree, and though there was a general likeness between them, each race had a character of its own.

In the legends of the heroic age, all the little states seem to have been under the rule of absolute kings of their own, but when history, deserving of the name, begins, the state of things was far different, almost all of them were governed by the people, and any supreme ruler was called a tyrant, a word which then only signified that he had taken an undue share of authority, not that he was necessarily cruel or oppressive. The popular government did not, however, include among those who had a voice in public affairs all the inhabitants, but only such as were free and noble; the rest were for the most part slaves, subject to no law but the will of their master.

All the chief tribes were subject to the council of the Amphictyons, persons chosen from among them, who met twice a year, once at the temple of Demeter, near Thermopylæ, and once at that of Apollo, at Delphi, there to decide disputes, take measures for the general defence, or ordain sacrifices to the gods. The Temple of Delphi was probably chosen as the place of meeting, because scarcely any spot was regarded with such general veneration. There, it was said, Apollo had slain the serpent Python, and there, by the mouth of his priestess, he returned prophetic answers to those who inquired of him. These replies, which were called Oracles, were without doubt sometimes fulfilled. Frequently, indeed, they were so artfully worded, that the event, be what it might, accomplished them, as when Crœsus was told that if he engaged in a war with Cyrus, a great empire would be overthrown. He understood this to mean the Persian, whereas it proved to be his own; but in some cases the prediction was so remarkably verified, that we cannot but wonder what voice it was which was permitted to speak.

The Greeks regarded as religious ceremonies the games which were celebrated every four years at Olympia, a small plain in Elis, whither they thronged to see their young men try their skill in races on foot, on horseback, or in chariots, as well as in wrestling, boxing, and throwing the disc. Before commencing these games, the gods were invoked, and at the conclusion the victor was raised on a brazen tripod, and crowned with a wreath from a sacred olive-tree, and this "corruptible crown" was deemed one of the highest honours to which man could aspire. Time was reckoned by the recurring seasons of these games, the first Olympiad, the second Olympiad, &c., the first being about the year 776. The Isthmian games, so called from being held on the Isthmus of Corinth, were likewise numerously attended, though not equally esteemed with those of Olympia.

The Greek cities were for the most part walled, and possessed a citadel, dedicated to the god who was thought to preside over the safety of the city, and strongly fortified, so as to afford a refuge to the inhabitants, when the rest of the town was in the hands of the enemy. The free inhabitants usually had both houses in the city and estates in the open country; all called themselves citizens; and it was from their word *polis*, a city, that our word politic is derived. The houses were suited to the warm climate, built round paved courts, often with a fountain in the middle, and with porticos on each side. Under these the family spent most of their time, only using the inner rooms at night. In this court there was usually an altar to some one of the gods, or to some hero forefather of the family, and before commencing a meal libations or drink-offerings were always here poured out.

The dress of the Greeks was a tunic, a long white loose robe gathered at the waist with a girdle, open at the sides for the arms, and fastened over the shoulder with a brooch. Those worn by women were long, and reached to the feet, while the men wore theirs no lower than the knee.

Their armour consisted of a helmet, adorned with a crest of horse-hair, a shield, and a cuirass, or breastplate, to the lower edge of which a number of broad strips of leather were fastened, and allowed to hang down as low as the knee, so as to protect the thigh from a sword cut Their legs were sometimes defended by greaves, sometimes by a high leathern buskin; but in general they only wore a sandal or sole, laced on by thongs of leather. They fought with swords and spears, the latter of which were sometimes thrown forward at the enemy.

Their ships or galleys were very small, and little better than boats; they were propelled by oars, of which there were one, two, three, or even five benches, according to the size of the vessel. The sails could seldom be used, and for want of the knowledge of the compass, the sailors never ventured out of sight of land. In front of the ship was a beam, armed with iron, called the beak, which in a sea-fight was thrust violently against the opposing vessel in order to sink it.

The Greeks, for the most part, burnt their dead, laying them on a pile of wood, together with a quantity of spices, and setting fire to it with great solemnity. The ashes were afterwards placed in an urn, and preserved with great care and reverence.

Almost all the Greeks were educated, and could both read and write on scrolls of parchment, or of the paper-rush. It was usual to study in the schools of the philosophers, and the cultivation of the mind and taste were highly esteemed. Thus in Greece we see the perfection of what can be accomplished by the intellect of man. Within a short time there lived in that little country, the authors, the sculptors, architects, orators, and warriors, who have ever since been the models of the world; but in their several kinds of excellence have never been surpassed, and seldom even approached. Decayed as are the remains which have come down to our time, they enchant us by their beauty and greatness, and to us it is given to look deeper and further than their outward beauty, so as to discover the spirit, yearning after truth, which dwelt in those mighty men of old, and the Hand which guided them to shadow forth His honour, goodness, and glory, unconsciously indeed and fitfully, but surely, to the eyes which are now unveiled and enabled to trace it aright.

PART IV. SPARTA. B.C. 1104—817.

The two leading cities of Greece were the Ionian Athens, and Doric Sparta, also called Lacedæmon. The first was considered as the favoured city of Pallas

Athene. Standing in the midst of its little domain of Attica, overlooking the Saronic Gulf, the most beautiful and the most gifted of the Greek cities, where learning and grace were found in their perfection; it strongly contrasted with Sparta, the stern capital of the rocky Laconia, whence was banished everything soft and elegant, all art or luxury, all that could charm the eye or the taste, and the whole soul and body of each citizen was devoted to war, and war alone.

The Spartans claimed their descent from Hercules, and had two kings, descended from the twin sons of the eldest of his children, both reigning with equal rights at the same time. One of them always had the command of the army, while the other remained at home; but within the city they had very little power, the government being almost entirely in the hands of certain judges called Ephors. Their government was called an oligarchy, from *oligos*, the Greek word for a few; sometimes, also, an aristocracy, from *aristos*, the best; and these names are given to states where only certain persons have a right to meddle with public affairs.

The Spartans had become idle, effeminate, and luxurious, when in the year 852, Lycurgus, a prince of the Heracleid line, took the government in the name of his infant nephew, Charilaus, whom he had saved from being killed by his wicked mother. He resolved to bring about a great reform, and to establish a discipline, which, as he hoped, would render his fellow-citizens the hardiest and most resolute warriors in the world.

He divided the lands among them, took away their gold and silver, so that they might have no means of obtaining luxuries from elsewhere, and gave them, by way of money, weights of iron, so heavy and worthless, that no merchant would receive them in exchange.

Men were not permitted to spend their time at their homes, but from early childhood to old age were exercised in warlike sports all day, and ate together in large rooms, where only the plainest fare was provided. Their black broth was one article of food which their neighbours, the other Greeks, greatly disliked and despised, and which they themselves allowed was only made palatable by hunger. When a child was admitted for the first time to the public table, the elders warned him against repeating the conversation by pointing to the door, and saying, "Nothing said here goes out there." They always used as few words as possible, and thus Laconic speech has become a term for brevity of discourse.

Nothing was deemed so important as the use of arms and the power of bearing pain. So strict and harsh was the discipline to which the Spartans were subjected within the city when at peace, that the time of war was comparatively full of ease and liberty; and so shameful was any expression of pain or token of cowardice considered, that a boy who had hidden a young wolf under his tunic, allowed it to bite him to death, without letting it go, or uttering a cry. Boys were beaten before the statue of Artemis, with their mothers looking on, till they sometimes expired without a groan; and Spartan mothers sent out their sons to battle with these words, as they gave them their broad shields, "With it or upon it." Either bring it home in honour, or be carried home on it a dead man, but never cast it away in flight.

The necessary arts and manufactures, and the cultivation of the soil, were carried on by the Helots, a miserable race of slaves, who were treated without mercy, ill-used and insulted, intoxicated in order to disgust the young Spartans with drunkenness, and ruthlessly slaughtered whenever their numbers were thought to render them dangerous to their masters.

PART V. ATHENS. B. C. 1104–510.

Athens stood at some little distance from the coast, at the foot of the rocky hill of Acropolis, on which stood the citadel, and a temple, the court of which contained a sacred olive, said to have sprung from the ground at the command of Athene, the guardian goddess of the city. On another point of the hill was her temple, called the Parthenon, (the temple of the virgin goddess,) of which one beautiful range of marble pillars still exists.

On the other side of the city rose the Areopagus, or hill of Ares, the place of judgment. The town was strongly fortified, and full of beautiful buildings, interspersed with groves, fountains, and porticos, the resort of the philosophers and poets. The harbour was called the Piræus, and was well fortified, and the fleet was the most numerous possessed by any of the Grecian states.

Athens was an Ionic city, and was anciently ruled by kings, of whom the hero Theseus was the most renowned. The royal line ended with Codrus, who nobly devoted himself to death in obedience to an oracle that declared that a king must perish for the good of the country.

Nothing certain is known of the government till 621, when a philosopher, named Draco, framed a code of laws so severe, that it was impossible to put them in practice, since death was the penalty even for the slightest offence. In 594, Solon, one of the seven wise men of Greece, drew up another table of laws, which he said were not the best he could devise, but the best the Athenians could bear. The government was placed in the hands of nine chief magistrates, called archons, who were chosen by lot from among the citizens; but no measure could be adopted without the consent of a majority of the citizens. Such a government, carried on by the people themselves, was called a democracy; but the free citizens did not include all the inhabitants, there were many who, being of foreign birth, or unable to prove an honourable descent, had no voice in the affairs of state. There were also many slaves, who were, however, in a much better condition than the Helots, and whose lives were protected by the law. Here there prevailed none of the unnatural rules for the training of the citizens which Lycurgus had established at Sparta, yet the Athenians were at least equal in warlike fame to the Lacedæmonians, and immeasurably their superiors in everything else. It seems to have been the great object of Solon's institutions to prevent any one man from becoming too powerful, and he therefore enabled the citizens to banish a person whom they thought dangerous to the state, even though no crime was laid to his charge. An urn stood in one of the places of assembly, into which any citizen might throw a shell or piece of tile, bearing the name of him whom they desired to exile, and if these shells amounted to six thousand, he was declared to be ostracised, and obliged to leave Attica for a certain term of years.

All these precautions did not, however, prevent the democracy from suffering a great danger soon after the first institution. Pisistratus, an able man, much loved by the people, wounded himself, and then by pretending that his enemies had tried to murder him, persuaded the citizens to give him a guard of soldiers, by whose means he made himself chief ruler. He was once banished, but he returned in a splendid chariot, accompanied by a tall handsome young girl, dressed as the goddess Athene, who presented him to the citizens, commanding them to obey him as her favoured servant.

The more ignorant Athenians were deceived by this profane trick, and received him joyfully; he was soon after driven away again, but returning, firmly established himself as tyrant of Athens. He was a merciful ruler, and is noted for having formed the beautiful garden called the Lyceum, where the philosophers taught, and the young men contended in all exercises which could strengthen the body or mind; and he also first caused the poems of Homer to be collected and transcribed.

At his death, in 527, he was succeeded by his two sons, Hippias and Hipparchus, who governed more harshly, and the people became impatient of the yoke. Two young men, named Harmodius and Aristogiton, whose family had been insulted by them, resolved to murder them at a festival, but only succeeded in killing Hipparchus. The two assassins were put to death, and Hippias reigned alone; but his brother's death had made him so cruel and suspicious, that his tyranny grew worse and worse. At last his life was threatened by the Athenians; he was obliged to leave the city in secret, and after several years of wandering, found a refuge at the court of Darius. The flight of Hippias took place in the year 510, when the democracy was restored to Athens, and statues were raised to Harmodius and Aristogiton, as the deliverers of their country.

PART VI. OTHER GREEK STATES AND COLONIES.
B. C. 1313–499.

The southern peninsula of Greece was called the Peloponnesus, or island of Pelops, from one of the ancient Kings of Mycæne, and it contained several small states besides that of Laconia.

North of the Isthmus of Corinth, and of Attica, lay the territory of Bœotia, where a number of cities leagued together, and yearly elected as their governor a magistrate called the Bœotarch. The chief of these cities was Thebes, which claimed to have been founded by Cadmus, one of the first settlers in Greece, whose history is one of the wildest of the Greek legends. He was said to have come from Egypt in search of his sister Europa, whom Jupiter, in the form of a bull, had carried off to Crete. On arriving at the site of Thebes he encountered a dragon, and having slain it, was instructed to sow its teeth in the earth. The dragon's teeth sprung up as fully armed warriors, who fought together till all were slain except five; these assisted Cadmus in founding the city of Thebes, and were believed to be the ancestors of the chief citizens. Cadmus was the grandfather of the hero-god, Dionysos, and was believed to have been changed into a serpent.

Œdipus, the last King of Thebes, slew his father, without knowing him, and was banished; but he was attended in his old age and blindness by his faithful daughter Antigone. His two sons killed each other, and the crimes and misfortunes of this unhappy house were next to those of the family of Agamemnon, the favourite subject of the Greek poets.

In historical time the government was, as has been said, elective. The Bœotians were despised by the other Greeks as being of dull intellect, although Pindar, one of the greatest of poets, was of their nation.

Thessaly was the most northern Greek state; and Epirus, Macedon, and Ætolia, which lay beyond it, were considered as barbarous. All the true Greeks did not, however, live within the narrow bounds of their own country; many colonies had been sent out by all the chief tribes, both to the islands and to Asia. The Æolians held the north-west of Asia Minor, and the Ionians had settled between the rivers Hæmus and Mæander, where the chief town was Ephesus, famed for the splendid Temple of Artemis or Diana, which contained a black image of the goddess, said to have fallen from heaven. They had also many islands in the Ægean Sea, and those on the western side of Greece, still called the Ionian Isles. The Dorians had a few towns to the south of Asia Minor, but their principal settlements were to the westward, in the island of Sicily, where stood their great city of Syracuse, with a number of lesser towns around it. In Italy there were so many Greeks, that the southern part was long called Magna Grecia, or Greater Greece; and here was the town of Sybaris, so famed for its sloth and luxury, that the inhabitants were said to have killed their cocks for wakening them too early in the morning. All the colonies kept up their connection with the parent state, and considered the glory and good of Greece as their own. Homer himself was born either in Asia Minor, or in one of the isles, but no less than seven places disputed the honour between them.

After the conquest of Lydia, Cyrus subdued many of the colonies, and Darius Hystaspes followed up his successes, till the whole peninsula was under his power. He then made himself master of several of the islands, and formed designs for subduing Greece itself. In these he was much encouraged by Hippias, the tyrant who had taken refuge at his court, and who wished to see his fall avenged upon Athens. The Queen Atossa wished for Athenian and Spartan slaves; Darius himself had been much struck by the sight of a tall handsome Greek girl, who was at once spinning, carrying a pitcher of water on her head, and leading a horse by the bridle; and to his desire of conquest was added that of revenge, when he learnt that in 499 the Ionians of Asia Minor, with the assistance of the Athenians, had risen against his officers, and had burnt the town of Sardis.

CHAPTER V.

PERSIAN INVASION OF GREECE. B.C. 490–465.

PART I. MARATHON. 490.

In the year 490, Darius completed his preparations against Greece, and sent forth a considerable fleet and army, under the command of the satraps Datis and Artaphernes. It was against Athens that their attacks were especially directed, and they therefore sailed for Attica, and under the direction of Hippias, landed in the Bay of Marathon, which was only separated by a ridge of hills from Athens itself.

The Athenians sent to ask aid from the surrounding states, but the Spartans did not arrive in time, and the only allies who came to their support, were a little band from the small state of Platæa. The Athenians were greatly outnumbered by the Persian host, but they bravely prepared to meet the danger, and called out all their fighting men. According to the laws, the army was under ten generals, with equal rights, who each had the command for one day; but Aristides, knowing that a war thus carried on could not succeed, set the example of resigning his turn to Miltiades, the most able among them, and persuaded the others to do the same.

Miltiades led his little army across the hill, and came in sight of the glittering ranks of the Persians, drawn up in a long line stretching across the plain of Marathon. The battle was very short. Without giving the Persians time to use their darts and javelins, the Athenians suddenly rushed upon them, and fought hand to hand. In the centre, the Athenians were broken, but their two wings were victorious, and then closing on the enemy's centre, totally routed it. The Persians fled in utter confusion, only attempting to reach the ships; but they were so closely pursued, that seven ships were seized by the Athenians, and there was an immense slaughter of the troops left on shore. The rest of the fleet escaped, and rounding the bay, appeared about to make a descent on Athens, but Miltiades, hastily marching back, arrived as soon as they did, so that they could attempt nothing, and sailed away to carry home the news of their defeat.

There were great rejoicings at Athens, and Miltiades at first was held in great honour; but he was not a man of high character, and he was soon suspected of double dealing. He led an expedition to conquer the Isle of Paros, and was there wounded and forced to retreat to Athens, where he was brought to trial for his want of fairness in conducting the enterprise, and was sentenced to die. In consideration of his services, the penalty was changed into a fine of fifty talents, but he was unable to raise the sum, and was therefore thrown into prison, where he soon died of his wounds.

The confidence of the Athenians was at this time divided between two great men, Aristides and Themistocles. Aristides was called the Just, from his unswerving uprightness and unselfishness; he was only desirous of the good of his country and her true honour and welfare, with scarcely a thought, in comparison, of his own wealth or advancement. Themistocles was more acute and clever; he loved Athens much, but he served her chiefly with a view to his own greatness and power, and he tried to win the favour of the people by presents and flatteries, instead of by uprightness and honourable conduct. For a time these plans succeeded; and when he found that Aristides stood in the way of his views, he was able to raise so strong a party against this just man, that they ostracised him, and sent him into exile. It is said that a freeman of Athens, coming in from the country, met Aristides, and not knowing him, and being unable to write, begged him to set down on his shell the name of the person whom he wished to ostracise. The name was that of Aristides himself, who, after writing it, only asked why this Aristides was to be exiled. "I cannot tell," said the man; "for my part, I would only get rid of him because I am tired of hearing him called the Just."

By votes given probably for no better reason, Aristides was sent into exile, while Themistocles became the most influential man in the Athenian state.

It was at this time that Æschylus, the first great composer of tragedies, was living at Athens. At the feast of Dionysos or Bacchus, the wine god, it had always been customary to have songs and dances in honour of him, and speeches were made in the character of the gods or heroes. These speeches became dialogues, and thus commenced the acting of tragedies founded on the legends of early Greece. Some of those of Æschylus, which have been preserved to our time, contain some of the sublimest poetry ever composed, and show more than any other writings of the classic times, the disposition of these early Greeks to seek for the unknown Ruler of events.

PART II. THERMOPYLÆ. B. C. 485–480.

THE repulse at Marathon only made the Persians desirous of revenge, and Darius made great preparations for another invasion of Greece, but he died in the year 485, before they were completed. He is believed to be the king mentioned in the book of Ezra, who forbade the Samaritans to molest the Jews in the rebuilding of the Temple.

He was succeeded by his son Kshayarsha, called by the Greeks, Xerxes. Daniel had predicted of him, "The fourth (king after Cyrus) shall be far greater than they all, and by his strength through his riches he shall stir up all against the realm of Grecia." The fulfilment of that prophecy is now to be shown.

Xerxes prepared eagerly for the war. In the voyage round the coast (since the fleet never ventured directly across the Ægean Sea) vessels were often in danger from storms, while rounding the rocky promontory of Mount Athos, and Xerxes gave orders that a canal should be cut between the mountain and the main land, wide enough to allow his ships to pass. It is said that he sent a message to the mountain god, bidding him not to put rocks or stones in the way of the workmen, otherwise his mountain should be cut down and cast into the sea. Xerxes also threw a magnificent bridge across the Hellespont, a mile in length, formed of a double line of ships, lashed together, anchored down, and covered by two causeways. When these works were injured by a storm, in his passion he caused the waves to be beaten, and fetters to be thrown into them, while the chief workmen were either put to death or scourged.

He sat on a lofty throne to watch his army cross the bridge, while a scribe read to him the name of each nation as it passed. Multitudes were there; the 10,000 Persian infantry, called the Immortals, glittering with gold and silver; the Assyrians with wooden clubs; the Indians with cotton vests; the Lydians armed in Greek fashion; the Arab horsemen with their bows; the Ethiopians, their dark skins painted half red and half white, and bearing lances tipped with the horn of the antelope; while in the open sea the most skilful Phœnician sailors were manœuvering the fleet in the light of the rising sun. As Xerxes looked on these hosts of living beings, he burst into tears at the thought that in a few short years not one of all these would remain alive; but this was but the emotion of a moment, nor did it cause him to spare one man from the fate to which his ambition was hurrying them.

In the meantime the Greeks, encouraged by the victory of Marathon, had united to face the danger, under the orders of a council which met at Corinth. The first post which they resolved to defend was Thermopylæ, a narrow pass of Mount Œta, the only entrance to Greece on the land side, since the mountains beyond it were impassable; and on the side towards the sea was a morass which could not be crossed.

Leonidas, one of the Kings of Sparta, was charged

with the defence of this post, with 300 of his own subjects and several bands from the other states. When the Persians arrived before the pass there they found the Spartans, some polishing their weapons, others combing their long hair, as they always did before a battle. Xerxes sent orders to them to come and deliver up their arms, but Leonidas, true Spartan as he was, only returned for answer, "Come and take them."

For three days the Persians vainly attacked the gallant defenders of the pass. In so narrow a space but few could fight at once, so that their numbers were of no avail, and the slavish troops of the Eastern despot were only scourged on to the assault to perish under the blows of the brave men who fought for their homes and their children. Xerxes was full of rage and despair; but at last a traitor, one of the inhabitants of the country, came in secret to his camp, and offered to guide his forces up a winding path which led over the mountain, so that the Spartans might be attacked on both sides at once.

Early in the morning tidings were brought to Leonidas that the path had been betrayed, and the enemy would soon be upon him. There was still time for retreat, but no Spartan ever turned his face from the foe, and Leonidas, with his own 300, and with 700 Thespians who would not forsake him, took leave of his allies, and remained devoted to certain death. On came the Persians, pouring at once from the fatal path, and from the camp in front, and in upon the brave thousand closed that double tide, overwhelming them with darts, javelins, and clubs. Leonidas fell among the first; his Spartans rushed to guard his corpse, and around it every man of them was slain; but not unavenged, for there too fell whole piles of Persians, heaped up in hosts around the brave devoted men, whose constancy has been honoured through every succeeding age.

PART III. DEFEAT OF XERXES. B. C. 480–465.

When the tidings of the loss of Thermopylæ arrived, the council at Corinth resolved to build a wall across the Isthmus, so as to defend the Peloponnesus, and leave the rest of Greece to its fate. Athens, thus deserted, sent to ask the oracle at Delphi, how it best might meet the coming danger. The answer was thus: "The city is doomed to ruin, but a wooden wall shall shelter the citizens, and at Salamis shall women be made childless."

Some thought that this meant that the citizens should take shelter in the Acropolis, which had once been guarded by a palisade of stakes; but Themistocles persuaded them that their wooden walls meant their ships, and that they were to escape in them; and every Athenian therefore embarked, except a few who chose to trust to the Acropolis. The women were landed at Ægina and Trœzene; and the men, with their ships, joined the rest of the Greek fleet at the Isle of Salamis.

The land army of the Persians ruined and burnt Athens, and carried off the statues and other ornaments, and the fleet proceeded to Salamis in such numbers, that the courage of some of the Greeks began to fail, and they proposed to sail away before the Persians could enter the Gulf of Sunium. While they were deliberating, a knock was heard at the door, and Themistocles was called to speak to a stranger. It was the banished Aristides. "Themistocles," said he, "let us still be rivals, but let our strife be, which best may serve our country. I am come to say that you are wasting words in debating whether to leave Salamis. We are encircled, and can only escape by cutting a way through the enemy."

Xerxes's fleet had, in fact, arrived, and so completely shut up the opening of the gulf, that Aristides had with difficulty made his way through it by night to bring the tidings. Xerxes had caused a throne to be raised on the neighbouring hills in order that he might see the battle, but the sight was far otherwise from what he had expected. The Greeks made the first attack, and quickly gained a complete victory, taking and sinking no less than 200 vessels, and dispersing the rest. His loss was so great, that he became alarmed for his own safety, and hurried back to Persia as fast as he could, leaving behind him a part of his fleet and army, under the satrap Mardonius.

After spending the winter in Thessaly, Mardonius advanced towards the south of Greece, but was met at Platæa, slain, and his army routed by the Spartans, led by their king, Pausanias, and the Athenians, under Aristides. Here the Greeks, for the first time, saw and laughed to scorn the quantity of gold and jewels, the cushions, carpets, and eastern luxuries with which the Persians encumbered their marches. The miserable remains of the invading army retreated through Thessaly and Thrace, and at last, after dreadful sufferings and heavy losses, returned to their own country.

The Athenians came back to their beloved city, which they raised from its ruins in greater splendour than before. Themistocles assisted much by his advice in restoring and beautifying it; but the citizens were becoming sensible of his dangerous ambition, and in the year 741 he was ostracised. About the same time

Pausanias of Sparta, discontented with his own scanty and divided power, was found to be plotting to bring Xerxes to Greece. He fled to a temple, whence the Spartans did not venture to remove him by force, but they shut up all the approaches, so that he was starved to death. Themistocles was engaged in the same plot, and was obliged to fly to the country of the Molossi, on the coast of the Adriatic. Admetus, the king, was his enemy, but Themistocles, nevertheless, entered his house, and sat down on the hearth among the household gods, and holding the king's little son between his knees, asked protection, which, claimed in this manner, could not be refused.

He afterwards escaped to Persia, where the king received him with favour, and listened eagerly to the plans which he was base enough to propose for the conquest of Greece. Honours were lavished on him, and he lived in the midst of wealth and magnificence; but he felt himself all the time a miserable, traitorous exile, and at length put an end to his own life by poison.

Far otherwise was it with Aristides the Just, who had so differently borne the ill-will of his fellow-citizens. He lived to convince them of their injustice by his own generosity, and returning to his own home, aided by his steady uprightness in establishing the greatness of his country. He there closed his life, after a peaceful and honoured old age, having shown how pure and steadfast might be the life of one who really strove to be a law unto himself.

Xerxes died in 465, and was succeeded by his son Artaxerxes, called Longimanus, or Long-armed. Both these kings are called in the Bible Ahasuerus; and one or other of them was the husband of Esther, but it is not certain whether it was the father or the son. From this time there is little worthy of note in the history of the Persian kings, as their vigour died away in the effeminacy of their palaces; and the monstrous cruelties to which they were impelled by their unrestrained passions became more frightful, till they were ripe for vengeance, and their empire was destroyed. Henceforth, therefore, we shall find the tide of invasion flowing back again, till, instead of a Persian monarch at Athens, we find a Greek prince at Babylon.

CHAPTER VI.

THE GREEK STATES. b.c. 432–361.

PART I. THE PELOPONNESIAN WAR. B.C. 431–404.

The Greeks, as has been shown in the history of the Persian invasion, were almost unconquerable when united; but divided as they were into a number of little states, and these again rent by party factions, without any one head to guide, any one principle to be obeyed, they wasted their powers in dissensions, did nothing worthy of their great talents, and at length were reduced to subjection.

The period immediately succeeding the retreat of Xerxes was the brightest in Athenian history. The three great tragedians, Æschylus, Sophocles, and Euripides, then composed their works. Herodotus had just completed his history, Thucydides was commencing his, Phidias was carving his exquisite sculptures, and Pericles, one of the most able men that ever lived, was the director of public affairs. He was indeed ambitious, but he had a true love for his own city and for Greece, and so well was he able to win and keep the hearts of the Athenians, that he directed their councils, with little intermission, for forty years.

A jealousy had long been growing up between Athens and Sparta, and it was only the wise forbearance of Aristides, and other Athenians of like wisdom, that had prevented a struggle for the chief power. In 432, however, a quarrel arose between Corinth and the Isle of Corcyra, one of the Ionian isles, now called Corfu. The Spartans took the part of the city, and Pericles induced the Athenians to take up the cause of the island.

The contest thus commenced, and known in history as the Peloponnesian war, lasted twenty-seven years; but Pericles did not live to see the ruin it occasioned. A dreadful plague broke out at Athens, where it raged for two years; and not only the houses, but the streets and temples, were filled with dead. Pericles lost all his family, and at length fell sick himself, and died after lingering longer than usual. A little before his death, some of his friends were gathered round his couch. They were recounting his great deeds, his victories, and the benefits he had conferred upon Athens, adorning her with buildings to such an extent, that it was said that he found her of brick, and left her of marble. Pericles exerted his failing strength to tell them that they had forgotten what he considered as his chief glory, namely, that he had never caused any Athenian to put on mourning; meaning that in all his struggles for power he had always spared his rivals.

There was no one of equal merit to supply his place. His young ward, Alcibiades, was not his inferior in talent, but too vain, haughty, and unstable, to keep the confidence of the people. Alcibiades early lost his father, and being very rich, had always been surrounded by flatterers, who did much to spoil his really noble character. He loved virtue, and would sometimes be a most earnest pupil of the great philosopher Socrates; but, on the other hand, he so loved pleasure, that next he would be the foremost in some mad frolic of the dissolute youth of Athens; but everywhere his vanity was conspicuous. His personal beauty was great, and in the city his dress was costly and studied; while in the camp his arms were very rich, his helmet gilded, and his shield adorned with gold and ivory. Wherever he was in command the Athenians triumphed; but his imprudent conduct at home raised up many enemies against him. The most important attempt made by the Athenians in the course of the war was upon Syracuse, the Dorian colony in Sicily; and the army sent on this expedition was placed under the command of Alcibiades, Nicias, a good and brave old man, and a third general of less note. Just before his departure, the busts of Hermes, which were placed at regular intervals on the roads of Attica, so as to mark the distance, were one morning found to be defaced and injured. It was probably the work of some drunken revellers, and there is little reason to think that Alcibiades was concerned in it; but after he had sailed for Syracuse, his enemies stirred up the people to believe that he had been guilty of this profanity, and that it further showed that he had designs against the state.

Unreasonable as the charge was, the rage of the Athenians was excited to a great degree; they seized his property, condemned him to death, and called upon the priests and priestesses to curse him. One priestess alone refused, saying that her office was blessing, not cursing; and Alcibiades was obliged to leave the army in Sicily, where he had been greatly distinguishing himself, and going to Sparta, made friends with the enemies of his country.

In his absence, the Athenians in Sicily met with nothing but disaster under Nicias, whose talent was not equal to the occasion. Their fleet was at length totally defeated by the Spartans in a great sea-fight before Syracuse. This was their ruin; the land army was left without means of returning home, and after a vain struggle were made prisoners. Nicias was put to death, and the other captives cruelly allowed to perish from neglect. Some few Athenians who escaped wandered about defenceless and half-starved; and it is said that some of them owed their maintenance to the poetry of the tragedian Euripides, in which the Sicilian Greeks so delighted, that they afforded food and shelter to those who could repeat passages from his plays.

The Persians, perceiving how much advantage they might gain by the dissensions among the Greeks, gave their aid to the weaker party, in order to prejudice the stronger; and the Spartans were not ashamed to receive money from Cyrus, second son of King Darius Nothus, and at that time Satrap of Lydia. They thus gained several advantages over the Athenians, who were at length obliged to invite Alcibiades to return, and received him with high honours. He won three battles for them, but still without removing the general dislike and mistrust; and he was at length again obliged to leave Athens, and betake himself, with some armed followers, to a rocky stronghold in the Thracian Chersonesus, where he became an unwilling witness of the ruin of his country.

The Athenians were still much stronger by sea than their enemies; and their fleet of 180 ships pursued that of Sparta, under Lysander, as far as the Hellespont, where the Spartans drew up their vessels at the mouth of a little stream called Ægospotamos, or the Goat's River. The Athenians came up to offer them battle; but as they did not move from their position, rowed back again to a little distance, and then leaving their vessels, dispersed through the neighbouring country in search of food or plunder. For five days this was repeated, the Athenians offering battle every morning, and landing every afternoon. Alcibiades, from his mountain fortress, perceived the danger of their thus leaving the ships unguarded, and came down to warn them, but the generals bade him remember he was no longer their leader, and he was obliged to withdraw.

Their folly was soon punished. On the sixth day, as soon as all had left there galleys, Lysander with his whole fleet came suddenly upon them. Only eight ships were manned, and with Conon, one of the generals, sailed to Cyprus, and there remained, sending one ship to carry the tidings to Athens, where he himself could not bear to show his face. All the rest fell into the hands of the Spartans; and all the crews, who were scattered about the peninsula, were made prisoners, and cruelly massacred, Lysander setting the example by killing the chief general with his own hand.

The strength of Athens was so broken by this disaster, that the Spartans gained possession of the city after a short siege. They threw down the walls, burnt the remaining galleys, destroyed the fortifications of the Piræus, and even took away the old form of government, establishing, instead of the nine archons, a council of thirty, called by the unfortunate Athenians the Thirty Tyrants, who were so cruel, that more blood was shed by them in eight months than all the twenty-seven years of the Peloponnesian war had cost Athens.

PART II. SOCRATES AND GREEK PHILOSOPHY. B.C. 402.

DURING the rule of the Thirty Tyrants, Alcibiades was murdered in Phrygia, and it is thought at their instigation. His assassins set fire to his house, and not daring to come within reach of his sword, overwhelmed him with a shower of darts, and thus put an end to a melancholy life of wasted talents and disappointed hopes. Many of the noblest Athenians were banished by the Thirty; others left the city, unable to endure their rule; and all these uniting, entered Athens by force of arms, expelled the tyrants, and restored the constitution of Solon.

There was now a desire among the citizens to resume the old habits and ways of thought in which the great men of their fathers' times had been trained up, hoping thus to recover the superiority which they had lost; and in their wish to revive the spirit of former times, they turned in anger on the man who, as they thought, wished to lead them into other parts.

This man was Socrates, the best of heathen philosophers—scarcely indeed to be called a heathen, so nearly had his pure life, and his obedience to the feeble light vouchsafed him, brought him to a knowledge of the truth. He believed that there was one Great Being, ruler of all, Who loved virtue, protected the good, and gave each man a voice within himself, which would guide him aright if he would but listen to its dictates. He dwelt but little on the multitude of superstitions around him, for though his better sense revolted at them, they were the faith in which he had been brought up; and he had too much reverence to indulge in questioning unbelief. He said a man's life was not long enough to inquire into his own nature and into that of the great God; and so he lived, engaged in one constant struggle after the beams of a brighter light, acting in every instance by the rules of virtue, daily teaching in the porticos and temples, and striving to raise and refine the minds of his fellow-citizens.

He had fought with great honour for his country, and had once saved the life of his pupil, Alcibiades, by carrying him out of the battle when severely wounded; but unfortunately one of the Thirty had once been his pupil, which occasioned an idea among the Athenians that he approved their measures. A dislike of him thus arose: the comic poet, Aristophanes, held him up to ridicule in a comedy, where he was represented as teaching young men to disobey their fathers; and he was at length brought to trial, and condemned to die as a corrupter of youth, and setter forth of a new worship.

In the space between his sentence and execution, he applied himself to console his friends. One of them lamented that he should be put to death an innocent man. "What!" said he, "would you have me die guilty?" They arranged all the means of his escape, but he would not consent, because he would not break the laws, only asking, with a smile, if they had found any place out of Attica where people did not die. Above all, as his death came nearer, so the conviction came more strongly upon him that life was beyond it. It was his outer case, he said, and not Socrates that was to perish; and he warned his friends again and again that the soul would carry nothing with it save its good or bad deeds, for which it would be requited with happiness or misery.

Hemlock had been appointed as the means of his death; and when the draught was brought him, he received it with calmness, and lying down on his bed, drew his last breath in peace, while his spirit went to have all its doubts set at rest for ever.

His philosophy was in great part carried out by his pupil, Plato, many of whose works have come down to the present day, but who never seems to have equalled his master.

It may be as well to mention here the principle systems of philosophy that were current among the Greeks. The earliest was that of Pythagoras, who lived about the year 600, and whose real history is lost. The most remarkable part of his belief was, that the soul, instead of dying, animated the bodies of different animals in succession. The practice he inculcated was a life of self-command, truthfulness, and uprightness; and it was this principle that led most of the better Greeks to their noble actions.

In after days there were the Stoics, so called from their teaching in porticos, called in Greek *stoa*. They taught a stern disregard for the ills of life, as what must soon be at an end: while, on the other hand, the disciples of Epicurus held that the gods did not concern themselves about the actions of men, and that as life is short, it should be enjoyed as much as possible; and thus, according as their minds were base or refined, they sought their pleasures in low or high pursuits. "Let us crown ourselves with rose-buds before they are withered," might well have been the motto of an Epicurian. In the disputes of these different schools of philosophy, the Athenians found their chief interest and amusement during the decay of their city, while their chief desire was daily "to tell or to hear some new thing."

PART III. RETREAT OF THE TEN THOUSAND. B.C. 401–400.

THE son of Xerxes, Artaxerxes Longimanus, or the Long-armed, called in Persia Ardisheer Dirazdust, died in 424, and was succeeded by Darius Nothus, who, at his death, left two sons, Artaxerxes Mnemon, and Cyrus, Governor of Sardis.

Cyrus, having been born after his father was king, imagined that he had a better right to the throne than his elder brother, and soon after his father's death resolved to seize the crown. He collected all the troops he could obtain at Sardis, and wrote to Lysander at Sparta, desiring him to raise for him a body of Greeks, with whose help, as he pretended, he wished to subdue the revolted province of Pisidia.

About 11,000 Greeks, under the command of a Spartan, named Clearchus, accepted the invitation, joined Cyrus at Sardis, and had marched with him as far as Tarsus before they learnt that his real design was against his brother. At first they refused to proceed; but Cyrus induced them to accompany him, and led them across the Euphrates without meeting an enemy. At Cunaxa, about seventy-five miles further, they encountered Artaxerxes at the head of all his forces, and a battle took place, in which, as usual, the Greeks easily overcame the barbarians, but Cyrus fell in a combat hand to hand with his brother. It is uncertain whether Artaxerxes himself killed him, but he was so bent on having what he thought the credit of having done so, that he put to death two of his servants for laying claim to it.

The army of Cyrus, thus left in the heart of the enemy's country, began at first to enter into negociations with Artaxerxes, who, by pretending that he would allow the Greeks to return home another way, induced them to cross the Tigris on a bridge of boats, thus placing a second great river between them and Greece. Here, however, they became convinced that the Persians of Cyrus's army were betraying them to

Artaxerxes, and stood upon their guard; but at their encampment, on the banks of the river Zab, Clearchus and the other chief officers having gone imprudently to the tent of one of the satraps, were all seized, some immediately put to death, and others reserved for torture at the Persian court.

Their enemies doubtless expected that the soldiers would fall an easy prey to them, but they little knew the temper of the Greeks. An Athenian, named Xenophon, once a pupil of Socrates, rose up to cheer the spirits of his countrymen. "If they were to die," said he, "they should at least die like men, and there was no need to despond. If the Tigris was here too wide to be crossed, why not trace it upwards, till it dwindled to a rivulet?"

All were encouraged by his bold counsel; and now commenced the famous retreat of the ten thousand Greeks, so noted for unshaken courage, endurance, and discipline, in circumstances where most armies would have lost hope, given way, dispersed, and thus have been ruined. The enemy's horse hovered on their skirts, and pursued them along the banks of the river; then they were harassed by the barbarous tribes of the mountains; and when they entered upon the mountains of Armenia, their sufferings from cold and hunger were dreadful. They had to struggle through snow six feet deep, where many lost their toes and fingers from the frost, and their eyesight from the glare of the snow; while the natives attacked them, and they had neither guides nor provisions. Still they kept up a bold and hopeful spirit; and at last, as they were ascending a mountain named Theche, Xenophon, who was in the rear, perceived that the van had stopped, and as he rode forward to learn the cause, was greeted by a loud and joyful shout, "The sea! the sea!"

There lay glittering in the distance the Euxine, a branch of the same sea whose waves dashed and foamed in the gulfs and bays of their own homes, whose waters every Greek might well hail as the friend of his childhood. Loud were their cries of joy as they wept, embraced each other, gazed upon the bright waters, and finally heaped up a pile of stones to mark this happy spot, and crowned it with their best offerings.

Their worst troubles were now over; and Xenophon at length arrived at the Greek city of Byzantium, with no less than 8,600 still remaining of the army, which he had conducted through so immense a tract of the enemy's country. This expedition proved to the Greeks how weak the unwieldly Persian empire was at its heart, and how easily its best forces might be overcome.

Xenophon wrote an account of his retreat, together with several other works; and he is the chief historian of this period whose works still remain.

PART IV. THEBAN SUPREMACY. B.C. 394–362.

An attempt was made against Persia in 394 by Agesilaus, King of Sparta, who was invited by the Greek colonies in Asia Minor to attempt their deliverance. Agesilaus was small in stature, and lame from his childhood; but he was one of the ablest commanders Sparta ever produced, and a very strict observer of the discipline of Lycurgus. A Persian satrap, who was invited to a conference with him, was much surprised to find him very plainly dressed, sitting on the ground, eating dry bread and vegetables; and the son of the satrap so admired his simplicity and the straight-forwardness of his answers, that he lingered behind his father, begged for the king's friendship, and exchanged swords with him.

Agesilaus had gained several successes in Asia during the two years he remained there, but these were rendered fruitless by a league which was at that time forming against his own country.

Conon, that single general who had escaped from Ægospotamos, went to the Persian satrap, and by representing to him that the safety of Asia would be best secured by raising up enemies against Sparta at home, obtained from him a sum of money sufficient to restore the walls of Athens; and returning home, obtained the help of the Thebans, built up the fortifications, and enabled Athens once more to lift up her head.

Thebes, which had of late become very powerful, was at the head of the league against Sparta; but the allies were all defeated at Coronea by Agesilaus, and the Spartans followed up their success by persecuting all the lesser towns depending on Thebes, and at last by treacherously seizing the Cadmea, or citadel, and putting in a garrison, which was much dreaded by the citizens.

The two greatest men then living in Greece were Epaminondas and Pelopidas, two Thebans, who had saved each others' lives in battle, and had since been united by the most generous friendship. Pelopidas, who was rich, while Epaminondas was poor, used to say that Epaminondas was the only man whom his friend did not entreat him to assist with his wealth; and Epaminondas, when his enemies gave him offices in the state which were considered as the meanest, was said to ennoble them by his wise and complete performance of them.

Pelopidas formed a plot for introducing forces into the city in secret, and surprising the Spartan garrison; but as it involved a dishonourable stratagem, Epaminondas, who would not speak an untrue word even in jest, did not choose to have anything to do with it. By the help of more unscrupulous persons, the plan, however, succeeded. The Spartan garrison were invited to a feast, where the Theban conspirators meeting them in the disguise of revellers and of women, slew them, and regained possession of the Cadmea.

Thebes was again free, and Epaminondas, taking the command of the army, routed the Spartans at Leuctra, under their other king, Cleombrotus; and while all around were praising him for his victory, said that his chief pleasure was in thinking how happy it would make his father and mother. From that time Thebes became the ruling city; and as long as he was at the head of affairs, her measures were wise, just, and prosperous, but her greatness lasted no longer than his life.

In 362 a dispute arose respecting Mantinea, in Arcadia; and before its walls a battle was fought between the Spartans and Thebans, where Epaminondas gained the victory, but early in the day his breast was pierced with a javelin. He was carried out of the battle to a little hill, where his first question was, whether his shield was safe; and when it was shown to him, he allowed his wound to be examined. The weapon still remained in the wound, and it was thought that when it was extracted, the excessive bleeding would probably cause his death. His attendants stood weeping round, without resolution to attempt to draw it out; but he, remaining calm and patient, waited only to hear that the victory was gained, and then grasping the shaft, drew it out himself with a firm hand, and died in a few minutes, leaving behind him a character which is a reproof to many who enjoy a clearer light.

The next year, Agesilaus, though eighty years old, led an expedition against the Persian power in Egypt, and there was attacked with an illness, of which he died.

CHAPTER VII.

THE MACEDONIAN EMPIRE. B.C. 359-334.

PART I. PHILIP OF MACEDON. B.C. 359-336.

AFTER the Battle of Mantinea, the struggle continued between the Greek cities, and Athens at length regained the first place; but in the meantime Macedonia, that northern kingdom which had hitherto been deemed almost barbarous, was acquiring a power dangerous to them all. The reigning monarch was Philip, who had succeeded to the crown in 359, after a long exile, spent for the most part at Thebes, where he had learnt the arts of war and policy from the example of Epaminondas. He was very desirous of being considered as a Greek; invited distinguished men to his court; and ordered public rejoicings in his kingdom when his chariots had won the prize at the Olympian games. He was very clever, and cared little about the justice and honour of the means by which he attained his ends, which were to hold in subjection all the rest of Greece, and to conquer Persia. In the first design he succeeded; for the latter he only prepared the way for his son. He had both to form his officers and his army. The first he attempted by bringing the young nobles to his court, and there instructing them; and in the last he succeeded in a remarkable manner. The chief strength of the army, as he constituted it, was in the phalanx, a body of 6,000 foot-soldiers, fully armed in the Greek fashion, with spears twenty-four feet long.

When drawn up in order of battle, the four front ranks held their spears pointing outwards, and stood at such a space apart, that the foremost line had four spear points between each man and the enemy; or on occasion they marched with their shields touching, so as to form an almost impenetrable wall.

As soon as Philip's designs against Greece were apparent, a strong spirit of resistance showed itself, and chiefly at Athens, where the great orator, Demosthenes, never ceased to rouse his countrymen to maintain their freedom. Demosthenes had trained himself in eloquence under great difficulties; he naturally either stammered, or had an indistinct pronunciation—a defect which he cured by speaking with pebbles in his mouth; and he used to rehearse his speeches to the roaring sea, in order to nerve himself against the clamours of a tumultuous assembly. He so far succeeded, that he often swayed the minds of the Athenians; his name stands as the first of orators; and his Philippics, as his discourses against Philip are called, are considered as models of rhetoric.

At Cheronæa, in 338, a battle was fought by Philip against the allied forces of the Athenians and Thebans. At one time the Athenians gained some advantage; but they used it so ill, that Philip, calling out to his troops, "They do not know how to conquer!" made a sudden charge, and routed them with great slaughter. The Battle of Cheronæa was the end of the independence of Greece, which from that time forward became subject to Macedon, in spite of its many struggles to shake off the yoke, and recover the liberty which had been lost for want of a firm, united, settled government.

The King of Macedon next commenced his arrangements for his other favourite scheme—the invasion of

Asia; but in the year 336, in the midst of the feasts in honour of his daughter's marriage, he was murdered by a young Macedonian noble, who was slain in the first anger of the surrounding guards, without having time to disclose the motive of his crime.

PART II. ALEXANDER IN ASIA MINOR. B.C. 334–333.

ALEXANDER, son of Philip and his Epirot queen Olympias, was twenty years of age when he came to the throne. On the night of his birth the great temple at Ephesus was burnt to the ground by a man named Erostratus, in the foolish desire of making himself notorious; and this Alexander liked to consider as an omen that he should himself kindle a flame in Asia.

He traced his descent by his father's side from Hercules, and by his mother's from Achilles; and throughout his boyhood he seems to have lived in a world of the old Greek poetry, sleeping with Homer's works under his pillow, and dreaming of deeds in which he should rival the fame of the victors of Troy. He was placed under the care of Aristotle, the great philosopher of Stagira, to whom, when Philip had written to announce Alexander's birth, he had said that he knew not whether most to rejoice at having a son, or that his son would have such a teacher as Aristotle.

From him the young Alexander learnt to think deeply, to resolve firmly, and devise plans of government; by others he was instructed in all the graceful accomplishments of the Greeks; and under his father he was trained to act promptly. At fourteen he tamed the noble horse Bucephalus, which no one else dared to mount; two years later he rescued his father in a battle with the Scythians, and he commanded the cavalry at Cheronæa; but he was so young at the time of his accession, that the Greeks thought they had nothing to fear from him.

There were very ungenerous rejoicings at Athens at the murder of Philip. Demosthenes, though he had just lost a daughter, crowned himself with a wreath of flowers, and came with great tokens of joy to announce it to the Athenians so soon after the event, as almost to excite a suspicion that he must have been concerned in the crime. But they found that their joy was unfounded; for no sooner did Thebes take up arms, than Alexander marched against it, destroyed the walls, killed many of the citizens, and blotted it out from the number of Greek cities. The other states did not dare to make any further opposition, and he was thus at leisure to prepare for the invasion of Persia.

Leaving Antipater as Governor of Macedon, he set out in the spring of 334, at the head of 30,000 infantry and 4,500 cavalry, and bade farewell to the native land which he was never to see again. He crossed the Hellespont, and was the first man to leap on Asiatic ground; then, while his forces were landing, he went to visit the spot which had so long been the object of his dreams—the village which marked the site of Troy. He offered a sacrifice at the tomb of Achilles; hung up his own shield in the temple; and took down one which was said to be a relic of the Greek conquerors, intending to have it always borne before him in battle.

His march was at first towards the east, along the shore of the Hellespont, until at the river Granicus he met the Persians drawn up on the other bank of the river, under the command of the satrap Memnon. Alexander himself, at the head of his cavalry, charged through the midst of the rapid stream, won the landing-place, and followed by the phalanx, quickly gained a complete victory.

All the neighbouring country fell into his hands; and after taking possession of it, he changed his course, marching along the shores of the Ægean, and taking all the towns. It was his first object to cut the Persians off from their seaports, and thus deprive them of the use of their fleet, which was so superior to his own, that he never ventured on one sea-fight.

This march round the western and southern coasts of Asia Minor, together with an expedition into the interior, occupied a year; and in the early part of the summer he arrived at Tarsus, in Cilicia. Here, on entering the city, overwhelmed with heat and fatigue, he bathed in the cold waters of the Cydnus, and the chill brought on a violent fever, which nearly cost him his life. A letter was sent to warn him that his physician, Philip, had been bribed by the Persian king to poison him. While he was reading it the physician himself brought him a draught of medicine; the king put the letter into his hand, took the cup, and drank it off, even before Philip could profess his innocence. In three days' time, he was again able to appear at the head of his troops, and not before he was needed, for the enemy's army was near at hand, under King Darius Codomanus himself.

The Persians advanced in great state. First came a number of persons bearing silver altars, on which burnt the sacred fire; then followed the Magi, and 365 youths robed in scarlet, in honour of the days of the year. Next came the chariot and horses of the Sun, with their attendants, and afterwards the army itself, the Immortal Band, with gold-handled lances, white robes, and jewelled corslets, and a host of others of less note, all far more fit for show than for battle. Darius himself, arrayed in purple robes and glittering with jewels, was in the midst, in a chariot covered with gold ornaments; and with him came his mother, Sisygambis, his principal wife, his daughters, a number of other ladies, and a multitude of slaves. This unwieldy and useless host took up their position on the hilly ground above the city of Issus, where they were so entangled among the rocks, that their numbers were of little profit to them; and it was an easy victory for the Macedonians. No sooner did Darius see that the day was against him, than he turned his chariot and fled, leaving his family to fall into the hands of the conqueror, whilst he himself hastened to Babylon to collect another army.

Alexander treated the mother, wife, and children of Darius, with great kindness and courtesy, sending an officer to assure them of his protection, and going the next morning to visit them, accompanied by his friend, Hephæstion, a young man of his own age. Alexander, though of beautiful and noble countenance, and well formed for strength and activity, was rather short in stature, and as his dress was very simple, Sisygambis mistook Hephæstion for the King of Macedon, and threw herself on the ground before him; and she was greatly confused and distressed when she discovered her error; but Alexander said, as he raised her, "You were not deceived, for he is Alexander's other self." He gave her the name of mother, never sat down in her presence except at her request, and showed in every point a respect and courtesy such as she had probably never before received from the Asiatic princes, who always held women in contempt.

PART III. CONQUEST OF PALESTINE AND EGYPT.
B. C. 334–332.

PURSUING his intention of first destroying the naval power of the Persian empire, Alexander next entered Phœnicia, and readily received the submission of Zidon; but Tyre refused to admit him within the walls. New Tyre, which was built after the seventy years' desolation which followed the conquest by Nebuchadnezzar, stood upon an island about half a mile from the shore, and was inhabited by a numerous and brave people, who thought themselves secure from an enemy who had no fleet to bring against them.

Alexander was, however, not to be daunted by any difficulty. He at first attempted to build a causeway from the shore to the island, and when the Tyrians destroyed his works he went to Zidon and there obtained a fleet, by means of which he at length took the city after a seven months' siege. He stained his victory by a cruel slaughter, and made slaves of all whose lives were spared, excepting a few whom the Zidonians contrived to conceal in their ships. This was the final fall of the great merchant city, so often predicted by Isaiah and Ezekiel.

He then marched through the rest of Palestine, intending to punish Jerusalem, which had stood loyal to Darius, and refused to send him supplies. The Jews, on his approach, prayed for guidance and protection, and it was revealed to Jaddua, the high-priest, that he should open the gates and go forth in his sacred robes to receive the Grecian conqueror. It was accordingly done; and Jaddua, in the vestments of Aaron, came forth at the head of the choir of priests in white garments as Alexander and the Greeks mounted the hill towards the city. No sooner did the king meet the procession than he bent down to the ground in adoration, and walked in the midst of the priests to the Temple, where a sacrifice was offered; and he not only spared the Jews, but showed them much favour.

He told his generals that before he left Macedon he had seen in a dream a figure exactly resembling that of the high-priest, which had foretold all his conquests. And surely there is little reason to doubt that such a revelation might be made to a conqueror marked out as clearly by prophecy as Nebuchadnezzar or Cyrus, before he set out on the work appointed for him. Both his predecessors in conquest, as soon as they came in contact with the chosen people, were taught that they were the subjects of prophecy; and Alexander in his turn, was shown by Jaddua the prediction of Daniel, which spoke of him as a he-goat, (the actual ensign of Macedon,) "who came from the West, and smote the Ram, and brake his two horns, and cast him down and trampled on him." "And the rough goat was the King of Grecia."

He then proceeded southwards, besieged and took Gaza, after a brave resistance, which he cruelly requited, and entered Egypt, subduing it with little difficulty. On one of the peninsulas formed by the mouth of the Nile, he founded a city, called after his name Alexandria, which became the capital of Egypt under its Greek rulers, and one of the most famous cities in the world. He made an expedition to the temple of Jupiter Ammon, on an oasis in the Lybian desert, and consulted the oracle there, and then after appointing a Macedonian satrap in Egypt, retraced his steps towards the Holy Land, and marched towards Babylonia, where Darius was again collecting his forces to oppose him.

PART IV.   CONQUEST OF PERSIA.   B. C. 331–327.

ALEXANDER crossed the Euphrates and Tigris without opposition, and the decisive battle did not take place till he reached the plain of Arbela, close to Gaugamela, (the city of Darius Hystaspes' camel,) where the Persians were drawn up to receive him.

The Macedonians wished to make a night attack, but Alexander would not permit it, saying that he disdained to steal a victory; and the combat took place the next day.

The present army of Persians was drawn from the more remote regions of Bactria and Parthia, where the men were more warlike, and they fought better than any whom the Macedonians had before encountered; but Darius himself fled early in the day, leaving behind him his bow and shield; his men lost courage, and followed him, and Alexander was left master of the field of Arbela.

This battle placed in his power all the western part of the Persian Empire, and he had only to march to the great cities of Babylon, Susa, Ecbatana, and Persepolis, to take possession of the huge stores of treasures there heaped up by the Persian kings, which he now distributed among his followers with royal bounty. The unfortunate Darius escaped into Bactria, where two satraps, in whom he had confided, treacherously seized him and made him prisoner, carrying him along with them as they fled before Alexander, until at length, being closely pressed by the Greeks, they threw their darts at him, and left him lying on the ground mortally wounded.

He was still alive when some of the Greeks came up,

but died before the arrival of Alexander. The conqueror wept as he beheld the corpse of the last of a line of such great princes; he threw his own cloak over it, and sent it to Sisygambis at Babylon, where it was buried with great magnificence.

The wife of Darius had died a prisoner, but Sisygambis still remained with her grandchildren at Babylon. Only once does Alexander seem to have hurt her feelings, and this was through ignorance of Persian customs. He showed her some robes of his sisters' own weaving and embroidery, and offered to have her granddaughters instructed in the same art; at which she wept, since Persian ladies deemed such employments work fit only for slaves and captives, and Alexander was obliged to explain how honourably the loom and needle were esteemed by his own countrywomen.

Alexander was much attached to his own mother, Olympias; and portions of his letters to her have come down to our time. She was a proud and violent woman, who often interfered with Antipater, governor of Macedon, and caused him to send many complaints to the king. "Ah!" said Alexander, "Antipater does not know that one tear of a mother will blot out ten thousand of his letters."

Alexander had indeed an open and affectionate heart, but he was fast becoming too much uplifted by his successes. On Darius's death, he took the state as well as the title of a king of Persia, wore the tiara and robes, and claimed from the Macedonians the same servile tokens of homage as were paid by the eastern nations, thus causing perpetual heart-burnings among them, since they could neither endure to see their king exalted so much further above them, nor to be placed on the same level with the barbarians whom they despised.

Their jealousies troubled Alexander from the time he assumed the tiara of Persia. He found it impossible to raise the condition of the Persians, and treat them with favour, without offending the Macedonians, and his temper did not always endure these provocations. The worst action of his life was the sentencing to death, on a false accusation, the wise old general, Parmenio, and his son; and in a fit of passion at a riotous banquet, he slew, with his own hand, his friend Clitus, his nurse's son, who had saved his life at the battle of the Granicus. It was the deed of a moment of drunken violence, and he bitterly lamented it, shutting himself up for several days without allowing anyone to approach him, and paying all honours to the memory of his murdered friend.

His pride and vain-glory went so far, that he imagined himself the son of Jupiter, and sent to Greece to desire to be enrolled among the gods in his life-time. Some of the Greeks were shocked at his profanity, others laughed at him; but all the Spartans said was, "If Alexander will be a god, let him."

PART V. INDIAN EXPEDITION, AND DEATH OF ALEXANDER. B. C. 330–325.

The four next years were the most laborious of Alexander's life. He pursued the murderers of Darius into Bactria and Sogdiana, avenged his death, and reduced the numerous hill-forts as far as the frontier of Scythia. Fierce insurrections broke out among the wild tribes of Sogdiana, which it required all his activity and judgment to quell, and more than once provoked him into cruelty, though in general, conqueror as he was, he was no spoiler, but wherever he went founded cities, and tried to teach the Persians the civilized arts of Greece.

In 326 he set out for India, as the region was called round the river Indus. Here the inhabitants were warlike, and Porus, king of a portion of the country, made a brave resistance, but was at length defeated and taken prisoner. On being brought before Alexander, he said he had nothing to ask, save to be treated as a king. "That I shall do for my own sake," said Alexander, and accordingly not only set him at liberty, but enlarged his territory.

All these Indian nations brought a tribute of elephants, which the Macedonians now for the first time learnt to employ in war. Alexander wished to proceed into Hindostan, a country hitherto entirely unknown; but his soldiers grew so discontented at the prospect of being led so much further from home, into the utmost parts of the earth, that he was obliged to give up his attempt, and very unwillingly turned back from the banks of the Sutlej.

While returning, he besieged a little town belonging to a tribe called the Malli, and believed to be the present city of Mooltan. He was the first to scale the wall, and after four others had mounted, the ladder broke, and he was left standing on the wall, a mark for the darts of the enemy. He instantly leaped down within the wall into the midst of the Malli, and there setting his back against a fig-tree, defended himself until a barbed arrow deeply pierced his breast, and after trying to keep up a little longer, he sunk, fainting, on his shield. His four companions sprung down after him—two were slain, but the others held their shields over him till the rest of the army succeeded in breaking into the town and coming to his rescue. His wound was severe and dangerous, but he at length recovered, sailed down to the mouth of the Indus, and sent a fleet to survey the Persian Gulf, while he himself marched along the shore. The country was bare and desert, and his army suffered dreadfully from heat, thirst, and hunger, while he readily shared all their privations. A little water was once brought him on a parching day, as a great prize, but since there was not enough for all, he poured it out on the sand, lest his faithful followers should feel themselves more thirsty when they saw him drink alone.

At last he safely arrived at Caramania, from whence he returned to the more inhabited and wealthy parts of Persia, held his court with great magnificence at Susa, and then went to Babylon. Here embassies met him from every part of the known world, bringing gifts and homage; and above all, there arrived from the Greek states the much-desired promise that he should be honoured as a god. He was at the highest pitch of worldly greatness to which mortal man had yet attained, and his designs were reaching yet further; but his hour was come, and at Babylon, the home of pride, "the great horn" was to be broken.

In the marshes into which the Euphrates had spread since its channel was altered by Cyrus, there breathed a noxious air, and a few weeks after Alexander's arrival, he was attacked by a fever perhaps increased by intemperance. He bore up against it as long as possible, continued to offer sacrifice daily, though with increasing difficulty, and summoned his officers to arrange plans for his intended expedition; but his strength failed him on the ninth day, and though he called them together as usual, he could not address them. Perhaps he thought in that hour of the prophecy he had seen at Jerusalem, that the empire he had toiled to raise should be divided, for he is reported to have said there would be a mighty contest at his funeral games. He made no attempt to name a successor, but he took off his signet-ring, placed it on the finger of Perdiccas, one of his generals, and a short time after expired, in the thirty-third year of his age, and the twelfth of his reign.

There was a voice of wailing throughout the city that night. The Babylonians shut up their houses, and trembled at the neighbourhood of the fierce Greek soldiery, now that their protector was dead; the Macedonians stood to arms all night, as if in presence of the enemy; and when in the morning the officers assembled in the palace council chamber, bitter and irrepressible was the burst of lamentation that broke out at the sight of the vacant throne, where lay the crown, sceptre, and royal robes, and where Perdiccas now placed the signet ring. More deeply than all mourned the prisoner, the aged Sisygambis, who covered her face with a black veil, sat down in a corner of her room, refused all entreaties to speak or to eat, and expired five days after Alexander.

Nor did the Persians soon cease to lament the conqueror, who had ruled them more beneficently than their own monarchs had done; their traditions made Alexander a prince of their own, and adorned him with every virtue valued in the east. That he had many great faults has already been shown, and of course, by the rules of justice, his conquests were but reckless gratifications of his own ambition; but he was a high-minded, generous man, open of heart, free of hand, and for the most part acting up to his knowledge of right; and if unbridled power, talent of the highest order, and glory such as none before or since has ever attained, inflamed his passions and elated him with pride, still it is not for us to judge severely of one who had such great temptations, and so little to guide him aright. The first monarch who was ever called the Great, well deserved that title.

CHAPTER VIII.

THE FOUR HORNS. B. C. 323-191.

PART I.   PARTITION OF THE EMPIRE.   B. C. 323-266.

"Therefore, when the he-goat waxed very great, and when he was strong, the great horn was broken, and for it came up four notable ones towards the four winds of heaven."

At the time of Alexander's death, his dominions were entirely without a head, for his son, Alexander Ægos, was not born till some weeks after his death, and Babel once more became the scene of dispersion. The chief officers of his army were, for the most part, men who had been instructed in all the learning and philosophy of Greece, and possessed much cultivation of mind and manners; but their example showed how little power merely human learning has to soften the heart, or promote nobleness of feeling. Their power of intellect served only to make them more dangerous, while the love of wealth, of splendour, and of luxury, they had acquired in the East, was an additional incitement to them to grasp at all which they could obtain, without respect to justice, mercy, honour, love of their country, or gratitude to their late master.

As were the officers, so were the soldiers, puffed up with conquest, haughty and merciless, greedy of prey and plunder, and without faith towards their chiefs, whom they deserted or murdered whenever they saw their cause likely to fail. The time of confusion and crime which succeeded the death of Alexander shall be passed over slightly, though some leading names and events must be recorded for the sake of tracing the fulfilment of prophecy, and understanding the after course of affairs.

Perdiccas was appointed Regent for the infant Alexander, and gave the four great satrapies of Thrace, Egypt, Syria, and Asia Minor, to four generals, Lysimachus, Ptolemy, Antigonus, and Eumenes. His authority was, however, disputed by Antipater, the governor of Macedon, and his son Cassander, who were exercising a stern rule over subject Greece, and caused Demosthenes to be put to death for his steady resistance to the pretensions of Macedon. Ptolemy, allying himself with Cassander, was attacked in Egypt by Perdiccas, and defended himself with great ability. Perdiccas tried to cross the Nile by night to attack him, but the river suddenly rising when a part of his men had crossed, they were cut off from their companions, and, in attempting to return, were swept away by the river, many drowned, and many others devoured by the crocodiles. The rest of the army, discontented at their ill success, and hating Perdiccas, who was a very cruel and wicked man, slew him, and went over to Ptolemy.

Ptolemy had it in his power to have become Regent, but he thought it wiser and safer to content himself with his rich province of Egypt; and the poor little Alexander fell into the hands of Cassander, one of the worst and most treacherous of all the Macedonians. Eumenes, the only general who had any loyalty or principle, struggled hard for the young king in Asia Minor, and at one time gained considerable ground; but he was shamefully betrayed by his own soldiers to Antigonus, who, not liking to shed the blood of an old comrade, spared his own feelings by having him starved to death.

After the death of this only true friend to the royal family, Cassander murdered Olympias, the mother of Alexander the Great, and kept the poor young king in captivity till he reached his sixteenth year, when, thinking he might become dangerous to him, he caused him to be put to death.

Antigonus had now become the most powerful of the Macedonian generals, although he had lost Persia and Babylon, which had revolted in favour of the former Macedonian satrap, Seleucus. He possessed Syria and Asia Minor, and his son Demetrius, called Poliorcetes, or the Besieger, obtained the adherence of the Greeks by promising them liberty, though he did nothing in effect but remove the Macedonian garrisons from the citadel.

How little Athens in particular was fit to enjoy freedom, was shown by the manner in which the citizens received Demetrius on his visits to them. All they seemed to desire was to devise the greatest honours that could possibly be paid to him, not only giving him and his father the title of kings, but adding a double portion of those divine honours so reluctantly granted to Alexander; and so far did their baseness reach, that they decreed sacrifices and festival days for him, lodged him in the secret shrine of the Parthenon, and even wrote verses in honour of his profane revelries there.

Cassander, Lysimachus, and Seleucus, who had all likewise taken the title of kings, grew jealous of the power of Antigonus, and formed a league against him. A battle was fought at Ipsus, in Asia Minor, where Antigonus was slain, and Demetrius obliged to fly to Greece, where he learnt how little trust could be placed in people who could descend to such servile flatteries as the Athenians, for they closed the gates of their city against him whom they had just been worshipping as a god. He contrived, however, to keep up a small army until the death of Cassander, when he succeeded in obtaining possession of the kingdom of Macedon.

In trying to recover Asia Minor, now in the hands of Seleucus, Demetrius was made prisoner, and died in captivity. Lysimachus added Macedon to his kingdom of Thrace, but likewise invading Asia Minor, was there defeated and slain. Seleucus, in his turn, crossed to Macedon, and was there murdered by an outcast son of Ptolemy, and at last, after many reverses, Antigonus, called Gonatas, son of Demetrius, succeeded in establishing his family on the throne of Macedon.

The four greater kingdoms, therefore, which arose from the fragments of the Macedonian empire, were Egypt, Syria, Macedon, and Thrace, but after the death of Lysimachus, Thrace was included in Macedon. There were several very small states also, which gradually obtained their independency, and became kingdoms, of which the most noted were in Asia Minor—those of Pergamus, under kings alternately named Eumenes and Attalus, and Pontus, where reigned the House of Mithridates, while further eastward was Armenia, and afterwards Bactria and Parthia.

PART II. THE KINGDOM OF EGYPT. B. C. 323–205.

"The King of the South shall be strong."

PTOLEMY, called Lagus, from his father's name, was, as has been said, wise enough to content himself with Egypt, without grasping at anything further, and thus was the only one of the Macedonian kings who lived and died in prosperity. The Isle of Cyprus and the Holy Land formed part of his kingdom, and Alexandria, the new capital, founded by his great master, was fast becoming a great merchant city, and acquiring the trade hitherto absorbed by Tyre. He wished also to render it equal to Athens in art and literature; he collected around him a number of philosophers, founded a museum, or collection of works of art, and a library, the most famous which ever existed. He himself wrote a history of his master's campaigns, which unfortunately has not been preserved.

He died in 284, and was succeeded by his son, Ptolemy Philadelphus, a peaceful and merciful prince, but a lover of luxury and pleasure, and so little inclined to put any restraint on his wishes, that he married his own sister Berenice, setting an example which was followed by many of his successors. He had, like his father, much taste for art and literature. He greatly enlarged the library of Alexandria, and one work which he set on foot for this purpose is most valuable to us.

During his reign the Scriptures were translated into Greek; as it is said because he wished to have a copy in his library. Seventy-two scribes were employed, and though they worked separately, their versions are said to have exactly agreed. From the number seventy, the translation is called the Septuagint, and as Greek was fast becoming the prevailing language, it was much used by the Jews themselves; from it the Apostles quoted, and it has always been considered as of great authority in explaining doubtful passages.

In 246 Ptolemy Philadelphus was succeeded by his son, Ptolemy Euergetes, a more warlike though not ess learned prince. His wife, whose name was Berenice, cut off and consecrated her hair as a votive sacrifice for his safe return when he went on a dangerous expedition into Syria, and the hair being shortly after lost out of the Temple, was said by some flatterers to have been raised to the skies, where a circle of small stars still bear the name of Coma Berenicæ. He met with great success on his journey, penetrating as far as Persia, and bringing back certain Egyptian idols which had been carried away in the time of Cambyses. He likewise visited Jerusalem, attended a sacrifice in the Temple, and was esteemed a friend of the Jews.

He was the last great king of his family. His successors were weak and wicked men; given up to indolence and pleasure, they gradually lost their dominions, and were at length only saved for a time from total ruin by the protection of the Romans.

PART III. THE KINGDOM OF SYRIA. B. C. 312–205.

Seleucus, called Nicator, or the Victor, had, as has been related, revolted from Antigonus, and obtaining the aid of the Persians, made himself master of Assyria, Persia, and great part of Asia Minor. He found his dominions much wasted by war; and to make up for the losses it had sustained, he founded a great number of new cities, of which no less than sixteen were named after his son Antiochus, and nine called after himself. The erection of Seleucia on the Tigris is thought to have been the occasion of the final desertion of Babylon, since the people flocked to inhabit the new city, leaving the old one, which became more and more unhealthy from the stagnant pools of water. At last it was so desolate, that one of the successors of Seleucus turned it into a hunting-ground, bringing a number of foreign animals to be turned out there; and thus it came to pass "that the wild beasts of the desert met with the wild beasts of the island;" the satyrs, or apes, danced there, and it was a habitation for owls. Antioch, in Syria Proper, became the capital of the kingdom, and one of the most celebrated towns of ancient times.

Seleucus was murdered in 281, and his son Antiochus reigned prosperously after him. The next king, Antiochus, who profanely called himself Theos, the god, married in fulfilment of a treaty, Berenice, daughter of Ptolemy Philadelphus; in the words of Daniel, "the king's daughter of the south came to make an agreement with the king of the north." But on the death of her father he put her away in order to take back a former wife, Laodice, who, fearing that her favour might not last, poisoned him, after having persuaded him to acknowledge her son Seleucus as king. She then murdered Berenice and her children, but was in her turn slain by Ptolemy Euergetes, who overran the whole kingdom.

Her son Seleucus reigned but a short time, and his brother Antiochus, called the Great, coming to the crown, attacked the weak and vicious Ptolemy Philopator of Egypt, and took from him the whole of Palestine, a change which was the cause of great suffering to the Jews.

Ptolemy Philopator died young, and his son, Ptolemy Philometor, being a mere child, Antiochus pursued his conquests, and even had designs of invading Egypt, when he was checked by the interference of the Romans.

PART IV.   THE ACHÆAN LEAGUE.   B. C. 266–191.

The royal line, founded by Antigonus, after many reverses, obtained the kingdom of Macedon, with its supremacy over Greece. Antigonus Gonatas, son of Demetrius Poliorcetes, was the first who enjoyed any settled authority there, and of his history very little is known.

During all the changes that followed the death of Alexander, the Greek states might, it would have seemed, have found some opportunity of recovering their independence; but the armies of the contending parties were too large to be withstood by any single city, and jealousy and party feelings prevented union among them. It is remarkable, too, that after the death of Demosthenes, during the eighty years that ensued upon the breaking up of the Macedonian empire, there was not one man distinguished as a statesman or soldier among all the cities where great talents had hitherto been so frequent. At last something of the old spirit began to stir in the Peloponnesus. The little towns of Achaia, anciently bound together by a league, had their share in the general disasters of Greece, each being held by a Macedonian tyrant, whose cruelty was, of course, more sensibly felt where the numbers were so small, until at length the oppression became unbearable, and first one and then another shook off the yoke, and renewed the league to aid each other in war and peace.

Sicyon, a large and wealthy town on the coast, was delivered from its tyrant by an ably conducted attack of a young citizen named Aratus, who joined it to the league, and from that time forward had the full direction of the councils of the Achæans. He succeeded in freeing Corinth, and after many vain attempts, at last rescued Argos; and though, as a general, he was not very successful, always preserved the attachment and confidence of his fellow-citizens.

In Sparta, too, there was something of a revival. Agis, one of the kings, a noble youth of twenty, strove hard to restore the laws of Lycurgus, setting the example himself by giving up his wealth, and living in the stern old Spartan simplicity. He was vehemently opposed by the other king, Leonidas, who had spent his youth in the palace of an Asiatic satrap, and could not endure a change; and at length, after a fruitless struggle, the brave young Agis was betrayed into the hands of his enemies, and condemned to be strangled. He died like an ancient Spartan, saying that even in death he was superior to his enemies. In his infant son, who died soon after, ended one line of the kings.

His wife, Agiatis, being a great heiress, Leonidas obliged her to marry his own son Cleomenes, a young boy, who became much attached to her, delighted to hear her speak of Agis, and learnt both to revere and imitate him. On the death of his father, Cleomenes became sole king, and applied himself with all his might to bring about the reform which had been begun by Agis.

Aratus and the Achæans wished to bring all Peloponnesus to join the league, and on the refusal of the Spartans, had the folly to make war upon them.

Aratus showed how the spirit of party can overcome patriotism, for in his hatred of Sparta, he gave up that independence of Achaia and all Greece for which he had all his life been striving, and called in the aid or the Macedonians. Cleomenes, on his side, asked help from Egypt, but could only obtain it on condition of sending as hostages to Alexandria his mother and his two young children, (he had lately lost his beloved Agiatis.) His mother cheered him, and bade him farewell with admirable firmness, and no sooner had she arrived, than she sent him a letter, desiring him to act for the good of his country without regard to the safety of a useless old woman or a helpless child.

In 224 Cleomenes was defeated at Selasia by the Macedonians and Achæans, who advanced upon Sparta. He thought his people might obtain better terms in his absence, and therefore sailed for Alexandria, where he spent several years, often entreating to be sent to his own country; but to this Ptolemy Philopator would not consent. He was regarded with fear and dislike by the soft luxurious Alexandrians, who said that to their eyes, the stern, grave, silent Spartan, with his self-denying habits, and brief truthful speech, was like a lion stalking about among a flock of sheep. At last fear rendered Ptolemy cruel; and he caused Cleomenes, with all his Spartans, to be slain, not sparing even his mother and child. And thus ended the two lines of Heracleid Kings of Sparta, each with a man whom Lycurgus would not have been ashamed to own.

Aratus was justly punished for having degraded his country. Philip, King of Macedon, at first regarded him as a friend and counsellor, but at length finding him interfere with his measures, put an end to his life by a slow poison.

Philopœmon, a citizen of Megalopolis, became the leading spirit of the league, and showed so much courage, wisdom, and uprightness, that he is often called the last of the Greeks. Both Achæans and Macedonians were at this time constantly at war with the Ætolians, a piratical nation, which often made unjust attacks on their neighbours, and at length, finding themselves hard pressed by Philip, called in the aid of the Romans.

CHAPTER IX.

ROMAN CONQUEST IN ITALY. B.C. 753-272.

PART I. ROMAN MYTHOLOGY.

SEPARATED from Greece by the Adriatic Sea, a second peninsula stretches far into the Mediterranean, the Apennine mountains forming, as it were, the spine, and numerous lesser ranges spreading out on either side. It was called by the Greeks Hesperia, or land of the evening star, and was inhabited by a number of native tribes, of whose origin little or nothing is known beyond their descent from Japhet.

From one of these tribes was derived the name of Italy, from another that of the Latin language, and the Tusci, or Etruscans, who lived in the territory still called Tuscany, seem to have influenced the manners and habits of all. The remains of the Etruscan walls and monuments show that they had made considerable advances in civilization, but their history, and almost their memory, has passed away. Upon their ruins arose the fourth great power, prefigured in Daniel's vision by the great and terrible Beast with teeth of iron.

Nearly in the centre of the peninsula, on the west side of the Apennines, the river Tiber flows along a valley, shut in by hills, off-shoots of the great range, which recede as it reaches the sea, leaving a wide level plain. About seventeen miles from the mouth of the river, just below the meeting of the Anio and Tiber, rise seven little hills, divided by narrow valleys; and here stands the city of Rome, once the mistress of the world. All the seven hills were inclosed by her wall, and on the most precipitous was the Capitol, or citadel, while all around the fertile country was divided into little farms, cultivated by the Romans.

The character of this nation seems, in early times, to have been grave, earnest, and upright; very warlike, and with a certain harshness and haughtiness—with a love and pride in Rome which amounted to idolatry. The Greek philosophy and love of beauty had no place in the mind of the stern practical Roman, wrapped up in his own self-respect, and his devotion to the glory of his "Respublica," or common cause. To Rome, and to his own ideas of virtue and endurance, he would sacrifice his hopes, his life—all that was dear to him, and all mercy or justice to other nations.

Of the religion of the early Romans we know very little. They afterwards adopted the mythology of the Greeks, and tried to identify their own original gods with theirs, which has caused great confusion, since the Greek deities have become familiar to us by Roman names, and the attributes of the Roman gods have been lost in those of the Greeks. Jupiter and Juno were thus made King and Queen of Heaven; Minerva, the goddess of school-boys, was made the same with Pallas;

Diana, the moon, was thought another name for Artemis; and Venus took all the stories about the Greek Aphrodite. Janus and Vesta are the only genuine Roman gods of whom any special account has been preserved.

Janus was the protector of the gates, and for this reason the doors of his temple were kept open in time of war, and closed in peace ; and it is to be noticed that so constantly was Rome in a state of warfare, that the doors were only shut three times in the course of the whole Roman history. Janus was always represented with two faces ; his name is preserved in that of the first month, the entrance of the year, and in the word janitor, a porter.

Vesta was the goddess of the sacred fire, on which the safety of Rome was thought to depend. It burnt in a circular temple, and was watched by six maidens consecrated to a life of purity, and regarded with great respect. The first seats on all great occasions were set apart for the Vestal Virgins, and they had the privilege of saving the life of any criminal whom they met on his way to execution.

The Romans likewise thought that each man had a Genius, or guardian of his life, and every house its penates, or protectors of the hearth, where libations, or drink-offerings, were poured out to them at every meal. The Etruscans certainly, and probably the Romans, expected to be rewarded after death according to their deeds, and it is evident that this religion, in its earlier and simpler form, when perhaps it had more remains of truth, had a strong effect upon their actions. It was not till they had lost their trust and reverence, amid the wild and foul legends and confused philosophy of later Greece, that their old honest faith gave way, and with it all restraint to their dark and blood-thirsty passions.

PART II. FOUNDING OF ROME. B.C. 753–640.

NOTHING is known of the early history of Rome excepting from traditions preserved by word of mouth, of which much must of necessity be fable.

According to these, Æneas, a Trojan prince, escaped from the burning of Troy, carrying his aged father, Anchises, on his back, holding his penates in his arms, and leading his young son, Ascanius, or Iulus. After long wanderings, the protection of the goddess Venus, said to be his mother, safely led him to Italy, where he married the daughter of the King of Latium, and his son Ascanius founded the city of Alba Longa.

Several centuries after were born the twins, Romulus and Remus. Their mother was Rhea Silvia, a vestal virgin, and a niece of the King of Alba, Amulius, a descendent of Æneas, and their father was said to be the god Mars. For breaking her vows Amulius condemned the mother to be buried alive, and the infants to be placed in a basket and drowned in the Tiber. The river had overflowed its banks, and as it subsided again, the basket, with the two children still living, was left on dry land, where they were found by a she-wolf. Instead of devouring them, the creature guarded and fed them until they were discovered by a shepherd, who brought them up as his own sons. The babes, with their foster-mother, the wolf, became one of the favourite emblems of the Roman power; and Mars was the patron god of the city, to whom was consecrated the third month in the year.

When Romulus and Remus grew up, they discovered their relationship to the royal family, and after overthrowing Amulius, resolved to found a city for themselves on the spot where they had once been exposed.

To determine after which of them it should be called, each took his stand on a hill to watch for some omen from the gods. Romulus saw twelve vultures, and Remus only six, and the former being therefore chosen king by his followers, commenced his building on the Palatine Hill; upon which Remus grew discontented, took no share in the work, and at last, in derision, leapt over the low mud wall which his brother was raising round the new city. In a rage Romulus killed him on the spot, exclaiming, "So perish all who dare leap over my walls."

The foundation of Rome is fixed at 753 B.C., and was the date from which the Romans reckoned; it is distinguished by the letters A. U. C., *anno urbis conditæ*, the year of the building of the city. Romulus and his followers were looked upon by the other nations as little better than robbers, and could not obtain their daughters in marriage. At last the king proclaimed a festival, to which he invited his neighbours, the Sabines, to bring their whole families; and at a given signal, each Roman seized upon a Sabine maiden, and bore her away to his own house, easily overcoming the resistance of the unarmed fathers and brothers. This outrage was followed by a war, in the course of which the Citadel was betrayed to the Sabines by Tarpeia, the daughter of the governor. She asked, as a reward for her treachery, what the Sabines wore on their left arms, meaning their golden bracelets; but they chose to misunderstand her, and threw at her their shields, by which she was crushed to death. The top of the precipice where she was killed was called the Tarpeian Rock, and criminals were usually put to death by being thrown from it.

The war was ended by the mediation of the Sabine

women, who had grown attached to their Roman husbands; the two nations were united, and the kings were for the future to be chosen from each in turn.

Romulus suddenly disappeared in the midst of an assembly of his army. It was said that his father, Mars, had carried him off to Heaven; he was worshipped under the name of Quirinus, and the same name was given to one of the seven hills.

Numa Pompilius, the next king, was a Sabine, a peaceable man, a lawgiver, and believed to receive inspiration from the wood-nymph Egeria.

Tullus Hostilius, a warlike Roman, reigned next, and made war upon Alba Longa. It was proposed that the quarrel should be decided by a battle between three champions on each side, those of the Romans being three brothers of the family of Horatius, those of the Albans, three of the family of Curiatius, cousins of their opponents. They fought long and well, and at length all the three Curiatii were wounded, but Publius Horatius, though unhurt, alone remained alive of the three Roman brothers. Slowly retreating, he contrived that his three wounded cousins should overtake him one by one, and thus killed them singly, and obtained the victory. As he returned to Rome to offer up their arms in the temple, he was met by his sister, who had been betrothed to one of them, and recognizing her lover's robe, which she had wrought with her own hands, she broke out into loud wailings, which so incensed her brother, that he killed her, crying out, "Away with thy unseasonable grief, forgetful of thy dead and of thy living brothers, forgetful of thy country. So perish every Roman woman who mourns the death of an enemy."

Publius was sentenced to death for the murder, but

was spared in consideration of his services, and that he was the only surviving child of his parents. He was obliged, however, to pass under a yoke, consisting of three spears set up like a doorway, which remained long after, and was called by his name. Alba Longa was afterwards taken and destroyed.

PART III. THE TARQUINS. B. C. 640–507.

The fourth king of Rome was Ancus Martius, after whom reigned Lucius Tarquinius, usually called Priscus, or the Elder, who seems to have been of Etruscan birth. He rebuilt the walls of Rome, which had hitherto been of mud, with large hewn stones, and carried off the water from the swampy valleys between the hills, by cloacæ, or drains, so solidly built, that they are still the wonder of all who behold them. The valley between the Palatine and Esquiline Hills was called the Forum, or market-place, and was by him fitted up with seats, as a place of judgment and of assembly for the people.

Though Tarquin left two sons, he was succeeded by a servant in his own household, Servius Tullius, who gave his two daughters, both called Tullia, from his family name, in marriage to the two young Tarquins. In his old age, Servius Tullius was cruelly murdered by Lucius Tarquin, and as his corpse lay neglected in the street, his unnatural daughter forced her slave to drive her chariot over it, so that her robes were stained with his blood.

Lucius Tarquinius, called Superbus, or the Proud, was very wicked, and much hated; and his sons were equally haughty and cruel. Sextus, the eldest and worst, was once taken by his cousin Lucius Tarquinius

Collatinus, to Collatia, his house in the country, where they found Lucretia, his beautiful wife, sitting among her maidens, late at night, spinning and carding wool. Sextus afterwards went alone to Collatia, and there so ill-treated Lucretia, that she killed herself in despair, after calling on her husband and father to revenge her wrongs. Lucius Junius Brutus, Tarquin's own nephew, joined with them, and going to Rome, so excited the indignation of the people, that Tarquin and all his family were obliged to fly. Such was the end of the Roman monarchy, in the year 510 B.C., the same year that the sons of Pisistratus were expelled from Athens.

The Tarquins made many attempts to regain their crown, and at one time had a secret understanding with some of the young nobles at Rome, among whom were the two sons of Brutus. Their connexion was, however, discovered, and the youths were sentenced to death by the stern Brutus himself, who looked on while they were first scourged, and afterwards beheaded, without a change of countenance, only the rigid grasp with which he clenched the arm of his seat of office betraying the anguish of his mind. Shortly after Brutus and his cousin Aruns, one of the sons of Tarquin, killed each other fighting hand to hand.

Lars Porsenna, an Etruscan prince, took up the cause of Tarquin, and suddenly marching against Rome, surprised and captured the gate Janiculum, the only one on the further side of the Tiber. The river was crossed by a single wooden bridge, on which Horatius Cocles stood as guard, when the multitude of surprised citizens came hurrying on to escape into the town. He told them the only hope of saving Rome was to break down the bridge, and undertook singly to defend the entrance to it whilst they crossed, and then destroyed it. Two warriors joined with him, and these gallant three stood at the end of the bridge, keeping back, by their dauntless bravery, the whole Etruscan host. The foundations of the bridge were in the meantime cut down or burnt by the Romans, who at last called to their three champions to come back while it could still bear their weight. Back hastened the other two, but Horatius kept his post; and the next moment down went the last timbers, leaving him with the enemy in front, the river behind. The crash caused the enemy to cease their attacks for one moment; he stretched out his arms, exclaimed, "Father Tiber, receive me, thy soldier, into thy merciful stream," leapt into the river, and, heavily armed as he was, safely reached the opposite bank, amid the joyful cries of his fellow-citizens whom he had saved.

Porsenna proceeded to blockade the city, and Caius Mutius, a young Roman, resolved to attempt the deliverance of his country by assassinating him. He gained entrance to Porsenna's tent, but not knowing his person, mistook for him one of his attendants, whom he stabbed to the heart. He was overpowered, and disarmed, when he freely avowed his intention of killing Porsenna, who, thinking he might know of some further plot, commanded that he should be tortured in order to make him disclose it. Upon this Mutius stretched out his right hand to a fire which burnt on an altar, and held it in the midst of the flame, without the least sign of pain, while he looked at Porsenna, and bade him learn how little those who sought glory esteemed their bodies. Porsenna was so struck by his fortitude as to set him free immediately, and Mutius then said that this generosity should obtain the information which torture could never have drawn from him, namely, that he was but one of three hundred youths of equal resolution, who had all sworn Porsenna's death, he being the first on whom the lot had fallen. This intelligence decided the Etruscan prince immediately to offer peace to Rome, and to draw off his forces. Mutius was highly honoured for the constancy which, in our eyes, assorts so ill with his purpose of assassination; and having lost the use of his scorched right hand, he obtained the name of Scævola, or the left-handed, as an honourable distinction.

Tarquin's last effort to regain his kingdom was in the year 495, when he had gained a party among the Latins, and a great battle was fought on the banks of the Lake Regillus, in which his hopes were so completely ruined, that he gave up all thoughts of again reigning, and spent his old age at the town of Cumæ.

PART IV. THE REPUBLIC.

The new form of government established at Rome, which continued the same, at least in name, if not in substance, for the next four hundred years, placed all power in the hands of the Roman Senate and people, as was signified by the four letters, S. P. Q. R., which marked all their acts and public buildings.

The Roman people consisted of two great orders: the patricians, or nobles, who alone were capable of holding any high office in the state, and the plebeians, who, though free and independent, and with a vote in the election of magistrates, were not in these early times allowed to rise to any dignity. The distinction depended on birth, not on wealth; a patrician, however poor, could not lose his rank, nor could a plebeian, though very rich, ever become a patrician. There was a certain class of plebeians, however, which served in war on horse-back, and were therefore called equites, or horsemen, sometimes translated into English by the word knights, who enjoyed some of the same privileges as the patricians.

There was another order of men, who, though their persons were free, had no vote or political power, and these were the clients of the patricians, who were bound to support and assist the patricians whom they served, while he, on his side, was obliged to protect them from oppression. Besides all these, there were the slaves who had no rights, and whose very lives were at the disposal of their master. Sometimes their liberty was given them, and they were then called freedmen, and remained attached as clients to the service of their lord.

The senate was the council, chosen at first solely from among the patricians and equites, though others were afterwards admitted. Without its consent no measure could be adopted, and no higher authority was acknowledged in the state.

The chief magistrates were the two consuls, who were elected every year by the people, and came into office on the 1st of January. Their dress was royal, except that they had no crowns: they sat on a throne called the curule-chair, carried in their hands sceptres of ivory, surmounted by a golden eagle, and were attended by lictors or executioners, bearing the instruments of their office, an axe and bundle of rods. The first pair of consuls were Lucius Junius Brutus, and Lucius Tarquinius Collatinus, and from that time forward the years were distinguished by the names of the two consuls in office. The prætors were the judges, and likewise had a right to the curule-chair; the censors apportioned the taxes, and inquired into the rank and political rights of each citizen; and the quæstor was the public accuser. These offices were all held by the patricians; and after a hard struggle the plebeians succeeded in obtaining for themselves ten magistrates of their own rank, called tribunes of the people, who could stop any measure of the senate by withholding their consent.

In times of great danger to the republic, when there was a necessity for promptitude and vigour, a single person was chosen as dictator, who possessed supreme authority both in the city and camp, as long as the danger lasted.

It must be remembered that the word citizen in those times conveyed the idea not of an inhabitant of a town, but of a free man of the commonwealth; and these early Roman citizens for the most part lived in what is now called the Campagna di Roma, spending their time in cultivating their little farms, when they were not called on to serve in war.

The Roman legion, so called from *lego*, to choose, because the soldiers were chosen by the consuls and other officers, consisted of about 6,000 men, all plebeians, possessed of a certain amount of land, which was supposed to be a pledge that they were to be depended upon. They all served on foot, the patricians and equites being on horse-back. The standard of the whole legion was the famous Roman eagle, made either of silver or bronze, and borne upon a pole; the cohorts or subdivisions had ensigns of their own, and each century, or hundred men, was commanded by a centurion, whose helmet was taller than the rest, and had some distinguishing badge, so that every man might know exactly where his own place in the army was. The discipline was thus most exact, and however unruly the Romans might be in the city, their obedience in the field was complete.

A victorious general received the title of Imperator, signifying commander, and on his return entered Rome in a chariot, with a laurel crown on his head, his troops marching in procession, carrying their spoils, and dragging their prisoners along in chains; the temples were thrown open, the streets strewn with garlands, the people observed a holiday, and the Senate conducted the conqueror to the temple of Jupiter, where a white ox was sacrificed. This entrance was called a triumph, and was regarded as the highest honour; but it too often ended by the slaughter of the unhappy captives, when they reached the Capitol, after being thus made a spectacle in their misery; and often royal prisoners put themselves to death, rather than endure the degradation of a Roman triumph.

The proper dress of a Roman, which none but a citizen might wear, was a long, loose, folding gown, termed a toga, of white edged with purple. Young boys wore a tunic, and a golden ball called a bulla hung round their necks, and it was a great festival day, when they reached their seventeenth year, and first were allowed to put on the toga and lay aside the bulla. Persons who wished to be elected to any office, went about asking votes, with their toga rubbed with chalk, and were therefore called candidates, from *candidus*, white. Senators had a broader stripe of purple on their togas, and those which the Consuls wore on great occasions were entirely purple, and covered with embroidery. It is not, however, quite certain whether the colour called purple in Latin, was that to which we now give that name, or whether it was scarlet.

Every Roman had two names; the first his own

individual name, such as Marcus, Publius, or Lucius, and the second the surname, or name of the clan to which he belonged, such as Mutius, Cornelius, &c., and which was inherited by all his sons and daughters, the latter being called by the feminine, Mutia, Cornelia. Some families had likewise a third name, derived from some one ancestor. Thus of the Cornelii, there was one family whose third name was Scipio, another whose third name was Rufinus, though both alike belonged to the Cornelian gens or clan; and of the Mutii, those alone who were descended from the left-handed Caius Mutius bore his other name of Scævola.

PART V.   EARLY WARS OF ROME.   B. C. 508–447.

It would take too long to describe the feuds between the patrician and plebeian orders, and the wars between Rome and the other Italian states; all that here can be attempted is to give a few of the stories which were most dwelt upon, and the names which were the watchwords of the Roman citizen.

The two neighbouring nations of Volsci and Veientes were great enemies of the Romans. Every summer there was an inroad, either of them into the Roman territory, or of the Romans into theirs, when the peasants, with their cattle, took refuge on the hills, the army was called out, and a battle was fought. If the invaders were defeated, they retreated; if they were victorious, they besieged the enemy's capital; but as they had no means of breaking down the walls, the siege usually lasted only till the approach of winter, when they returned to their own country.

In a war with the Volsci, the town of Corioli was, however, taken from them, chiefly by the valour of a brave young patrician, named Caius Marcius, who received for that reason the surname of Coriolanus. His pride soon after led to a quarrel with the tribunes of the people, who banished him; and in his anger at their injustice, he joined the Volsci, and appeared before Rome at their head. So much was he dreaded, that the Romans in despair applied to his mother and wife, who had been left in poverty and neglect, begging them to use their influence to turn him from his revenge. They went forth to his camp, and there his mother, Veturia, so powerfully pleaded the cause of her country, that he yielded to her persuasions, gave up his purpose, and left the Volscian camp. His after history is uncertain. Some say that the Volsci killed him for deserting them, others that he spent the rest of his life in exile.

The Romans built the fort of Cremera on the frontier, as a protection against the Veientes, and Cæso Fabius, the head of a patrician gens, took the charge of it, at the end of his year of consulship, with the title of Proconsul, and assisted by his whole clan. He maintained his post with great valour, but in the year 477, was taken at unawares by the enemy, and slain, with all the other Fabii, to the number of three hundred and six, so that the name of Fabius only survived in one little boy, who chanced to be at Rome at the time of the massacre.

The plebeians were always struggling to gain political power, and the patricians always striving to repress them. Cæso, the eldest son of the old patrician Lucius Quinctius Cincinnatus, murdered a plebeian, and afterwards fled from the country; and the fine which was imposed upon his family was so heavy, that his father had no property left, excepting a farm of four acres. An incursion of the Etruscans placed the Romans in such danger, that they were obliged to choose a Dictator, and fixed upon Cincinnatus, who had ably filled that office once before. The messengers sent to inform him of his appointment, found him at his farm driving his plough; he called his wife to bring him his toga, washed the earth from his hands, and accompanied the deputies to Rome, where the Senate was ready to receive him in state, and the four-and-twenty lictors awaited his orders. He placed himself at the head of the army, and meeting the enemy on the hill of Algidus, totally defeated them; and resigning the Dictatorship after possessing it sixteen days, returned to his cottage and his plough.

His son soon after made an attack on Rome, together with some other lawless young men, and was beaten off and killed. Cincinnatus never forgave the plebeian party for his exile, and when made Dictator a third time, is said to have made an unworthy use of his power in order to punish Cæso's enemies.

The disputes between the patricians and plebeians ran so high, that it was agreed that the laws should be revised, and ten persons called Decemvirs were appointed for the purpose, with extensive powers of government. They at length fell, through the wickedness of one of their number, Appius Claudius, who, while sitting at his office in the Forum, cast his eyes on Virginia, a beautiful girl of fifteen, who daily passed on her way to a booth at the side of the Forum, where writing was taught. Wishing to have her in his power, he caused one of his clients to claim her as the child of a female slave of his, who had given her when an infant to the wife of Virginius, who had made her pass for his own daughter. Poor Virginia was accordingly seized on her way to school, and declared to be the slave of his client; but as she shrieked aloud for help, her cries were heard by her betrothed, Icilius, and her uncle.

Numitorius, who rescued her for the time, and sent to the camp for her father, who was a centurion. A day was fixed for the trial, and Appius, with his fellow Decemvirs, in spite of the clearest evidence, declared that she was the property of the client. Her father begged to be allowed to embrace her for the last time, and putting his arm round her, drew her aside towards the booth of a butcher, wiped away her tears, kissed her, and said, "My own dear child, there is no way but this to save thee from dishonour!" then snatching up a knife that lay on the stall, plunged it into her heart. A great uproar followed; Appius escaped with difficulty from the indignation of the people, and the Senate were obliged to give up the Decemvirate, allow the former government to be restored, and grant further privileges to the plebeians. This was in 447.

PART VI. THE GAULS IN ITALY. B. C. 449–367.

THE country north of Italy, surrounding the Alpine mountains, was inhabited by a tribe of the great Keltic race, which seems to have been gradually retreating before the still fiercer Teutons, from the borders of the Caspian to the west of Europe.

Everywhere these Kelts had the same features, language, weapons, and even garments, which in many respects are still retained by their remote descendants in the mountains and moors on the borders of the Atlantic. Wherever we hear of them, as Kelts, Gael, Gauls, Galatians, Welsh, Belgi, Cymri, Cimmerians, Cumbrians, or Britons, they always are evidently of the same stock. Dark eyes, black or red hair, a bold, hasty, and warlike temper, impatient of control, and unapt for peaceful arts, seem to have distinguished them from the first; the Welsh or Gaelic tongue was their speech; the checquered plaid, woven of wool of different colours, was their dress; and the huge two-handed broadsword their chief weapon. They believed in one unknown God, whom they worshipped in temples consisting of huge stones ranged in mystic forms, and whose will was revealed to them by their priests, the Druids.

The Galli, or Gauls, as the Romans called the first of them who came under their notice, came over the Alps, and waged war with the Etruscan nations, thus weakening them so much that the Romans, on their side, gained greater successes than they had ever before done, and at last, in the year 395, the town of Veii was taken by the able general, Lucius Furius Camillus. His triumph was remarkably splendid; his chariot was drawn by white horses, and his face coloured with vermillion, as was the custom with the images of the gods when carried in procession, so that this was thought a piece of overweening presumption on his part. He was of a haughty temper, and soon gave offence to the plebeians, who called him to account for his division of the spoil of Veii, and obliged him to go into exile. He prayed as he went that his ungrateful country might soon be taught to know his value; and his wish was soon fulfilled.

In 390 the Gauls, under their chieftain Brennus, as the Romans called him, from his Keltic title of Bran, a king, broke into Italy, and spread themselves over the whole of Etruria. The Romans marched out to meet them, and were totally defeated on the banks of the Allia, only a few escaping to bring the tidings to Rome, whither the enemy was fast following them. It was impossible to man the walls, and all that could be done was for the strongest men to shut themselves up in the Capitol, with such provisions as could be hastily collected, while the rest either sought refuge in flight, or remained to die in their own homes.

In two days' time the enemy were upon them, entered the city, and dispersed themselves through it to plunder. In the Forum they found eighty aged senators, seated on their chairs of state, in their white and purple robes, their long beards descending to their girdles, and their ivory staves in their hands. The savage Gauls stood still for a moment, struck with the majestic appearance of the old men: and one of them began to stroke the beard of the nearest, as if to discover whether he was a living man or a statue. The senator struck the barbarian with the staff, and thus broke the charm; the wild fury of the Gauls was let loose, and in a short time the whole of the old men were slaughtered.

Rome was completely sacked, the houses and temples burnt, the great wall overthrown, and the Gauls encamped in the midst of the smoking ruins that remained to mark the streets; but still the little garrison in the Capitol held out bravely, although sorely pressed by famine, till at last hopes began to dawn upon them. One night there appeared among them a youth named Pontius Cominus, who had swum across the Tiber, crept through the Gallic camp, and scaled the Tarpeian Rock, hitherto believed inaccessible, to bring them word that Camillus, the exile, only waited for powers from the Senate to put himself at the head of the other Romans who had escaped, and attempt their rescue.

The Senate, or rather the remains of it, hastily assembled, restored Camillus to the rights of a citizen, and appointed him Dictator, and Pontius safely returned to him at Veii. The broken boughs and trodden grass on the Tarpeian Rock showed, however, that the ascent had been performed, and Brennus appointed a party of the best cragsmen of the Alps to climb up by night and surprise the Capitol. They had so nearly succeeded that they were close to the summit, when Marcus Manlius, the last year's Consul, was awakened by the cackling of some frightened geese, which being sacred to Juno, had been spared in spite of the scarcity. Hastening to the spot, he was in time to hurl downward the first Gaul, who had just finished his perilous ascent; and the rest of the troops coming to his aid, the Capitol was saved.

The Gauls were growing weary of the siege, and at last agreed to allow the Romans to ransom their city. When the required treasure was weighed out, the Romans complained that the Gauls had brought unjust weights; upon which Brennus, in defiance, cast his sword into the scale, which was already too heavy, only saying, "Woe to the vanquished." His boast was soon at an end, for Camillus had by this time collected his forces, and coming suddenly on the enemy, totally defeated them, took from them the ransom, and forced Brennus to retreat discomfited to his own hills.

The city of Rome was rebuilt, according to the best abilities of the citizens; but it was long before they could again encircle it with a stone wall, and the new streets were much more narrow, irregular, and inconvenient than the former ones; besides which, they disregarded the direction of the cloacæ, and the water, not being carried off as before, occasioned Rome to be much less healthy.

A great jealousy remained between Camillus and Marcus Manlius, called Capitolinus, from his brave defence of the Capitol. Each thought himself the hero of the defeat of the Gauls, and would endure no rival; and as Camillus had always been one of the proudest of the patricians, so Manlius now connected himself with the plebeians. He began at first from compassion, but party spirit soon mingled with his motives, and he was led on further than he intended. The patricians, thinking him a deserter from their order, pursued him with deadly hatred; and at last, he who had saved the Capitol, eight times rescued fellow citizens from death, twice being the first to scale the walls of a besieged city, and had besides redeemed four hundred debtors from slavery at his own expense, was condemned to be thrown headlong from the Tarpeian Rock, the scene of his greatest glory; and his name was held in such aversion, that it was decreed that no son of the Manlian gens should ever bear the name of Marcus.

Every great victory of one party at Rome was, however, immediately followed by a corresponding one of the other; and in 367, Caius Licinius Calvus Stolo, the tribune, obtained certain laws for the people, which were of great effect in the subsequent course of affairs at Rome. The chief of these Licinian laws, as they were called, were that one of the two Consuls might henceforth be a plebeian, and that no person should be allowed to possess more than five hundred acres of land. A law relating to the distribution of land was called an agrarian law—from *ager*, a field.

PART VII. INVASION OF PYRRHUS. B. C. 327–270.

The Gallic invasions, by crushing the forces of the Etruscan nations, rendered it easy to the Romans to subdue them entirely; but the territory to the south was occupied by a warlike people, of whom the

Samnites were the leading tribe, and the war with them was long and fierce.

The Roman army once suffered at their hands a great disaster, allowing themselves to be surrounded by the enemy, and entangled in a narrow pass of the Appenines, called the Caudine Forks, whence it was impossible either to advance or retreat, so that they were forced to submit to whatever terms the Samnites chose to dictate. The Samnites sent to ask the advice of the wise old general, Pontius Herennius, as to the terms. His first answer was that they should let all the Romans go freely; but not choosing to do this, they sent to ask his counsel a second time, when he replied that they had better kill them all. When they desired to know the meaning of such contradictory advice, he explained that by freeing the Romans without a ransom they would obtain their friendship, and make a bond with that powerful nation for ever; but if they were determined in their hatred, and resolved on war, it was for their interest to cut off at once such a large number of their enemies as were now in their hands. The Samnites, however, decided on a half measure, which was in fact the worst for themselves. They did not kill the Romans, but they made them suffer a humiliation, in their eyes worse than death, by obliging them to lay down their arms and pass under a yoke, after which they allowed them to return to Rome in their full strength, and burning to revenge their disgrace.

At last, in 289, the Samnites were completely reduced, and the Romans were acknowledged as masters of all the centre of Italy. They now began to come into collision with the Greek colonies of the southern part of the peninsula, who on their side turned to the mother country for aid against the barbarian robbers, as they termed the Romans. Tarentum, a Spartan colony at the head of the gulf that still bears its name, had long since lost all the severity of manners of the elder city, but without losing its pride; and after provoking a quarrel with the Romans, the inhabitants sent to ask aid from Pyrrhus, King of Epirus.

Through Olympias, Pyrrhus was nearly related to Alexander the Great. His father had been slain and his throne usurped in his infancy, and his youth had been spent in the courts and camps of the generals of Alexander, where not only had he acquired the desire to emulate the fame of his kinsman, but had learnt much of the art of war. When, by the assistance of Ptolemy Lagus, he recovered his own kingdom of Epirus, a mountainous nook on the coast of the Adriatic, he chiefly valued it as the means of supplying the men and money with which he hoped to effect his conquests. He was not, however, sufficiently steady of purpose to succeed in anything, and his whole life was but a course of great half-finished undertakings.

He gladly accepted the invitation of the Tarentines, and with a great force of horse and foot, and twenty elephants, which now were used by the Greeks in all battles, he landed on the southern coast of Italy in the summer of 279. A great battle was fought on the banks of the river Siris, in which the horses of the Romans were so frightened at the elephants, that Pyrrhus won the day; but it was so hardly contested, that he said another such victory would be his ruin. On his proposal to treat with the Romans, they sent three ambassadors to his camp, of whom the chief was Caius Fabricius, a complete specimen of the upright simple-mannered ancient Roman.

Pyrrhus, a polished Greek, with a great contempt

for barbarians, was surprised to find in the untaught warrior the greatness of soul which had belonged to Greece in her earlier ages, and he put him to several trials. One day he offered him a greater store of gold than Rome had yet seen, in order to induce him to enter his service; but the Roman replied that he valued his poverty and the honest fame he enjoyed at home, above all riches. Another time he thought to startle him by causing the curtains of the tent to be suddenly withdrawn, so as to display an enormous elephant standing close to him, waving its trunk and trumpeting through it. Fabricius only smiled, and told the king he cared for his great beast as little as for his treasures. Pyrrhus next tried whether he could be bewildered in the mazes of Greek philosophy, and caused a learned man in attendance to expound the doctrines of Epicurus, namely, that the end of man's existence was to please himself. "O Hercules!" exclaimed Fabricius, "grant that Pyrrhus and the Tarentines may be heartily of this faith as long as they are at war with us."

The king and the citizen parted with much respect for each other; and when the physician of Pyrrhus sent to offer the Senate to poison his master, Fabricius wrote a letter to warn him, beginning, "You choose your friends and enemies badly." Pyrrhus, to show his gratitude, released all his Roman prisoners; and the Romans, not choosing to feel themselves under an obligation, sent him back those of his subjects and allies whom they had taken. The before-mentioned philosopher went to visit Rome, and reported to his master that the city was a temple, and the Senate a tribunal of kings.

Pyrrhus afterwards left Magna Grecia, and made an attempt on Sicily, but not succeeding so well as he had expected, he came back to Italy, and there was totally defeated at Beneventum by the Consul, Marcus Curius Dentatus, who, by causing his soldiers to attack the elephants with lighted torches, so terrified these animals as to render them quite unmanageable, and thus they did as much harm to the Epirots as to their enemy. The camp of Pyrrhus was taken by the Romans, who learnt from this pattern the Greek fashions of encampment, which were very superior to what they had hitherto practised.

By this defeat Pyrrhus was obliged to leave Italy, after having spent five years on this expedition. He had hopes of the conquest of Macedon and Greece, and for this purpose engaged in a war with Antigonus Gonatas. In the year 271, during a fierce combat in the streets of Argos, a woman on the top of a house, seeing her son engaged with Pyrrhus, threw a tile upon the king's head, and as he fell stunned from his horse, he was killed by a Macedonian soldier.

Dentatus received the honour of a splendid triumph after his victory, the spoils of Pyrrhus's camp being carried behind him, and the elephants he had taken marching in the procession with towers on their backs, a sight such as had never before been seen in Rome. The Senate wished further to reward him with a grant of land, but he refused it, saying that his present estate of seven acres was sufficient for the wants of any citizen.

The retreat and death of Pyrrhus put an end to the hopes of the Greek colonies, and all of them yielded to the Romans. So much silver was found in Tarentum, that it was coined for use as money, nothing but brass having been hitherto used at Rome. Thus, in the year 270, the Romans became lords of the whole of Italy.

CHAPTER X.

PERIOD OF THE PUNIC WARS. B. C. 264-202.

PART I. CARTHAGE AND SYRACUSE. B. C. 878–356.

The Phœnician city of Tyre had in ancient times sent out a colony which had settled on the north coast of Africa, nearly opposite to Sicily. The legends of Carthage related that Dido or Elisa (said to be a niece of Jezebel,) fled thither from the cruelty of her wicked brother Pygmalion, and obtaining from the natives as much land as could be surrounded by a bullock's hide cut into strips, made it the foundation of her city. The Roman poet, Virgil, afterwards added a story that she had there been visited by Æneas in the course of his wanderings; and that when he forsook her, she raised a funeral pile, mounted it, and there, while it was set on fire, she stabbed herself to the heart.

It is said that an inscription was once found recording Carthage to have been a settlement of the Canaanites expelled by Joshua; but be this as it may, they were in every respect complete Canaanites—with the same cruel worship of the idol Moloch, the same perfidious temper, the same love of gain and ability for commerce, as were to be found in their brethren in Syria. Carthage was by far the largest Phœnician settlement; the city was magnificent, and its commerce had spread into every part of the known world, even beyond the Pillars of Hercules, which guarded the entrance of the Mediterranean, and to the shores of the distant land of frost and fog, then called the Isles of Tin.

The Carthaginians had sent out many colonies, both to the coasts of Africa and Spain, and the islands of the western Mediterranean, and they held under their power a large district of the surrounding country. Their government was not unlike that of Rome, excepting that theirs was a commercial, not a warlike republic; and they esteemed wealth far above glory, not fighting their own battles, but committing their defence to paid soldiers—Greeks seeking their fortune, Moorish horsemen, and slaves of all descriptions—who were regarded by the merchant princes, their employers, with mingled dread and dislike.

So great was the power and influence of Carthage, that it might easily have become dangerous to Rome in her earlier days, had it not been weakened and kept in check by the Greek colonies, which divided with it the possession of the island of Sicily.

After the Athenian expedition, which ended so unfortunately, in the course of the Peloponnesian war, a man named Dionysius rose to great power at Syracuse, and ruled as king from 405 to 367. He was of a stern and harsh temper, and was guilty of so many cruelties, that his name stands as the very type of tyrants; but he was possessed of great abilities, and by uniting the other Greeks of Sicily with the Syracusans, was able several times to defeat the Carthaginians, and almost to drive them out of Sicily. The most noted stories told of him are those of his Ear, and of his friend Damocles. His Ear was a chamber in his state prison, which was said to be so constructed that he could hear from it all that his unfortunate captives said to each other, and make use of their unguarded speeches against them. Damocles was a courtier, who once expressed a wish to be one day in the place of the king.

Dionysius told him his desire was granted, and accordingly Damocles, the next day, was placed on the throne, and attended with the utmost state and splendour; but in the midst of the feast, when he raised his eyes, all his delight was turned into terror at the sight of a naked sword, the point immediately over his head, only suspended by a single slight thread. Such, according to Dionysius, was the life of a king; but it was only true of that of an unlawful tyrant, reigning only by terror, not by right, or by the love of his people.

Dionysius said at his death that he left his son an empire cemented with bands of iron; but Dionysius the younger was much inferior to him in ability, and after leading an indolent life, was dethroned in 356 by his nephew Dion, and was afterwards obliged to maintain himself by keeping a school.

At Syracuse, as well as elsewhere, the valour of the Greeks was fast declining; this barrier to the Carthaginian power was much weakened; and now, sixty years after the death of Alexander, while the wars between the lesser powers into which his empire was broken up, were raging fiercely, the Romans, rulers of their mountainous peninsula, and the Carthaginians, lords of the sea, first began the struggle which was to decide which of them should be the dominant power, ignorant alike of the prophecy which had given the foremost place to Japhet, and declared that Canaan should be a servant.

PART II.   FIRST PUNIC WAR.   B. C. 263–240.

THE beginning of the dispute between Rome and Carthage, seems to have been the aid which the Romans sent to the Mamertines, a settlement of Italian soldiers in Sicily, where first commenced what was called the Punic War, from Pœnus, the Latin for a Phœnician.

The contest was at first entirely in Sicily, till at length the Romans, finding the disadvantage of having no power by sea, built a fleet of their own, after the model of a Carthaginian war galley, which had been stranded on their coast. They furnished their ships with machines to grapple with and sink those of the enemy, and by this means so compensated for their inferiority in skill, that they were victorious in several sea-fights, and at last landed a considerable force, under the command of the Consul, Marcus Attilius Regulus, on the Carthaginian territory in Africa.

Regulus gained several successes at first, and the Senate continued him in the command there after his year of consulship was over, though he entreated to be allowed to return home to his own little farm, as a slave had stolen his implements of husbandry, and he feared that his wife and children would be in want if he continued absent. The Senate promised to provide for them, and he remained in Africa, where he had made great progress, when Xantippus, a Spartan general, who chanced to be at Carthage, placed himself at the head of the army, defeated him, and made him prisoner.

Knowing the manner in which the cruel and jealous Carthaginians were wont to requite the services rendered to them, especially by strangers, Xantippus fled for his life immediately after his victory, and indeed it is said that he did not escape, being thrown into the sea by the master of the ship in which he sailed, by orders of the Carthaginian Senate.

After a long captivity, Regulus was sent home by the Carthaginians to carry proposals of peace, which they hoped to make him urge upon his countrymen, by forcing him to swear that he would return to his prison, if the terms were not accepted. He arrived before the walls of Rome, but he would not enter the city, saying that he was no longer a senator, no longer a man of consular rank, but only a slave of Carthage. The Senate met without the walls to hear him, and highly did they esteem him, when he spoke exactly contrary to his own interest, advising them by all means to persist in the war, explaining to them the weak points of Carthage, and begging them not to waste one thought on the safety of himself, an old man, who could be of little further benefit to the state. He even dissuaded them from exchanging prisoners, by which means he might have been saved, saying that they would thus be the losers, since no less than thirteen Carthaginian generals were in their hands, and he was the only Roman commander who was a prisoner.

The Senate, almost against their will, were thus persuaded to continue the war, and tried to induce him to disregard the oath extorted from him by force, and remain at home instead of returning to chains and death; but this noble-minded man stood firm against their entreaties, and the tears of his wife and children. The sacredness of his word, and the good of his country, were dearer to him than life and liberty, and without setting foot either within the walls of Rome, or on his own beloved estate, he went back to his enemies. The Carthaginians, unable to appreciate his greatness, and enraged at him for disappointing their plans, put him to death with cruel tortures; but the glory of his name has never been forgotten.

The continuance of the war obtained for the Romans a more favourable treaty than had been at first proposed. The Carthaginians, weary of a war which had lasted twenty-three years, and was doing much injury to their commerce, gave up to the Romans the islands of Sardinia and Sicily, with the exception of Syracuse, which still continued independent, at least in name, and a peace was concluded in 240, putting an end to the First Punic War.

PART III. HANNIBAL IN ITALY. B.C. 219–203.

AFTER the close of the First Punic War, there was an interval of peace, and for the second time since the foundation of Rome, the temple of Janus was closed. Meanwhile, the losses that Carthage had sustained were deeply felt in that city, and Hamilcar, the most able of her statesmen, declared that he was bringing up his four sons to be lion-whelps against Rome. He tried to compensate for the loss of Sicily, by extending the power of Carthage over Spain, then called Iberia, whence much wealth was derived from the rich silver mines; but the Kelts and Iberians, who inhabited Spain, were a warlike race, and Hamilcar at length fell in battle with them, leaving the command of the army to his youngest son, Hannibal, who at nine years old had been led to the altar of Baal, and there made to swear eternal hatred to Rome.

No sooner had Hannibal trained his army to obey him implicitly, than he sought a quarrel with Rome, hoping to strike a blow which must be fatal to her. In 219 he took Saguntum, a Spanish town in alliance with the Romans, and as soon as they complained of his breach of the treaty, set off to invade Italy itself. His march was one of the most celebrated that was ever made. At the head of a force, consisting partly of

Carthaginians, partly of Gauls, and Spanish Kelts, with a body of Moorish, or Numidian horse, and twenty-two elephants, he crossed the Pyrenees, marched round the Gulf of Lyons, and entered upon the passage of the Alps, which had hitherto never been trodden excepting by the Gauls. The hardships and difficulties with which he had to contend, were dreadful; he had to fight his way through treacherous Gauls, to climb precipice after precipice, to struggle with snow and ice, and even in one instance to cut out a way through the solid rock; but at length his perseverance was rewarded by seeing the fair plains of Italy lie extended at his feet, and he entered on the beautiful country on the banks of the river Eridanus, or Po.

Publius Cornelius Scipio, the Consul who first led his troops against him, was totally defeated on the river Ticinus, and so severely wounded, that he was with difficulty saved by his son Publius, who gallantly defended him, and led him out of the battle. Before he had recovered from his wound, his colleague, Tiberius Sempronius Longus, fancying he should enjoy the sole credit of the victory, again offered Hannibal battle, and met with a disastrous defeat at Trebia.

During the winter which now set in, Hannibal made his way through the marshes of the Arno, where both he and his army suffered dreadfully from the unhealthy atmosphere, which caused him to lose an eye, and such were the difficulties of the march, that his life was said to have been saved by the last remaining elephant, which carried him safely through the swamp.

He again defeated the Romans at the lake Thrasymene, and entered upon the plains of Campania, without having experienced a check, until Quintus Fabius

Maximus was appointed Dictator. Fabius never offered battle, but acquired the name of Cunctator, or Delayer, by always keeping encamped near the enemy, harassing the stragglers, and preventing them from obtaining provisions, by which means he reduced them to great straits; but when he went out of office, and Lucius Æmilius Paulus, and Caius Terentius Varro, became consuls, the rashness of Varro prevailed over the counsels of his wiser colleague, and involved them in the battle of Cannæ, the most ruinous of all. Æmilius did his utmost to retrieve the day, but in vain; the slaughter was immense, and very few saved themselves by flight. The tribune Lentulus, in the course of his flight, found Æmilius sitting on a stone, bleeding fast, and offered him his own horse to escape; but the Consul refused, desiring him to save himself, and saying he had no mind either to have to justify himself or to accuse his colleague before the Senate. The pursuers here approaching, Lentulus was obliged to fly, and looking back, saw the Consul fall pierced with darts. So great was the loss, that Hannibal sent to Carthage a bushel of the rings, worn by the equites, collected from the field of battle.

Cannæ was the point of Hannibal's chief success, and it has often been matter of surprise that he did not instantly march upon Rome; but his own losses had been considerable, and the Carthaginians, with their usual base jealousy, would not send him fresh supplies; besides which, the army that he still possessed was rendered less prompt and vigorous, by the pleasures to which they were tempted by the wealth and delicious climate of Campania.

His brother Hasdrubal was in Spain, collecting troops for him, but was there opposed by Scipio and his brother, until at length he succeeded in defeating them in a battle, in which they were both slain, and he then marched in Hannibal's track to enter Italy. At the river Metaurus he was met by the Consul, Caius Claudius Nero, and killed in battle, after which Nero returning to the south, ordered his head to be thrown down in front of his brother's camp, and sent two prisoners to carry the news of the defeat to Hannibal. After this disaster, Hannibal was never able to attempt any great thing against the Romans; but he would not leave Italy, and remained with his army in Bruttium, the extreme south of the peninsula, waiting, in the vain hope of some turn of affairs to his advantage, and seeing plainly that the only chance for Carthage was in weakening Rome in her own neighbourhood.

PART IV. CONCLUSION OF THE SECOND PUNIC WAR.
B.C. 214–201.

THE Carthaginians had all this time been endeavouring to stir up enemies against Rome. They entered into an alliance with Philip, King of Macedon, the same who poisoned Aratus, and he began to entertain projects of crossing the Adriatic Sea, and invading Italy; but the Romans stirred up the Ætolians to attack him, and by this means gave him sufficient occupation at home.

The Carthaginians next induced the Greek city of Syracuse to shake off the alliance with the Romans, and declare in their favour. Marcus Claudius Marcellus, a fierce and impetuous soldier, who had served against Hannibal with great distinction, was sent to reduce the city, but he met with great difficulties, for the town was well fortified, and within it was Archimedes, one of the most famous mathematicians that ever existed, who invented machines which the besiegers exceedingly dreaded. At last, after a two years' siege, Marcellus discovered a weak place in the walls, by which he succeeded in surprising the citizens and taking the town by assault. He gave up the city to be plundered, and his troops exercised great cruelties. Archimedes was slain by a soldier who did not know him, although Marcellus had given especial orders that he should be spared. It is said that he was so intently occupied with a mathematical problem, that he never heard the storm of the city, and was first roused by a soldier, who rushed with a drawn sword, and held it over his head. "Wait," said Archimedes, "till I have finished my demonstration;" but the man not understanding him, killed him on the spot. Syracuse was taken in 212, and thenceforth became part of the Roman province of Sicily.

The young Publius Cornelius Scipio, who had saved his father's life at the Ticinus, was appointed, at twenty-four years of age, to the command in Spain. He was one of the best as well as the greatest of the Romans, with an earnest belief in the protection and guidance of the gods, and never undertaking anything without prayer; and of a disposition so amiable, that he gained the affection of his army, and won many allies to the cause of Rome. In Spain he was completely successful, winning the whole of the Carthaginian possessions, and gaining the alliance of many of the Kelts, after which he returned to Rome, and represented to the Senate that the best hope of obliging Hannibal to leave Italy, would be to carry the war into Africa, so as to oblige him to return to the defence of Carthage.

The cautious old Fabius thought the enterprise too

dangerous, and prevailed on the Senate, instead of giving Scipio an army to invade Africa, only to appoint him proconsul of Sicily, with leave to cross to Africa if he thought it expedient. In Sicily, therefore, he collected a great number of Italians, trained them in the use of arms, and at length sailed for Africa, where, by winning to his cause Masinissa, King of Numidia, he deprived Carthage of the Moorish horse, which had hitherto been her great strength.

The Carthaginians were obliged to recall Hannibal to protect them, but even he was not equal in generalship to Scipio, and was totally defeated at the battle of Zama. The loss was so great, that the Carthaginians found it impossible to continue the war, and were forced to accept the hard terms which the Romans imposed. They were to give up all their war-galleys and elephants, and never to build any more ships, or train elephants for war; they were to pay an immense tribute, and never make war upon any ally of Rome; and thus, with a complete crushing of their power, ended the Second Punic War in 201.

Scipio was received at Rome with a magnificent triumph, and obtained the surname of Africanus. He was the first Roman who studied Greek literature and arts, which were at that time despised by most of his stern rugged countrymen.

Hannibal remained for some time longer at Carthage, doing his best to improve the institutions of his country, until his enemies accused him to the Romans of caballing against them, and he was obliged to fly to the court of Antiochus the Great, King of Syria.

CHAPTER XI.

GROWTH OF THE ROMAN POWER. B.C. 201-146.

PART I. MANNERS OF THE LATER COMMONWEALTH.
B.C. 201-146.

UNTIL the end of the Second Punic War, the continual warfare of the Romans might be regarded as necessary to secure their independence, since if they had not overcome the Etruscans, the Samnites, and the Carthaginians, they would assuredly have been crushed by them.* After this period, however, their wars were only for the sake of conquest, and for the most part, unnecessary and unjust; but the leading men in the state promoted them because they were the means of obtaining distinction; and the lower classes, because so much wealth was acquired from the conquered countries, that no taxes were asked from the Roman citizens.

The usual policy of the Romans was to find a pretext for war with the greater states, by undertaking the protection of some petty nation on the borders, which, whether justly or unjustly, complained of oppression; then to break the power of the unfortunate kingdom, and make a peace with it on terms so hard, that when the first effects of the defeat had slightly worn off, there was sure to be a rising against it, which the Romans chose to call rebellion, and thereupon to complete its overthrow, and turn it into a Roman province. Not unlike the manner in which a cat treats her prey, first laming it, and then letting it imagine itself free for a few moments, but on the first struggle to escape, completing its destruction, and devouring it at her leisure.

The allies who had first asked their aid fared no better, but were soon cast off, and a pretence found for subduing them, and at last no colour was even sought for such injustice, and Rome ruled only by the right of the strongest.

The Consuls usually spent the year of their consulate at Rome, and at its close took their choice of the provinces, where they were either to govern or to conduct the war, with the title of Proconsul, and more absolute authority than they had enjoyed at home. They continued there three, five, or even eight years, according to the will of the Senate, or the circumstances of the time. Lesser provinces were given to the Prætors after their year of office was at an end, with the title of Proprætor, and thus every Roman of rank was obliged in his turn to become a statesman and a general.

They often used their authority shamefully, cruelly oppressing the subject people, and gathering to themselves immense fortunes out of the public revenues. The days were gone by when a Roman patrician gloried in his honest poverty, and patricians and plebeians alike for the most part grasped at all they could acquire both of land and of slaves. The Licinian law against holding more than an estate of a certain size was evaded, and the captives taken in war being sold at a cheap rate, every rich man had his house and estate filled with multitudes of them. They were made to till the land entirely, so as to leave no employment for the poorer freemen who had hitherto been hired for the purpose; and not only this, but they manufactured all that their master required in his family, dresses, furniture, &c., putting the artizans of Rome out of work, while there were some who, being of Grecian blood, were capable of high cultivation of mind, and were often more learned than their masters, by whom they were employed as secretaries, and as tutors for their children. This upper class of slaves seem for the most part to have been well treated, and often were much attached to their lord, by whom they were often released from bondage.

The worst use to which the Romans put their slaves was to make them fight with each other for their amusement. These unfortunate fighting slaves were called gladiators, and kept in schools, where they were carefully trained in the use of arms, but without the slightest hope of ever using them for any purpose but the destruction of each other. Large buildings were erected, called amphitheatres, in the form of a circle, or of a horse-shoe, with an open space strewed with sand in the middle, and seats rising one behind the other around, where the spectators sat at their ease, watching sometimes fights between wild beasts, sometimes between beasts and men, and sometimes between gladiators, fights even to the death. When a gladiator was wounded, his antagonist, who had probably that very morning eaten of the same food and drunk of the same cup, turned to the spectators to demand what should be his fate; if they turned down their thumbs, the poor man's life was spared for the time, if they held them up, the victor was obliged to kill him, and the victor himself had nothing to expect but in his turn to be put to death when his strength or good fortune should depart.

Shows of gladiators were what the Romans chiefly

delighted in, and even at last almost required of candidates for the consulship. It is frightful to think of the multitudes thus "butchered to make a Roman holiday," and, as well might be expected, the pleasure they took in the sight of such spectacles, served above all things to harden their hearts and increase their indifference to human suffering.

With all this, there was much more of taste for literature at Rome than there had ever been before, that learning, be it remembered, which does not, of necessity, either improve or soften the disposition. Books, works of art, and teachers of every description, came from Greece, philosophy and eloquence were studied, the knowledge of the Greek language became a necessary accomplishment, and the Romans began to compose for themselves, though their works were in general but poor imitations of those of Greece. It was now, too, that the whole Greek mythology was adopted; some believed, some laughed at it, all earnestness of faith was fast becoming forgotten; the Epicurean philosophy was professed by great numbers, and with it came deadness to all the higher and better principles that had once served as motives of action.

Luxury and splendour were fast increasing with riches. Every wealthy Roman possessed a house in the city, and one villa or more at his country property, decorated in the richest manner he could afford, with the pavement of the court composed of tiles, in beautiful mosaic work, and the gardens laid out with great care and cost, with statues, beautifully-trained trees, and fish-ponds. The fish were kept for amusement, and indeed, one Roman Senator was accused in public of having shed tears for the death of a favourite fish, to which he retorted by saying his accuser had lost three wives without weeping for one of them.

The couches on which the Romans lay at meal-times were covered with cushions, and so arranged as to hold three persons; the feasts were of the most sumptuous kind, consisting of rich meats, vegetables cooked in different ways, varieties of fish, sometimes brought from a great distance, fatted dormice, and other delicacies, which to our taste would be equally strange.

Those who wished to maintain the severe old manners viewed this style of living with great displeasure, and did all they could, by edicts, to prevent it. Sometimes they forbade the having more than a certain number of guests, sometimes the dressing more than three dishes of meat; now there was a law against the fatting of dormice, and now against any poultry appearing at table except one old thin hen; but it was all in vain, the laws were evaded and disregarded, and the feasts continually grew more splendid and costly.

Dress, too, was becoming very different; the colour of the toga was varied, and at last other garments, considered more becoming, were adopted, and the toga itself was only used when it was necessary to appear in the official dress of a citizen. Ladies had at one time been prohibited from driving in a chariot, or wearing gold or purple, but at last they would submit no longer, and raised a great tumult for the repeal of the law. Marcus Porcius Cato, the censor, a stern, plain old Roman, opposed them with all his might. He said the poorer would be tempted to vie with the rich, and grow ashamed of their poverty. "And," most wisely said he, "she who once begins to blush for doing what she ought, will quickly cease to blush for doing what she ought not." However, the ladies gained their point, and soon were spending immense sums on gold and jewels.

All this time, however, the Roman army did not lose its effectiveness, and fought with much more knowledge of tactics than previously. Wherever they rested they threw up a rampart, and dug a deep ditch around the camp, which was always exactly square, with four gates, and often so firmly made, that the remains exist to the present day. So complete was the discipline, that it was impossible to take a Roman camp by surprise, and every soldier knew his own post without chance of a mistake. The winters were usually employed in strengthening the defences, or in constructing roads, so as to secure the communication with Rome, and from one station to another; roads so solid, that many are still in existence. The soldiers were often rewarded for their services by being allowed to settle in the conquered countries without losing their rights as citizens, and the colonies thus formed had privileges superior to those of the other towns in the provinces.

The changes here related were gradually coming on during the period upon which the history now enters, and as it is difficult to mark the commencement of each, it has been thought better to put them together at the beginning, so as to explain much that will follow.

PART II. WAR WITH MACEDON. B.C. 215–146.

BEFORE the end of the Punic War, the Romans had already made themselves known in Greece, by putting an end to the piracies of the Illyrians, whose country was their first possession on the eastern shore of the Adriatic. They had likewise formed an alliance with the Ætolians, whom they had stirred up against Philip,

King of Macedon, so as to prevent him from coming to the aid of Hannibal.

The Ætolians, being hard pressed by Philip, called upon the Romans for help, an invitation which they rejoiced in accepting, and in 196, Titus Quinctius Flaminius, defeated Philip at the rocks of Cynocephalæ, and obliged him to accept such terms as the Romans were willing to grant. In particular, Philip was forced to give up all the Greek towns, both in Europe and Asia, and Flaminius, going to Corinth, when great numbers of Greeks were assembled at the Isthmian games, declared to them that Rome bestowed freedom upon Greece.

The joy of the Greeks was excessive, their shouts rose so loud that it was said that birds high in the air fell down stunned by the noise, and no honours were deemed too great for Flaminius, their deliverer; but it soon proved that the promised freedom only meant that it was Rome, instead of Macedon, that held them in bondage, as the stern interference of their new masters made them feel, whenever they attempted any exertion of free will.

This surrender of the cities held by Philip in Asia, gave occasion to the Romans for interference there. They had likewise two allies, whose quarrel they chose to support against Syria, namely, the young King Ptolemy of Egypt, and Eumenes, King of Pergamus; nor was Antiochus the Great, King of Syria, disposed to avoid a war. Hannibal was at his court, and ever persevering in enmity to the Romans, was persuading him to go himself to invade Greece, whilst he gave another army to Hannibal, with which a second time to attack the Romans in Italy.

Antiochus was at first pleased with the project, and actually led an army into Ætolia; but his pride and jealousy of Hannibal prevented him from listening to his further proposals; he wasted his time in pleasure in the Isle of Eubœa, and at last, on the approach of the Romans, returned to Asia Minor. Lucius Cornelius Scipio offered to conduct the war; and his brother, the great Africanus, accompanied him as his legate. A great battle was fought at Mount Sipylus, in which Antiochus was totally defeated. Neither of the two great generals were present at this battle, since Africanus was absent in consequence of illness, and Hannibal was besieged in a town of Pamphylia, but it is said they met on friendly terms about this time, and Scipio, in the course of the conversation, asked Hannibal who he thought the greatest of generals. "Alexander," answered Hannibal; and Scipio asking whom he considered the next, he said, "Pyrrhus." "And the third?" "Myself," was the reply. "What would you have said if you had conquered me?" said Scipio. "Then," said the Carthaginian, "I should have placed myself before Alexander."

When peace was made, the Romans insisted that Antiochus should dismiss Hannibal from his court; Scipio remonstrated against this as ungenerous persecution of a brave enemy, but in vain, and Hannibal was obliged to seek protection from Prusias, King of Bithynia. Here again the Romans pursued him, insisting that Prusias should drive him away, and Hannibal, worn out with disappointment and vexation, put an end to his life by poison, saying that he would rid the Romans of their fears of an old man.

Lucius Scipio received the surname of Asiaticus, but the year after his return to Rome, Marcus Porcius Cato called him to give an account of his government in yria. Africanus was greatly indignant at the accusations laid against his brother, and rescued him by force from the hands of the tribune, but Cato proceeded to require of himself an account of the spoil of Carthage. Africanus, whose conduct had been perfectly upright, would not say a word in answer to the charges laid against him, and on the second day of his trial, just as the judges had taken their seats, he exclaimed, "This is the anniversary of my victory of Zama, let us return thanks to the gods, instead of sitting wrangling here." The senate were carried away by the recollection; Scipio led the way to the Capitol, and after the sacrifice had been performed, he left the city, no one offering him any opposition, going to his own estate at Liternum, where he spent the rest of his life, and desired to be buried there, that his ungrateful city might not possess even his bones.

He died in 183. In the same year died Hannibal, and likewise Philopœmon, the brave Achæan, often called the last of the Greeks, who was taken prisoner and shamefully murdered by the Messenians.

PART III.   PERSECUTION OF THE JEWS.   B. C. 167–107.

The wars of Antiochus the Great are predicted in the Book of Daniel. The Jews suffered much in his time, as their country was generally the battle-field on which he fought with the Ptolemies. He was killed while plundering the temple of Elymais, in Persia, in 187, and it was in the reign of his son Seleucus, called in Daniel a raiser of taxes, that Heliodorus was sent to carry off the sacred treasures from Jerusalem. Onias, the high-priest, assembled the people, and offered up the most earnest prayers for protection; and they were answered as of old, for just as Heliodorus was about to break into the treasury, there appeared a horse and his rider of glorious beauty, arrayed in glittering armour, and attended by two young men of equally marvellous appearance, who smote the spoiler to the ground, and scourged him, so that he was carried out speechless and senseless.

Onias, at the entreaty of the friends of Heliodorus, offered up prayers for him, and the two angelic forms once more visited him, told him that his life had been spared at the intercession of the high-priest, and bade him publish to all the world the mighty works of the Lord.

Thus the chosen people were once more visibly assured " that the angel of the Lord tarrieth round about them that fear him ;" and it was well for them that their faith should be thus strengthened, since heathenism was now about to make a great effort to overwhelm that single spot of light which shone in Judea.

Heliodorus poisoned his master Seleucus, and Antiochus Epiphanes, second son of Antiochus the Great, usurped the throne, "the vile person obtained the kingdom by flatteries." His wickedness and cruelty were great, and his folly and levity made him despised by all. After drinking to excess he would wander about the streets of Antioch, dressed in a white garment, and throw stones at all he met; and he behaved at the festivals of his own gods in such a manner as to make them more a jest than a solemnity. Nevertheless, he was resolved to force their worship upon all his subjects. The good high-priest, Onias, was supplanted by his apostate brothers, Jason and Menelaus, who supported the king's plans, set up an arena at Jerusalem for the practice of the Greek exercises, and allowed the priests themselves to leave the service of the altar, to contend in the games of wrestling, throwing the disc, &c.

Soon orders were sent that the Temple should be dedicated to Jupiter, and the king himself soon after coming to Jerusalem, broke into the Holy Place, offered swine's flesh on the altar, and sprinkled the whole building with broth of swine's flesh in order to desecrate it. Every Jew who refused to sacrifice to Jupiter, to carry ivy in a procession in honour of Bacchus, or to eat swine's flesh, was put to death with cruel tortures. Two women who had circumcised their children were thrown from the walls after their babes had been hung round their necks; and the venerable scribe Eleazar, and the mother with her seven sons, were the most noted of the other martyrs. Many Jews, however, submitted; an altar of Jupiter was raised in the very Holy of Holies, and never had the true worship seemed in so much danger as when the Temple was desecrated, and priests and people alike apostate.

At last at the little town of Modin in Judea, when the people were gathered together by an officer of Antiochus, and called upon to offer sacrifice, Mattathias, one of the seed of Aaron, firmly refused, and full of righteous zeal, struck down a Jew who was advancing to the altar of Jupiter, and then, with the aid of his sons, and some of the other Jews, overpowered and killed the Greeks.

They then fled with their families to the mountains, where they were joined by many other faithful Jews, and began to make war upon their enemies. Mattathias himself did not live long, and at his death he appointed to the command his third son, Judas, called, from his courage, Maccabæus, or the Hammerer.

Judas was one who trusted in the protection of God, and who therefore obtained it; with very inferior numbers he thrice routed the whole Greek army, and recovered the whole of Judea. He marched to Jerusalem, entered the city, and purified the Temple on the very day three years after it had been dedicated to Jupiter; but the fortress on Mount Zion was held by a garrison of apostate Jews, who greatly harassed their countrymen in the city.

Antiochus Epiphanes had made an expedition into Perisa, where he learnt the tidings of the success of the Jews. In great fury he set out to chastise them, but on his way he was siezed by an agonizing and loathsome disease, and suffered almost equal anguish of mind at the thought of his cruelty and sacrilege. He died in 163, and was succeeded by his son Antiochus Eupator, who followed up the war against Maccabæus and his brothers, until he was dethroned by his cousin Demetrius. Judas now sent to request the alliance of the Romans, but before the ambassadors returned, in a battle with the apostate Jews, he was defeated and slain, and the faithful were again reduced to the greatest distress. Rallying around his brother Jonathan, they again showed great courage, and gained more and more ground from their enemies, until they finally obtained, in the year 143, an acknowledgment both from Syria and Rome, that they were a free and independent people.

Jonathan was about this time treacherously murdered, but his brother Simon succeeded to the government, and was at once prince and high-priest of the Jews; his son succeeded him, and his grandson, Aristobulus, assumed the title of king.

Onias, the son of the former high-priest, who had

been banished by Antiochus Epiphanes, had founded a settlement of Jews in Egypt, with a temple, which had once been dedicated to Isis, thus fulfilling a prophecy of Isaiah, that five cities in Egypt should speak the language of Canaan.

PART IV   FINAL CONQUEST OF GREECE.   B. C. 196–145.

PHILIP, King of Macedon, remained subject to Rome after his defeat at Cynocephalæ, but nourished a bitter hatred against the Romans, which was inherited by his son Perseus, who coming to the throne in 179, made a last struggle for independence. After the war had lasted a considerable time, Lucius Æmilius Paulus, son of him who was killed at Cannæ, was sent against him, conducted the war with great skill, and at last defeated him at Pydna, in 168. Perseus fled, and wandered about in a miserable state, till at last he was captured at Samothrace. He sent to entreat the victor not to exhibit him in his triumph, to which all the answer that Æmilius vouchsafed was, "The favour he asks of me, he may obtain of himself;" meaning that Perseus had it his power to escape this indignity by suicide, for so perverted were the notions of the Rommans, that they esteemed self-murder as something brave and high-spirited, instead of looking upon it as a cowardly means of escaping misfortune.

Æmilius was generally esteemed a humane man, and he highly valued the learning and arts of the Greeks; yet he did not oppose an order which arrived from the Senate, that no less than seventy cities of Epirus should be given up to be plundered by his soldiers. On his return to Rome, he enjoyed a splendid triumph, being rowed from the mouth of the Tiber in Perseus's own state galley, and afterwards going in procession to the Capitol, followed by the unfortunate king, chained and in deep mourning, after which Perseus was sent to Alba, where he spent the rest of his life.

The Ætolians, the original allies of Rome, next rose against them, and were speedily crushed, and the Senate thinking the Achæan League had shown a disposition to join them, required a thousand citizens to be sent as prisoners to Rome. Of these the most noted was Polybius the historian, son of one of the chief men of Megalopolis. At Rome he became a great friend of Æmilius, who placed under his care his two sons, the youngest of whom, having been adopted by Scipio, the son of Africanus, bore the name of Publius Cornelius Scipio Æmilianus. These exiles remainded for seventeen years at Rome, all their entreaties to be allowed to return home being refused, until at last Æmilianus begged Cato, the censor, to use his influence in their behalf, and on the next debate Cato arose, and said, " It was a waste of time to question whether these wretched old men should lay their bones in Italy or Achæa." His unfeeling speech had the effect of exciting some contemptuous pity, and they were at length permitted to return.

The unjust yoke which Rome had imposed upon Greece was severely felt, and the Achæans at last began to struggle against it. Lucius Mummius came to oppose them, easily routed their forces, and entering Corinth, gave it up to be plundered and burnt. The various rich metal ornaments of the houses and temples, being melted together in the flames, formed a mass of metal, which was called Corinthian brass, and was considered as one of the best materials for statuary. Great numbers of choice pictures, statues, and other works of art, were captured. Mummius, a rough ignorant plebeian, only valued them because others thought them precious, and was much laughed at by the more cultivated Romans for telling the masters of the ships to whose care he committed them, that they must supply new ones if these were lost. He was, however, more honest than many who had more education, for he took no private property, and only sent that of the state to Rome; nor did he even help himself to the price of any of these spoils, but after exhibiting them in his triumph, gave them freely to adorn the public buildings of Rome.

The ruin of Corinth was in 145, and with it fell the last remains of Grecian independence. Greece became a Roman province under the name of Achæa, and therefore shared the fate of its Roman masters. Athens was still celebrated for its learning and beauty, and became a sort of college for the studies of the young Romans.

PART V   THIRD PUNIC WAR.   B. C. 149–146.

THE victory by which the Romans had broken the strength of Carthage had not contented them; they were resolved on the complete destruction of their ancient enemy, and only watched for a pretext for treading her underfoot.

It was not long before they found one. The old Numidian king, Masinissa, their ally, was constantly making inroads on the domains of Carthage and robbing the inhabitants, who took up arms to repel these incursions; the Romans called this a breaking of the treaty, which forbade them to make war on the friends of Rome, and prepared to punish them. If the unfortunate Carthaginians had been overcome when in possession of ships, trained elephants, bands of practised soldiers, and such a general as Hannibal, much less could they hope for success in their present weakened state, and they therefore declared themselves willing to do anything to avert the wrath of their oppressors.

They gave hostages, yielded up their arms, destroyed the fortifications of the city, but all in vain; the Romans were resolved to drive them to extremity, and sent them for answer that nothing would satisfy the Senate excepting that they should all leave their city, that it should be overthrown, and they transplanted to another spot at a distance from the sea. This last command was more than they could endure; all with one voice declared that death was better than such usage, and prepared to hold out to the last. Men, women, and children laboured to rebuild the walls; new weapons were made from the iron and brass used in the houses and furniture; even gold and silver were melted up for the purpose, and when ropes were needed for the machines, the women cut off their long hair and twisted it into cordage.

Scipio Æmilianus was appointed to subdue them, and landed with a large army, with which he began the siege of the city; but for a whole year all his attempts were baffled by the despairing inhabitants, who held out in spite of hunger, misery, and factions among themselves. When at length he forced the walls, each of the tall houses was defended against him like a fortress, and could not be taken till after much hard fighting, in which numbers of his soldiers perished, and day after day fire and slaughter raged in the streets. Scipio himself was struck with the overthrow of the once mighty city; he shed tears at the sight of the desolation around, as he reflected that in its turn Rome might be destined to decay and fall.

Carthage was by order of the Senate completely ruined and laid waste; the inhabitants who still survived were sold for slaves, and the country round formed into a Roman province. This was in the year 146, the same as witnessed the equally cruel destruction of Corinth.

Scipio returned to Rome, and was, as usual, honoured with a triumph, and with the surname of Africanus. He was afterwards sent into Spain, where the Kelts were making a brave resistance to the encroachments of the Romans. The town of Numantia held out against him for two years; and at last, after dreadful sufferings from famine, the unhappy people died by each other's hands rather than yield to the conqueror, and he a second time found himself the victor over a scene of desolaton. His personal character seems to have been kind, upright, and generous, but, like all other Romans, he unscrupulously executed the cruel decrees of the state, and did not spare the vanquished one humiliation that could conduce, as he thought, to his own glory.

About the same time, Attalus, the last King of Pergamus, bequeathed his dominions to the Roman state, thus giving them a firm footing in Asia Minor, which they did not fail to extend, though at the expense of long and dreadful wars.

CHAPTER XII.

FACTIONS OF ROME. b. c. 133-30.

PART I. THE GRACCHI. B. C. 133-122.

During the period that next ensued, Rome was reaping the reward of the misfortunes it inflicted on other nations, in the disputes between the Senate and people, which filled its streets with bloodshed, and finally destroyed the republic itself.

Tiberius Sempronius Gracchus, the first to awaken the spirit of faction, was the eldest son of an officer who had fought bravely in Spain, and of Cornelia, daughter to the first Scipio Africanus. Cornelia was beautiful, learned, and high-spirited, and when early left a widow, refused, which was then very unusual, all offers of a second marriage, for the sake of her children, whom she brought up with great care. A lady who was visiting her made a great display of ornaments, and in return begged to see hers, upon which Cornelia called her children, and said, " Behold my jewels!"

Cornelia was ambitious for her sons, and when her daughter Sempronia married Scipio Æmilianus, she used to say it was a reproach to them that she should be called the daughter of one Africanus and the mother-in-law of the other, instead of the mother of the Gracchi. Tiberus Gracchus, as soon as he obtained the tribuneship, proposed an agrarian law, so as to **make a** fresh distribution of land. The rich opposed him with all their might, but the measure was carried by the votes of the plebeians, and he went on to provoke the Senate more and more, till, when his year of office was over, and he stood for his election the second time, his supporters made a great uproar in the Forum, and it was reported in the Senate-house that he was going to make himself king. The senators rushed down into the Forum in great anger, the plebeians fled in confusion, and Gracchus, falling down, was struck on the head with a stick and killed. His body was thrown into the Tiber, and no less than three hundred of his partizans shared the same fate.

Caius, the brother of Tiberius, was nine years younger, and his mother tried to prevent him from engaging in the courses which had proved so fatal to his brother, but in vain. As soon as he was old enough to be elected tribune, he obtained that office, carried out his brother's law, and took other steps still more dangerous to the state. Scipio Æmilianus was the best supporter of the Senate until his death, which happened so suddenly, that Caius Gracchus and his sister were accused of having poisoned him, but this is very improbable. Caius at length went out of office, and the Senate proceeded to repeal some of his measures; upon which a great tumult arose, and a number of his supporters drew together on the Aventine Hill, threatening to maintain their cause by force of arms. For this Caius was not prepared, and unable to resolve actually to fight against his country, he joined them, without weapons, and tried to come to terms with the Senate. Instead of attending to his proposals, the Consuls sent an armed force, at sight of which all his followers dispersed and fled. He withdrew into a sacred grove, where he obliged a faithful slave, who alone had followed him, to kill him, after which the poor slave fell on his own sword that he might not survive his master. The Senate had promised the weight of Gracchus's head in gold to whoever should kill him, and the person who found his body cut off the head, and filled it with melted lead in order to obtain a larger reward. His followers were pursued and slaughtered without mercy, and three thousand were killed, ten times the number who suffered for his brother's sedition, so quickly were the Romans increasing in cruelty. Cornelia, after the loss of her "jewels," retired to her country-house, where she lived highly respected for many years. At her death a statue was raised in her honour, bearing the title she had coveted, and obtained at so dear a price—"The Mother of the Gracchi."

PART II. MARIUS. B. C. 106–86.

On the death of Masinissa, the old King of Mauritania, his throne was usurped by his nephew, Jugurtha, who waged a long war with the Romans. Caius Marius at length reduced him to take refuge with Boccus, another Numidian king, by whom he was betrayed to the Romans. Lucius Cornelius Sylla was the officer sent to arrange the affair, and, as if profiting by treachery was a thing to be proud of, caused a seal to be engraved with the representation of himself, recieving Jugurtha from Boccus, and always wore it as his signet-ring, thus giving great offence to Marius, who considered that he took all the credit of the transaction to himself.

Marius and Sylla had a great hatred and contempt for each other. The first was a plebeian, born of poor parents in a country village, but his valour and ability had, while only a common soldier, gained the favour of

Scipio Æmilianus, and had since gradually raised him to the highest offices in the state. He was ignorant, violent in his passions, with a great dislike both to the pride and the luxury of the patricians, and as it had been declared in his childhood that he would be seven times consul, he was determined, at any cost, to fulfil the prediction. Sylla, born of the Cornelian gens, one of the noblest in Rome, had all the vices into which the patricians were too apt to fall, but he was an active warrior, and very learned and accomplished.

The next war was with the Cimbri and Teutones, two savage races, whose origin is not known, though, from their names, it would seem that the first must have been Kelts, and the second a part of the great Teutonic nation, that was spreading westwards from the Black Sea. They broke into Italy, and the part of Gaul which the Romans had subdued, and for several years did fearful damage there, routing all the armies sent against them, until Marius defeated them, first near Aix, in Gaul, and then near Milan. After this last rout, the survivors killed themselves, their wives, and children, and Italy was delivered from them.

Marius had already been five times consul; when he obtained his next election, partly by bribery, and partly by promises to the factious plebeians, he behaved so disgracefully to the senators, that he who had hitherto been highly esteemed, began to be looked upon almost as a traitor to the state. The favourite project of the revolutionary party was at this time to make all the other Italians Roman citizens, and this was strongly opposed by the Senate, who feared that when so many new voters were admitted, they should lose all influence in the assembly of the people. At last the Italians took up arms to obtain what they desired, and Marius was obliged to fight against them. The Social War, as it was called, lasted three years, and at last ended, in 88, in the Romans granting to all the Italians, except the Samnites, who were still in arms, the rights of Roman citizenship, although under certain restrictions, which they hoped would prevent the actual Romans from being out-voted.

While this was passing, Mithridates, King of Pontus, was becoming very dangerous to the Roman power in the East, and an army was to be sent against him, of which Marius and Sylla were each determined to have the command.

Sylla, who had just been consul, was regularly appointed by the Senate, upon which Marius called an assembly of the people, and finding that even there he should not be made general, broke into the Forum with his soldiers, drove the patricians out with violence, and made the mob declare him general. But Sylla, escaping from the tumult, went to his army, who would not part with him as their commander, led them into Rome, overcame the plebeians, had his own appointment confirmed, and restored the Senate to their authority. Marius had fled at his approach, and Sylla, making the Consuls, Publius Cornelius Cinna, and Caius Octavius, swear to preserve affairs in the state in which he left them, had marched off with his army.

Marius tried to escape to Africa, but was detained on the coast of Italy by contrary winds, and was obliged to land and hide himself in a hole among some reeds. Here he was taken, and carried to Minturnæ, where he was thrown into prison, and as the Senate had sent orders that he was to be put to death wherever he was found, a soldier was sent to kill him. The prison was very dark, and as he lay on the ground, it seemed to the frightened soldier that his eyes flashed fire, while he cried with a voice of thunder, "Darest thou kill Caius Marius?" The man turned, ran away in terror, crying out, "I cannot kill him;" and the people of the town, beginning to remember the favour Marius had once shown the cause of the Italians, became willing to save him, and gave him a ship, with which he safely arrived on the coast of Africa. There he wandered about among the broken walls and columns of Carthage, where the governor of the province sent to warn him to leave the place. All the answer he returned was, "Tell him that you have seen Caius Marius sitting among the ruins of Carthage," as if he meant that greatness fallen like his own should be his protection.

In the meantime the two consuls left at Rome had a violent quarrel, which ended in Cinna being driven out of Rome, and sending for Marius to assist him in maintaining his power. Marius returned, burning with rage against his enemies, still wearing the ragged dress in which he had wandered, and with his beard and hair untrimmed. He gathered round him a great army of Italians, and of runaway slaves, and soon forced Rome to open its gates. And now he satisfied his vengeance. The friends of Sylla were murdered in great numbers, and among them the best and most upright of the senators; nor was this all, for as Marius proceeded along the street, he ordered his body-guard of slaves to kill all whose salutation he did not return, and multitudes were cut down at his very feet. Day after day the slaughter continued, and the slaves perpetrated every kind of atrocity, so that Rome was one scene of terror, till at last Quintus Sertorius, an upright and honourable officer, who had had the folly to connect himself with the party of Marius, was so shocked at these horrors. that, as the only way of stopping them, he fell upon the slaves with his soldiers, and in one night speared four thousand of them.

Marius now attained his seventh consulship, but he did not enjoy it long, being quite worn out by the fatigues he had endured during his exile. He died on the sixteenth day of his consulship, in the seventy-first year of his age, in the year 86. It would have been well both for Rome and himself if he had died ten years sooner.

PART III. SYLLA. B.C. 88–76.

MITHRIDATES, the King of Pontus, against whom Sylla had been sent, was the ablest adversary, excepting Hannibal, with whom the Romans ever had to contend. He was decended from the old kings of Persia, and had received a Greek education, could speak twenty-five languages, and had a great knowledge of the art of medicine; he was wonderfully active and persevering, and often restored his affairs when they seemed in the most desperate condition. At the same time, he was both treacherous and cruel; he began his reign by the murder of his mother and brother; he killed many of his subjects, and, among many other vices, was a great drunkard.

He seized a great part of the Roman dominions in Asia, and sent orders that in all the towns willing to shake off their yoke, every Roman or Italian should be put to death on one night. The Asiatics were but too willing to comply, since they had often been very ill-used by the Romans, and neither the women nor children were spared, so that no less than eighty thousand perished in this massacre. After this he sent his army to Greece, and was in possession of Athens, and many other of the chief towns, when Sylla arrived with his forces, recovered Attica, and gained so many victories as at last to reduce him to sue for peace.

Sylla was glad to grant it, for he received no supplies from Rome, and was forced to maintain his army by plundering the country round; besides which, he was eager to return home, to revenge the death of his friends, who had been slaughtered by Marius's party. He therefore, after obliging Mithridates to give up a great part of his conquest, signed a treaty of peace, and set out on his return to Rome. Cinna had been killed by one of his own soldiers, but the revolutionary party still continued in power at Rome, and were prepared to resist Sylla by force of arms. No sooner, however did he appear, than their soldiers, who were always willing to follow so distinguished a general, all went over to him, except an army of Samnites, who fought a battle with him under the walls of Rome, and were there routed, and three thousand taken prisoners.

And now came the time for Sylla's vengeance, when he stained the cause of law and order with as much bloodshed as had been perpetrated by Marius himself. He began by causing his troops to murder the three thousand prisoners; and when their shrieks and cries reached the place where the Senate was assembled, he bade the Senators not disturb themselves, it was only a few wretches whom he was chastising. He was appointed Dictator, and proceeded daily to command the death of so many of those he deemed his enemies, that at last one of the Senators begged that he would let them know who was to live and who was to die, that the suspense might last no longer. Sylla accordingly drew up a list, which he called a proscription, containing about nine thousand names, and hung it up in the Forum, saying that if he recollected any more, he would add them afterwards. It was not only the adherents of Marius who were included in this dreadful list, but all who were hated or envied by any friend of Sylla, or who possessed any property coveted by his party. "Ah!" said one poor man, who was horror-struck at seeing his own name, "my Alban villa is my destruction!" and before he had gone many steps he was stabbed by a party of Sylla's soldiers.

In every quarter of Italy the same destruction was going on, till whole districts, especially about Samnium, became perfect deserts. At last the thirst for blood seemed to be satisfied, and Sylla applied himself to restore the government which Marius and Cinna had overthrown, and so well and wisely did he do so, that it causes additional regret at the horrible crimes with which he had stained its re-establishment.

When all had been set in order, and the constitution adapted to receive the great increase in the number of citizens, Sylla quitted the Dictatorship, in order to give himself up to his favourite pursuits, the exercise of his intellectual powers, and at the same time, the gratification of all the worst propensities of his nature. He wrote his own memoirs, and only completed them two days before his death, which was brought on by breaking a blood-vessel in a fit of passion. It is said by some that he had long been suffering from a dreadful disease, regarded as the punishment of his crimes. He died in the year 76.

PART IV. POMPEY. B. C. 76–63.

THE state of things which Sylla had left at Rome continued for about twenty years, during which time

Marcus Tullius Cicero became very eminent. He was of the equestrian order, and his profession was the law. He possessed great learning, and his eloquence was second only to that of Demosthenes; it was, moreover, always employed on the right side, and for the good of his country; and in spite of a few faults, of vanity and wavering, there was scarcely a statesman of ancient times whose career was so blameless. While he was Consul he discovered and disconcerted a conspiracy against the state, contrived by a wretch named Lucius Sergius Catilina, and the orations he made on that occasion are the most famous of his works. His letters to his friends have likewise been preserved, and show us the Roman habits and ways of thinking at that period.

Marcus Porcius Cato was one of the most just and upright men of the time, but, like his ancestor, the Censor, he thought it a merit to be harsh and unpleasing in manner. He was very proud, and showed his pride in his ungracious demeanour, and the difference of his dress and habits from all those around him, which made him everywhere disliked, though at the same time he could not but be respected.

Neither Cicero nor Cato was a soldier, and at this time the armies of the Republic were directed by Cneius Pompeius Magnus, better known as Pompey the Great, who, while still very young, had begun to make himself distinguished under Sylla. He was sent to serve in Spain, in Sicily, and in Africa, and when only twenty-five obtained a triumph, before he had held any office in the state. Wherever he was governor, the provinces were prosperous, since he kept his hands perfectly pure from the exactions in which almost all other Romans indulged, and protected the tributary nations from injustice. He cleared the Mediterranean of a horde of pirates, who, from their strongholds in Cilicia, had long infested the seas, taking the Roman vessels as they sailed to Greece, and putting the prisoners to ransom, at the same time that they carried off men, women, and children from the surrounding coasts, and sold them as slaves.

Pompey overcame the pirates, pursued them into Cilicia, and obliged them to surrender their ships and themselves into his power; and then, instead of selling them for slaves, or putting them to death, he settled them in towns at a distance from the coast, and gave them employments, by which he converted them into peaceable citizens. After this, he obtained the command against Mithridates, who had been for some time struggling for the possession of Bithynia, with the Roman forces under Lucius Licinius Lucullus.

Pompey came in time to complete the conquest which Lucullus had begun. Mithridates, after fighting with indomitable courage, gathered fresh armies when his forces were thought to be destroyed, and showing wonderful talents and activity, found himself deserted and betrayed by his own son, Pharnaces, and took poison to avoid falling into the hands of the Romans. From constant fear of being poisoned by others, he had, however, so accustomed his constitution to antidotes, that the dose had no effect, and he was obliged to cause himself to be killed by a slave.

During this war Pompey exercised a great authority over all the East; and at one time held a court at Damascus, which was attended by no less than twelve suppliant kings. One of these was Antiochus Asiaticus, the last of the line of Seleucus Nicator, who had been driven out of Syria by Tigranes, King of Armenia, and now that his enemy had fallen with Mithridates, begged to be restored to his throne; but Pompey would not listen to him, and Syria became a Roman province. Ptolemy Auletes, or the flute-player, who had been dethroned in one of the many revolutions of Egypt, was at the same time restored to his own country, as an ally of Rome.

Two others were Hyrcanus and Aristobulus, brothers, who were disputing with each other for the kingdom of Palestine. Aristobulus endeavoured to gain Pompey's favour by a present of a golden vine, but, finding that his decision was likely to be for Hyrcanus, retired to Jerusalem, and prepared for defence. Pompey followed him thither, besieged and took the city, and even ventured to enter the Temple, and penetrate into the Holy of Holies itself. No immediate judgment fell upon him, but it was remarked that from the time of this profanation his prosperity forsook him. He made Hyrcanus prince and high priest, but set over him as procurator, or guardian, of Judea for the Romans, a man named Antipas, an Idumean by birth, but professing the Jewish religion.

PART V.   THE FIRST TRIUMVIRATE.   B. C. 63–48.

WHEN Pompey returned to Rome, he found that in his absence his popularity had been much diminished, and the favour of the people was shared between Marcus Licinius Crassus, called Dives, or the rich, who had just put down an insurrection of some escaped gladiators, and Caius Julius Cæsar.

Julius Cæsar was of high patrician birth, his family claiming its name and origin from Iulus, son of Æneas, but his aunt had been married to Marius, and he was thus connected with the revolutionary party; besides which, he perceived that it was by the favour of the lower classes that he must hope to gain the chief power in the state, and break down the authority of the Senate. He was a man of wonderful talent, very learned, an able writer, and one of the greatest of generals, but he led a very profligate and dissipated life, and though less personally cruel than many of his contemporaries, cared not how many lives he sacrificed to his ambition.

Pompey, finding that the Senate hesitated to confirm his acts in Asia, became impatient, and was thus led to commit the great mistake of his life. He made an agreement with Cæsar and Crassus that they should form a union, called a Triumvirate, and assist each other in gaining their own ends, thus lending his weight to overcome the government, and raising its greatest enemy. The Senate was obliged to yield to their united influence, and granted Cæsar the government of Gaul with an army, gave Crassus the province of Asia, confirmed Pompey's proceedings in the East, and made him Proconsul of Spain.

Crassus went to Jerusalem, where he robbed the Temple, and then set out on an expedition against the Parthians, who, since Syria had been made into a province, were the next nation to the frontier. They were a warlike race, excellent horsemen and archers, and their manner of fighting was not to stand the shock of the enemy, but to gallop away, and aim their arrows from a distance, with deadly effect. In the plains of Mesopotamia, Crassus and his army were hemmed in by the enemy, entangled in the morasses, and at length perished, all excepting a few who were led back to Syria by an officer named Caius Cassius Longinus. The head of Crassus was cut off by the

Parthian king, and his mouth filled with melted gold, in derision of his avarice. He left an immense fortune to his son, a spendthrift, who wasted it all, and in his poverty was often mocked with the name of Crassus Dives.

While this was passing, Cæsar was engaged in the conquest of Gaul, where he remained nine years, and after much hard fighting, entirely subdued all the brave inhabitants, and formed it into a province. During this time he made his two expeditions to the British isles, the first time only effecting a landing, and the second advancing as far as to the northern side of the Thames. His object all this time was not so much to serve the state as to train up an army devoted to him, which might enable him to overcome the Senate, and raise him to the sole dominion.

Pompey had meantime been living at Rome, his army near at hand, and his lieutenants governing Spain in his name. He entertained the people with splendid shows of wild beasts, in which a rhinoceros was exhibited for the first time, and five hundred lions were killed; there were also dramatic entertainments and shows of gladiators, for which he built an amphitheatre at his own expense. At first he held fast to his engagement to Cæsar, and used his influence with the Senate in his favour; but when Cæsar's ambitious projects showed themselves more plainly, he returned to his former principles, and zealously supported the government. When Gaul was completely subdued, Cæsar set out on his return, and caused a worthless friend of his, Marcus Antonius, who was one of the tribunes, to require of the Senate that Pompey should be obliged to dismiss his army before Cæsar came to Rome. This was refused; and Antonius, or as he is more commonly called, Mark Antony, fled to Cæsar, pretending to think himself in danger.

Upon this Cæsar advanced with his army, though the law forbade troops to be brought into the territory of the state without permission from the Senate. The province of Gaul was divided from Italy by the little river, Rubicon, and here Cæsar hesitated for some moments, before by crossing it he committed his first open act of rebellion; and from this it has become a saying, that the Rubicon is passed when the step is made by which an enterprise is irrevocably undertaken.

The Senate charged Pompey with their defence; and he, being unable to raise an army in Italy fit to compete with such soldiers as Cæsar's, retreated first into the south, and afterwards into Greece, all the Senate going with him, the Consuls, and almost every other person who was attached to the old form of government. After taking possession of Rome, and defeating Pompey's forces in Spain, Cæsar followed him to Greece, and with much difficulty at length forced him to give battle, and gained a great victory at Pharsalia, in Thessaly. Pompey fled, and sailed with his wife and son for Alexandria, where he expected to find friends in the children of the king whom he had raised to the throne. He entered the harbour, where a boat was sent to meet him, into which he descended, only accompanied by a freed-man. Just as he reached the shore, and was rising to step out of the boat, he was stabbed in the back by a treacherous Roman, and fell to the ground; his head was cut off, and his body left lying on the beach till night, when his faithful freed-man, with an old Roman soldier, raised a funeral pile with broken planks of ships, and burnt it. His wife and son, who had seen the murder from their ship, sailed away, and escaped. His son, Sextus, grew up to be a distinguished man, and inherited many of his virtues.

PART VI. JULIUS CÆSAR. B. C. 48–44.

Julius Cæsar pursued Pompey to Egypt, and on arriving there was presented with the head of his rival, over which he shed tears, as he remembered their former friendship.

He then took upon himself to decide the disputes of the Egyptian royal family. The last king, Ptolemy Auletes, had by his will desired that his son Ptolemy and daughter Cleopatra should reign jointly; but the young king had expelled his sister, who had raised an army to assert her claim. She came to Alexandria to plead her cause with Cæsar, and finding the entrance to his house forbidden her, hid herself in a bale of cloth, and was thus carried into his presence. Her surpassing beauty and sweet voice so captivated him, that he remained two years at Alexandria, and, her elder brother being drowned in the Nile, made her Queen of Egypt. He then went to Asia, and there in sixteen days conquered Pharnaces, the traitorous son of Mithridates, and afterwards sailed for the province of Africa, where Cato and the other staunch supporters of the old constitution had drawn together and obtained the alliance of Juba, King of Mauritania.

Cæsar gained another complete victory at Thapsus; and Cato, after trying in vain to persuade his friends to stand a siege at the city of Utica, did all he could to forward their escape; and then, seeing the liberty of Rome lost, too proud to submit to the conqueror, and having neither the hope nor the fear of Christians before his eyes, he stabbed himself. His friends found him still alive, and bound up the wound, but he tore off the bandages, and expired. "Cato," said Cæsar when he arrived, "thou hast grudged me the glory of saving thy life."

Cæsar was now complete master of Rome and its dominions; all the warlike supporters of government had submitted or were slain, and the Senate was obliged by fear to obey his will. He was appointed Dictator for life, and on returning home was honoured with four triumphs on four different days. At that for his victories in the East, a banner was displayed, bearing the words, *Veni, Vidi, Vici,*—I came, I saw, I conquered,—in allusion to the rapidity of his conquest of Pharnaces. He distributed a great quantity of corn and money, granted land to his soldiers, extended widely the rights of Roman citizenship, and thus added much to his popularity.

Julius Cæsar is noted, among other things, for the reform of the Calendar, so called from Calend, the Latin name for the first day of the month—for the days were known by different names, Calends, Nones, and Ides. The year, as the Romans reckoned it, had hitherto been too long or too short, so that the real mid-summer and mid-winter, instead of coming on the right days of the year, came in autumn and spring; and Cæsar, to remedy this, decreed that henceforth 365 should be counted as the number of days in a year, and as the real length is 365 and nearly 6 hours, that every four years when the hours had amounted to 24, another day should be added, so that the reckoning might not be behindhand with the sun. The sixth Ante-calend of February being counted twice to make up the number, these years of 366 days were called Bissextile. Cæsar rebuilt the cities of Carthage and Corinth, which had both been ruined by the Romans a hundred years before.

Every day added to the usurped power of Cæsar, and there were signs that he wished to obtain the actual monarchy. He always wore the laurel wreath of the Imperator or victorious commander; his friends decked his statue with signs of royalty; and though he said he would not be king, but Cæsar, and in the sight of the people refused a diadem offered him by Mark Antony, there was no doubt that he was grasping at the power, if not the name, of a king.

Cassius, the same who had led back the remains of Crassus's army, Marcus Junius Brutus, the son-in-law of Cato, and descended from the first Consul, his cousin Decimus, and some others, seeing the Republic thus overthrown by one man, resolved to destroy him by murder. Both Brutus and Cassius had recieved their lives from Cæsar's mercy; and Decimus had fought under him, was looked upon as his intimate friend, and had just received from him the government of Gaul; so that their crime had all the baseness of ingratitude. The day they chose for the execution of their plot was the Ides of March, the 15th as we should call it, when Cæsar was in his place at the senate-house. Some rumours began to get abroad, and a soothsayer warned Cæsar to beware of the Ides of March; his wife, too, was alarmed by a dream, and had almost persuaded him not to leave his own house, when Decimus Brutus came in, and prevailed on him to go, by saying it would be absurd to stay at home on account of a dream.

As Cæsar passed along the street, he saw the soothsayer, and said, "The Ides of March are come."

"True, Cæsar," was the answer; "but they are not past."

The fifteen conspirators crowded round their victim as he took his seat, and one of them offered him a petition; Cæsar refused it, and at the same moment was struck by a dagger. At first he struggled, and tried to break away, but they closed in on him and wounded him on all sides.

"*Et tu, Brute,*" (Thou too, Brutus,) were the only words he spoke, as he drew his robe over his face, sunk on the ground, and died, at the foot of a statue of Pompey the Great. So perished, on the 15th of March, 44, in his fifty-seventh year, one of the ablest, most ambitious, and most unscrupulous men that ever lived.

PART VII. THE SECOND TRIUMVIRATE. B. C. 44–42.

GREAT confusion followed the murder of Julius Cæsar; the old republican party, with Cicero at their head, rejoiced in it, and looked forward to a recovery of freedom; but Mark Antony stirred up the lower classes and the soldiers, to cry out for vengeance on the murderers. They were obliged to leave the country, Marcus Brutus and Cassius going to Asia, and Decimus to his government in Gaul; while Antony seized upon Cæsar's will, and all the property which Cæsar had bequeathed to his nephew, Caius Octavius, the grandson of his sister Julia.

Octavius, a youth of eighteen, came to Rome, and was adopted into his uncle's family, assuming the name of Caius Julius Cæsar Octavianus, and in his displeasure at finding that Antony had deprived him of his inheritance, at first took the part of the Senate.

Antony was now at the head of Julius Cæsar's old troops, in open rebellion, and Decimus Brutus, young Cæsar Octavianus, and Marcus Æmilius Lepidus, Governor of Transalpine Gaul, were each commanding an army of the state against him in the north of Italy.

Young Cæsar soon perceived that his real interest was to obtain the good will of his uncle's army, and as he was cool, wary, and perfidious, he resolved to betray the confidence of the Senate, and to go over to Antony. Lepidus, an officer of Julius Cæsar, saw that theirs was the winning side, and joined them. Decimus Brutus, thus forsaken by his fellow commanders, tried to escape over the Alps into Macedon, but was taken by a Gaul, and put to death.

Antony, Lepidus, and Octavianus, met on the banks of the Eridanus, and agreed to form themselves into a Triumvirate for five years; to cut off all those whom they esteemed as their enemies, to avenge Cæsar's death, and to ruin the old constitution. A proscription list was drawn up, longer than even that of Sylla, and the wickedness of which was even greater, for Sylla's massacre was, as he thought, for the good of the state, whereas the Triumvirs murdered to overturn the state. Lepidus wrote the name of his own brother in the fatal roll; Antony added that of his uncle, and insisted that Cicero should be one of the proscribed. He hated the great orator as a personal enemy, and the others disliked him as one of the best maintainers of the laws, so that they doomed him with one accord. Cicero was at his villa at Formium when the messengers of death approached; his slaves placed him in a litter, and tried to carry him away, but the soldiers overtook them, and he calmly presented his neck to their swords. His head was carried to Antony, whose wife Fulvia exulted over it, and pierced the tongue with her bodkin, in revenge for the orations it had spoken against the crimes of her husband.

Cicero was the most distinguished victim, but multitudes of others were relentlessly put to death by the Three. Rewards were offered to the slayers of the proscribed; and the slave betrayed the master, brother slew brother, and even children their parents. It was not only the enemies of the Triumvirate who thus died, but many of those whose lands or wealth they coveted, and among these were young children whose estates had excited their avarice. Distrust, terror, and bloodshed, prevailed throughout Italy.

At last, when the work of slaughter was over, Antony and Octavianus set out for Macedon, where Brutus and Cassius were at the head of an army. At Philippi a battle took place, in which Cassius's half of the army was defeated, and that of Brutus gained the advantage; and Cassius, fancying all lost, obliged a slave to kill him. The next day another battle was fought in the same place, where Brutus was also beaten, and retiring into a narrow valley as the evening came on, took leave of his friends, and threw himself on the point of his own sword.

PART VIII.   ANTONY AND CLEOPATRA.   B. C. 42–31.

AFTER their victory Cæsar and Antony parted; the first returned to Rome, and the latter went to take possession of the government of the East. Cleopatra, Queen of Egypt, had been accused of not supporting the Triumvirs against Brutus and Cassius, and Antony cited her to appear before him at Tarsus, in Cilicia, to answer to the charge. Insolent as was such a summons, Cleopatra, who well knew the power of her charms, was nothing loth to comply with it. She sailed into the mouth of the Cydnus in such splendour as was never equalled. Her vessel was of the most beautiful form, the oars inlaid with silver, and the sails of purple; whilst under a canopy of cloth of gold, the queen reclined upon the deck, robed as the Goddess Venus, with beautiful children in the character of Cupids fanning her, and her attendants representing the sea-nymphs and the Graces. Soft music sounded, and perfumes breathed around her; and Antony, who was at his tribunal, found himself deserted by all the people of Tarsus, who ran to look at the wonderful spectacle.

No sooner was she landed than he sent to ask her to supper; but she returned answer that he should come to her. The taste and richness of the entertainment surpassed all that the Romans had ever beheld; the discourse of the queen was most alluring, and soon Antony was completely enchanted with her, and forgot all his former plans in the delights of her presence. He accompanied her to Alexandria, and there the waste, the excess, and the magnificence, of their revelries, are almost beyond belief. The queen and Triumvir once laid a wager that she could not outvie him in the costliness of her banquet, when she, declaring that she would spend a million on one draught, took off her magnificent pearl ear-ring, threw it into a cup of vinegar, and drank it off when dissolved. The fellow ear-ring was so large, that it was afterwards made into two, to adorn a statue of Venus. Eight wild boars are said to have been found roasting whole at once in Antony's kitchen, so as to be ready at different times, that he might have his supper served up in perfection whenever he might choose to call for it.

Antony made an expedition against the Parthians, in which he met with no success; and during this time he raised to the throne of Judea, Herod, the son of that Antipas the Idumean, whom Pompey had made procurator for the Romans. Herod had married Mariamne, the beautiful daughter of Hyrcanus, last of the Maccabean line; but he had no other claims to the throne, which he obtained by violence and treachery; and as he could not assume the priesthood, he raised to the office of high priest such of the family of Aaron as he chose to appoint.

Antony was once obliged to return to Rome, where on the death of his wife Fulvia, he married Octavia, sister of Cæsar, a virtuous lady, who deserved a better fate than to be given to a coarse-minded selfish soldier, who never loved her, and who hurried back to Cleopatra at the first opportunity. On this second occasion they gave themselves up still more to every sort of dissipation, and Antony became more and more blinded by his passion for Cleopatra, so that, reckless of the danger of offending Cæsar Octavianus, he sent a divorce to Octavia, and gave out that he had long since been married to the Queen of Egypt.

Cæsar, who had all along been bent on obtaining such power as his uncle had enjoyed, wanted nothing but an excuse for overthrowing his rival, as he had already set aside the weaker Lepidus. A fleet was fitted out, and the Romans, indignant that the cruel, treacherous, and captivating eastern queen should cause a virtuous matron like Octavia to be deserted and disowned, willingly supported Cæsar in the war. Antony and Cleopatra both sailed to meet the Roman fleet; and near Actium, a promontory of Epirus, the ships met and engaged. Before the victory had declared itself on either side, Cleopatra was seized with a sudden terror, and fled, followed by the whole Egyptian fleet; and Antony, as soon as he perceived her flight, sailed after her himself.

They retreated to Alexandria, where they tried to lose in feastings the recollection that the enemy was fast approaching, and that hope there was none. Cæsar was soon at the entrance of the harbour, and managed so dexterously through his messengers, that the vain queen, fancying she might gain him likewise by the power of her beauty, allowed her fleet and city to fall into his hands without a blow. Then she fled with only two women into a tower, which, like other Egyptian monarchs, she had caused to be built for a tomb, and spread a report that she was dead. Antony could not bear to survive her, and tried to kill himself with his own sword; but while he lay dying on his couch, a message was brought that Cleopatra was alive, and begged him to come to her tower. He was carried thither on his bed; but Cleopatra, afraid to open the door, drew him up with cords through the window, and he died in her embrace.

Still Cleopatra did not despair till she had seen the new conqueror, when, having tried all her most seductive arts in vain, and finding that her charms had no power over him, she saw that there was no hope of her escaping the degradation of being obliged to make part of his triumphal procession, and rather than endure this, she resolved to die. Octavianus, on the other hand, was resolved to display this most beautiful and splendid of queens as his captive, and took every precaution to prevent her from destroying herself. One day, however, the guards allowed a countryman to pass to the queen's apartments carrying a basket of figs.

A few hours after Cæsar received a letter from her, begging him to spare her children, and allow her body to be placed in the same tomb with Antony's. Dreading that his prisoner had eluded his power, he hurried to her apartments. All was still; and entering, he beheld the queen, arrayed in her royal robes, lying on her state couch, one of her maids stretched at her feet, the other kneeling at her head, settling her diadem.

Cæsar saw that the silence was the silence of death. "Was this well done?" said he. "It was," replied the maid: "it was worthy of so great a princess;" and with these words she too sunk down and died. A small serpent, called an asp, whose bite was deadly, though but slightly painful, was found on Cleopatra's arm, having been brought to her in the basket of figs.

Egypt was now reduced to a Roman province; and Cæsar, loaded with treasure, returned to Rome. His triumph was splendid; a figure of Cleopatra asleep on her couch was carried in his train; and behind it walked her twin children, Alexander and Cleopatra, who had lately been called, in the profane pride of their father and mother, by the names of Apollo and Diana, and now were slaves and captives among their enemies. One kind hand was, however, stretched out to them, when the pride of Cæsar had been gratified by their humiliation—it was that of their father's neglected and injured wife, Octavia, who took them to her home, brought them up on equal terms with her own children, and finally obtained the marriage of the daughter with a Mauritanian king.

CHAPTER XIII.

THE TWELVE CÆSARS. B.C. 33–A.D. 86.

PART I. AUGUSTUS. B.C. 30–A.D. 23.

By the death of Antony, all rivals to the power of Cæsar Octavianus were removed, and he stood alone in the Roman state, at a higher pitch of power than his uncle had ever obtained. He took the surname of Augustus, which signifies something sacred or set apart, like a temple: and as the eighth month of the year had received the name of July from that of his uncle, so that of August was given in his honour to the next ensuing. He already bore the title of Imperator, or commander, though not as yet in the sense in which it was afterwards applied to his successors, and which the word Emperor conveys to our ears; and by taking to himself the powers of all the magistrates, he became in fact an absolute monarch, though he was far too cautious to call himself so. The people, worn out by a century and a half of civil discord, were willing to repose under his government; and in fact, it was not possible for the citizens all to have a voice in the affairs of state, now that their number was so much increased, and instead of all living in the immediate neighbourhood of Rome, they were scattered throughout Italy, and in all Roman colonies. The rights of citizenship, which had already been much extended by Julius Cæsar, was given by Augustus to many places beyond the confines of Italy, where the inhabitants ranked as citizens, and were thus free from taxation, and could not be punished by the governors of the provinces.

No more blood was shed by Augustus after he had obtained the supreme power, for he knew that his best policy was to win the affection of the people by the mildness of his rule, and he fully succeeded. Art and learning flourished in his time to such a degree, that an "Augustan Age" has since been used to express a time when many great writers were living. In his time Titus Livius wrote a history of Rome, of which unfortunately a great part has been lost. Virgil composed his beautiful poems on the occupations of rural life; and by desire of the emperor, commenced a poem on the wanderings of Æneas, and the first glories of the Julian race. Horace and Ovid were also living, and their works were much admired by the emperor himself, and his two great friends, Agrippa and Mecœnas, the last of whom so favoured poets, that his name has become a proverb for the patrons of literature.

Augustus engaged but little in foreign wars; and in his reign the Temple of Janus was closed for the third time since the foundation of Rome, whilst the people rejoiced in the unwonted peace which they enjoyed. Whilst they complimented the emperor on his wisdom and skill in silencing all wars abroad, and disputes at home, they little knew by Whose Hand it was, or for what cause, these wars and tumults were hushed into one silent awful lull.

In the 4004th year of the world, in the empire of Augustus, in the reign of Herod, King of Judea, a Child was born in the royal village of Bethlehem of Judea, and that Child was the Prince of Peace.

The time before appointed had fully come; the seventy weeks of years had passed since the rebuilding of Jerusalem; darkness covered the earth, and gross darkness the people; the Sceptre had completely departed from Judah, when the cruel and suspicious tyrant Herod murdered his wife Mariamne and her two sons, thus extinguishing the last remnant of the princely line of the Maccabean priests; even a heathen oracle had declared to Augustus, that the greatest foe of the Roman power was a child, to be born of the Hebrews; the aged Simeon, and doubtless all such as like him read the prophecies aright, were waiting till their eyes should see the promised salvation; when the decree was sent forth from Augustus, that each subject of the Roman power should be enrolled at his own proper abode, and the Blessed Mary and Joseph were thus led to the city of David.

The shepherds came to see "that great sight;" and the wise men from the East brought their offerings. It is said, too, that in China, where the memory of patriarchal religion had hitherto been preserved more fully than elsewhere, there was so strong a belief that "a great Saint should appear in the West" about that time, that messengers were sent to seek Him out, and pay Him homage; but these envoys never reached Judea, but met with some teachers of Buddhism, a new and false belief which had spread from Thibet, and, bringing them back to China, made it the prevalent belief there.

The massacre of the Innocents was one of Herod's last acts. He did not long survive it; and knowing how the Jews would rejoice at his death, when he found himself seized with a mortal sickness, he made the fiendish resolve that they should at least mourn for something, and therefore caused a great number of the principal men of the nation to be imprisoned, with orders that they should all be slain the instant he had breathed his last; but the command was not executed, and they were set at liberty. He died the second year after the birth of our Lord, the era from which the years are now always reckoned.

His son Archelaus now took possession of the kingdom, and went to Rome to obtain from Augustus the confirmation of his father's will; but his brother, Herod Antipas, who was already at Rome, disputed the possession with him, and the Jews sent to petition against him. Augustus, however, gave him the kingdom; but after ten years his cruelties were so great, that the entreaties of the Jews were listened to, and he was banished to Vienne, in Gaul. Palestine was then united to the province of Syria; and Herod Antipas, and his brother Philip, received the two small governments of Galilee and Ituræa, whilst a procurator, appointed by the Governor of Syria, ruled over Judea, usually living at Cesarea, and leaving the city of Jerusalem to the care of the high-priest.

PART II.   THE TEUTONES.   A.D. 2–13.

The peace which had spread over the world, lasted in the East throughout the thirty-three years that the earth was so marvellously favoured with that holy Presence of which it was so little conscious; but in the West fresh wars broke out.

The Teutonic race, who have been hitherto in this history called Scythians, appear, during the last five hundred years before the Christian era, to have been gradually driving the Kelts before them towards the West, and fixing themselves in their settlements. They were a nation of greater height and size than any that had yet appeared in the ancient world, of great strength, with blue eyes, light hair, and fair complexions, of a temper which, though enterprising, was firm and resolute, with steady persevering courage, and even in their early barbarous state, with great purity of manners, and respect for women, such as is seldom met with among uncivilized people. Their mythology, like that of all other nations, was not without some traces of ancient truth. Odin was their chief god, and they taught that his son Baldur had assumed a human form, and had been slain by Lok the Destroyer, who was now indeed chained, but would one day, with his pale daughter, Hela, overthrow the whole universe, with both gods and men, and all perishing together, new heavens and earth would be formed, and the good and brave would come forth purified, to enjoy complete happiness. In the meantime Hela ruled over the souls of the weak and timid dead, while the courageous feasted and hunted in the hall of Odin. Freya, goddess of the earth, was Odin's wife, and to her were offered human sacrifices. Thor was her son the Thunderer; and there were almost as many persons in their mythology as in that of the Greeks. Their language was called Teutske, that of the Teutes, or people, a word still preserved in the name Dutch.

These Teutonic barbarians were the forefathers of almost every nation of modern Europe; and their language is still used with comparatively but slight changes through the north-western countries. The tribe with whom the Romans came in contact called themselves Ger-mans, or Alle-mans, Spear-men, or All-men, the whole tribe priding itself on its manliness. They inhabited the forests to the north of the Alps, between the rivers Rhine and Elbe, which have since been known by their name; and the Romans, as usual, began to encroach upon their territory, build forts, form alliances, and set one tribe against another, so as to weaken them, and obtain excuses for conquering them. At last their insolence and exactions roused the Germans to revenge; and Arminius, a German prince, who had served in the Roman army, formed a secret combination with his countrymen, and drew the Roman army, with its general Publius Quinctilius Varus, into difficult broken ground, near the river Lippe, where they fell upon it, and completely destroyed it. Varus himself was slain, his corpse barbarously mangled, and his officers were sacrificed to the German gods.

This disaster threw Augustus into great grief; and he often broke into fits of violent weeping, crying out, " Quinctilius Varus, give me back my legions." Two years after, he died, A.D. 13, after ruling Rome for forty years, reckoning from the death of Antony.

PART III. TIBERIUS. A.D. 13–37.

Augustus had adopted as his heir his step-son Tiberius Claudius Drusus Nero, giving him the names of Julius Cæsar Augustus, which became, in fact, titles of the Emperor. The army which Tiberius had commanded in Germany accepted him as their general; and the Senate continued to pay him such homage, that he said of them, " What a set of willing slaves!"

He usually lived in his villas in the south of Italy; and his coming to Rome was much dreaded, as he cared not what sufferings he inflicted upon others, and was of a haughty, reserved, and gloomy temper. The heir whom Augustus had caused him to adopt, was his nephew, Drusus Cæsar, a young man of great promise, called from his victories in Germany by the surname of Germanicus, and much beloved; but he died early, much lamented by all except Tiberius, who was jealous of him.

By Tiberius, Annas was appointed High Priest of the Jews, and after a few years, deposed in favour of his son-in-law, Caiaphas. Pontius Pilate was sent as procurator to Judea; and in his third year, A.D. 29, John the Baptist began to prepare the way for his Master, by preaching repentance. The next year, A.D. 30, He Who had hitherto dwelt unknown, and in great humility, commenced His public ministry; and shortly after St. John, decreasing as He increased, was thrown into prison in the Castle of Macherus, for having rebuked Herod Antipas for his marriage with his brother's wife, and suffered death by the request of Salome, the daughter of Herodias. Antipas soon after suffered a total defeat from an Arab chief, whose daughter he had put away in order to marry Herodias.

The year of the Redeemed was at length come, the 4037th of the world, the thirty-third since the first coming of the Seed of the Woman; and now was bruised the head of the Serpent, just as he had most closely bound the world in sin and corruption.

The great Feast of the Passover arrived. Herod came from Galilee, Pilate from Cesarea, the rulers took counsel against the Anointed, His own familiar friend betrayed Him, the multitude clamoured for His death. Then was the Most Holy doomed to the death of a slave, His own title was set over Him in scorn, and the Cross, from the token of shame, became the most glorious of signs. The awful ninth hour came, "It is finished," was spoken, and the Victim gave up His life; the rich made His grave, the Sabbath passed, and very early in the morning the bands of death were broken, and He became the first-fruits of the Resurrection.

The forty days went by, and earth was no longer blessed with His bodily presence; but ten days after came the rushing wind and fiery tongues, announcing the arrival of Him Who is with us alway. Then was the Church set up on earth, and St. Peter gathered in three thousand at once to the fold.

The order of deacons was instituted the next year; and in 37 St. Stephen became the first of the glorious army of martyrs. It was in the course of that same year that Pilate was obliged to go to Rome to defend himself from numerous charges of cruelty and extortion brought against him by the Jews. He arrived just as Tiberius was dying, after having adopted as his successor Caius, son of Germanicus. His sickness was of itself mortal; but his death was hastened by his attendants, who, taking a swoon for death, proclaimed Caius as emperor, and on his giving signs of revival, smothered him rather than abide his terrific displeasure.

Pilate gained nothing by his death, being banished to Vienne, in Gaul, where he was so tormented by remorse, that he closed his wicked life by his own hand. Antipas was likewise banished, and his nephew, Herod Agrippa, received full power over Judea and Galilee.

PART IV. CALIGULA, CLAUDIUS, AND NERO. A.D. 37–68.

THE proper name of the new emperor was Caius Drusus Claudius Nero Cæsar Augustus. In his own time he was called Caius; but he has become known in history by his nickname of Caligula, from caliga, the sandal of the foot-soldier, which he had been used to wear when a child with his father in Germany.

He had always led a life of unrestrained indulgence; and just before he became emperor, had an attack of illness which destroyed his reason, so that all his acts were those of a madman. He would go about the streets as a beggar, and in his own house would lie down and roll on heaps of gold; he made his horse a consul, and gave him a golden manger; he set out with an army to conquer Britain, and when he came to the coast of Gaul, caused his men to fill their helmets with shells, and then returned to Rome, where he claimed a triumph as lord of the conquered ocean. His cruelties were frightful; he caused persons to be tortured to death for his amusement at his meals; in the middle of the sports in the amphitheatre, he ordered a number of the spectators to be seized at hap-hazard, and thrown to the wild beasts, after their tongues had been cut out, that they might not curse him; and once he cried out, "Would that the Roman people had but one neck!" meaning that he might be able to destroy them at one blow.

After a reign of four years, this unhappy madman was murdered, A.D. 41, and the army set up as Emperor his uncle, a brother of Germanicus, usually called Claudius.

In the course of these four years, the vision of St. Peter had announced that the Gentiles were to be admitted to the Church, and Cornelius, the first Roman convert, had received Baptism. Saul, the zealous persecutor, had become Paul the Apostle of the Gentiles, and the name of Christians had been given at Antioch to the believers. In 44, St. James the Great was put to death by Herod Agrippa, and St. Peter was delivered from prison by the angel. Herod soon after celebrated games in honour of the emperor at Cesarea, and in the midst of them was punished, for receiving the idolatrous flattery of the Phœnicians, by the deadly disease which suddenly struck him. He was the last King of Judea, though his son Agrippa had a small government under the Roman procurators.

St. James the Less remained as Bishop of Jerusalem, and most of the other Apostles travelled in different directions; but little is known of their labours, with the exception of the earlier journeys of St. Paul, which were recorded by his companion, St. Luke. His former fellow-workers, Barnabas and Mark, after parting with him, went to Cyprus, whence St. Mark afterwards crossed to Egypt, there founded a Church, and with the assistance of St. Peter, wrote his gospel. St. Thomas went to the East, and there are Christians in India who still bear his name; St. Andrew, to Arabia; St. John, to Asia Minor. Wherever they found converts they ordained elders, also called presbyters, or priests, to administer the Sacraments, and deacons to serve under them; setting over them in each principal place a Bishop, or Angel, on whom their own Apostolic power was conferred by the appointed means of laying on of hands; and everywhere they left in the mouths of the Christians the symbol, or watchword, the confession of faith, that is to say, in substance at least, if not in form, the same as our own Apostles' Creed; with certain rules and forms for the administration of the Sacraments, which have ever since been observed, and are the ground-work of all Liturgies.

The Roman officers were mostly careless of religion,

but as friends to order usually interfered to protect the Apostles from the violence of the Jews. They respected St. Paul's rights as a citizen; and when he appealed to the emperor, the procurator, Festus, had no power to try him, and was obliged to send him to Rome.

Claudius was a dull heavy man, not cruel by nature, but often led into crime by his wicked wives. Agrippina, the second, persuaded him to adopt her son by a former husband, Lucius Domitius Ahenobarbus, who, taking as usual the whole number of imperial names, was usually called Nero.

In the time of Claudius, the first actual conquest of a part of Britain was made; and he spent twenty-three days there himself, after which he assumed the surname of Britannicus, and returned home in triumph. In 54 he was poisoned by his wife Agrippina, lest he should change his intention of leaving the empire to her son; and about the same time St. Paul recovered his liberty, and was able to journey into Spain, Gaul, and perhaps Britain.

Nero was a weak, jealous-tempered man, and his great power had a fearful effect on his disposition. He began by suspecting a plot on the part of his brother, and put him to death; then he went on from crime to crime, till no one's life was safe. His wife, his mother, his tutor, the philosopher Seneca, were all killed by his orders; and he seems to have acquired a positive love for bloodshed almost like that of a wild beast. Coupled with this, he had a taste for literature and art, with much vanity in his own proficiency; he wrote verses, sung, acted in dramas, and drove in the chariot races in the amphitheatre, and woe to the man who grew weary of the emperor's performance, or dared to find fault with it.

At last, so reckless did Nero grow, that he set Rome itself on fire by way of seeing how Troy looked in flames; and then, when he found the people indignant, accusing the Christians of having lighted the fire, he commenced the first persecution. Great numbers of Christians were martyred in horrible torments, thrown to wild beasts, burnt; while some of them were smeared with combustible matter, fastened to a stake to keep them upright, and then set on fire so as to burn slowly, to light the arena where the emperor was entertaining the Romans.

In this persecution both St. Paul and St. Peter received the crown of martyrdom at Rome on the same day of the year 66. St. Paul had been for some time in prison, whence he wrote his last Epistle, the second to Timothy, Bishop of Ephesus; his citizenship saved him from torture, and he was beheaded with the sword. St. Peter, reckoned as the first Bishop of Rome, was, in the eyes of the world, only a Galilean fisherman, and he was sentenced to die by crucifixion as the basest mode of execution; but he deemed that death all too blessed and glorious for him, and entreated to be nailed to the tree with his head downwards, that so he "might change the Cross, yet suffer with his Lord."

PART V.   DESTRUCTION OF JERUSALEM.   A.D. 66–100.

"His Blood be upon us and our children!" had been the cry of the Jewish multitude; and the time of vengeance was come for the city which would not be gathered under the wings of the Almighty.

Gessius Florus, the procurator, was even more than usually cruel and rapacious; and in the year 66 the

Jews revolted, fancying that the time of their deliverance was come, and misinterpreting the prophecies. Yet the signs of coming judgment were not wanting: armies were seen fighting in the clouds; a man ran up and down the streets crying, "Woe to Jerusalem!" the heavy gate of the Temple, though bolted and barred, flew open of its own accord; and more awful than all, a voice was heard in the Holy of Holies, saying, "Let us depart hence." The Christians took the warning, as they had long since been taught to do, and fled from the city; but the Jews became still more determined in their rebellion.

An army was sent against them commanded by Titus Flavius Sabinus Vespasianus, an able officer, and a rough, straight-forward man, much disliked by Nero, and loved by the army. He had reduced all the lesser towns of Palestine, and was marching on Jerusalem, when he learnt that there had been a revolt in Italy, that Nero had killed himself, and that he had been chosen emperor by a portion of the army. He left the command to his son, of the same name as himself, and hastened to Italy. Three other emperors, Galba, Otho, and Vitellius, had been chosen, but as quickly set aside and slain; and both army and Senate were willing to receive Vespasian, who soon showed himself the best emperor that had yet governed Rome.

In the meantime his son Titus began to besiege Jerusalem, in the spring of A.D. 70, just when the Feast of the Passover had caused the Jews to hasten to the city from all quarters. The regular priesthood was at an end; Agrippa, the last of the line of Herod, was with the Roman army, and there was no legal ruler of the city, so that it was torn to pieces with dissensions, and the strong on either side fought against each other even more fiercely than against the enemy. The town was closely blockaded; and while war raged without, there was murder, robbery, and famine within, fulfilling to the letter the awful curses denounced when first the law was given. Thousands died of hunger; multitudes of prisoners were crucified by the Romans; the robbers in the city broke into the houses, and slew and pillaged without mercy, especially where, like ravenous beasts, they were attracted by the scent of food. In one instance they turned back in horror and loathing when they found that the food they had smelt was the flesh of a young child, slain and roasted by his own mother, a tender and delicate lady, who called on them, in her frenzy, to share it with her.

The ravines were so choked with dead, that Titus was struck with horror, and called Heaven to witness that the Jews, and not himself, were guilty of this destruction. After much severe fighting, the outer and inner walls were gained, and he ordered an assault on the fortifications of the Temple, desiring that every means should be taken for preserving the beautiful building; but it had been decreed that not one stone should be left upon another, and his precautions were vain. In the course of the attack, a Roman threw a firebrand through a golden window; the flames spread rapidly, and though Titus called repeatedly to his men to extinguish them, all were too busy fighting and pillaging to heed him, and the fire raged until the whole building was consumed, and in it 6,000 persons who had trusted to its shelter for protection.

On the 18th of August, Zion itself, the city of David, was taken, and found to be full of dead; the flames were quenched in the blood of the defenders, and the women and children lay dead with hunger in all the upper rooms. A million had perished by the sword and famine, ninety-seven thousand were made prisoners, and Titus's victory was at length achieved. When he looked at the strength of the walls and towers, he exclaimed that God Himself must have fought for him, since man could never have driven the Jews from such defences. He then caused them to be all thrown down, and the very foundations of the Temple were ploughed up and sown with salt.

He enjoyed a great triumph, leading great numbers of his captives in his procession, after which many were used as victims in the cruel sports of the amphitheatre, and the rest sold as slaves, and thus dispersed through the empire. An arch was raised in honour of his triumph, on which may still be seen sculptured figures of the seven-branched candlestick, and others of the sacred ornaments of the Temple.

Vespasian died in 79, the year of the first recorded eruption of Vesuvius, when Herculaneum and Pompeii were destroyed. Titus succeeded him, and was much loved for his generous disposition, which led him to say, "I have lost a day!" whenever he had spent one without doing some good.

His virtues shone more brightly from the contrast with the vices of his brother Domitian, by whom he was poisoned in 81, the second year of his reign. Domitian, called the Last of the Twelve Cæsars, reigned fifteen years, and if possible, outdid Nero in his cruelties, until, in 96, he was murdered by his freedman. It was he who condemned the evangelist St. John to be placed in a caldron of boiling oil, when by a miracle the saint was preserved from injury; upon which Domitian banished him to the Isle of Patmos, where a marvellous vision was vouchsafed to him, of what should befall the Church in her latter days. With this revelation, related in the form of an epistle of solemn exhortation to the angels or Bishops of the Seven Churches of Asia Minor, he closes the roll of inspired writings with his most awful warning to such as should dare to tamper with Holy Scripture.

He was the last survivor of the Apostles—the only one, it is believed, who did not meet with a violent death. He spent his latter days at Ephesus, where, when extremely aged and infirm, he still, as he was carried about in his litter, would repeat the exhortation, "Little children, love one another." He died about the year 100—the last of those who could tell of those great things of which they were chosen witnesses, which their own ears had heard, and their own eyes had seen.

CHAPTER XIV.

THE GREAT PERSECUTIONS. A.D. 86–325.

PART I.   THE PRIMITIVE CHURCH.   A.D. 86–180.

THE death of the last of the Twelve Apostles happened just when the faith of the Church began to be proved by systematic persecutions; for the martyrdoms which had hitherto taken place were either the effect of popular fury, or of the lawless cruelty of such tyrants as Nero and Domitian; and it was not till the time of Nerva, who was made Emperor in 86, that edicts were passed for the suppression of Christianity.

The Gospel had by this time spread wherever the Roman power had made itself felt. Each city had its own bishop; and these were, for the sake of order, subject to principal bishops, called patriarchs, of whom in early times there were four—of Jerusalem, Antioch, Alexandria, and Rome. The believers were chiefly inhabitants of towns; the villagers, called in Latin Pagani, had not in general yet heard the word, and it is from this that the word Pagan has come to signify a heathen.

The Christians were of all ranks—nobles, soldiers, and slaves; and there was nothing to distinguish them from the surrounding world, save the purity of their lives, their love for one another, and their refusal to join in aught that savoured of idolatry. It was at night, or whenever they were least liable to interruption, that they met to worship, and above all, to receive the Holy Eucharist. Their place of assembly was sometimes a room in a rich man's house, sometimes the ruins of a deserted temple, the depth of the forest, or the cave on the sea-shore; and at Rome it was in the excavations whence the materials of the city had been dug out, and which were used as burial-places for slaves and malefactors. Many of them toiled here in slavery, and were familiar with the long winding galleries, which might enable them to elude their pursuers; and hither came the flock from every part of the city. The Roman noble and tenderly nurtured ladies there met the slave of barbarian blood, and often bowed meekly before him as their pastor; and above the graves of the martyrs arose the voice of prayer and praise, when the Holy Communion was solemnized, for the sustaining of those who might soon themselves be called to endure the fiery trial of persecution.

The men and women were ranged on opposite sides of the place of assembly; and behind the baptized Christians were those who were as yet under instruction before being admitted into the Church, and who, therefore, used to depart before the administration of the Communion. Further off were those who were under penance, excluded from the Communion till they had shown full repentance for some fault, and those unhappy persons who had yielded to the terrors of persecution and denied their faith, and were now entreating for their restoration; but it was a very long time before they were again received, often not until their death.

Trajan, who succeeded Nerva in the empire in the year 98, was an admirer of the old Roman temper, which he sought to restore; and knowing nothing of Christianity, his pride made him look upon it as a silly superstition which ought to be put down, as likely to alter the ancient manners. He therefore enacted that all should be put to death who would not revile the name of Christ, nor offer incense to his own statue nor to Jupiter; and the law was carried into effect through the greater part of the empire. Multitudes were martyred in this persecution, among whom the most noted was St. Ignatius, Bishop of Antioch, one of the Fathers of the Church, whose writings are still preserved. It was by order of Trajan himself that he was thrown to the wild beasts.

Trajan adopted Adrian, his cousin, who succeeded him in 117, and in his turn adopted Titus Aurelius Antoninus Pius, a gentle amiable man, and a philosopher. The Greek philosophy, it should be remembered, was a feeling after the truth, and was the best guide that could be possessed in the days of heathenism, but now that light was in the world, it was wilful blindness to prefer these feeble guesses to the perfect truth; and Antoninus was no true follower of Socrates and Plato, when he permitted the persecution to continue, instead of laying hold of the faith they would have hailed so gladly. His nephew and successor, Marcus Aurelius Antoninus, was likewise a philosopher, and of sterner and more warlike mould, and he revived the fury of the persecution with still greater vigour. The chief of the victims now martyred, was St. Polycarp, Bishop of Smyrna, a disciple of St. John the Divine, and more than eighty years old. He was condemned to be burnt to death in the midst of the amphitheatre, and when bound to the stake, raised his voice in praise that he was counted meet to drink the Lord's cup of suffering, and be numbered among the martyrs. The wood was lighted, but the flame refused to touch him, and spread out around him in a circle of light, where his weeping flock beheld him standing as if already surrounded by the glory of heaven. At last the Proconsul ordered that he should be slain by the sword; and he thus obtained the crown of martyrdom, though he was spared the torture.

Even in the midst of this persecution, the Roman army itself contained many Christians. Marcus Aurelius was at war with the German tribe called Marcomanni, or Marchmen, the borderers on the frontier of the Danube, where his troops were reduced to the utmost distress for want of water. The Christian soldiers prayed for rain, and a shower was sent, to the relief of the whole army, for which reason their comrades called them the Thundering Legion; but Aurelius, choosing to ascribe the mercy to his own gods, set up a column at Rome, on which may still be seen sculptured a figure of Jupiter, with streams of water flowing from his head and shoulders, and the soldiers catching it in the hollow of their shields.

PART II. POWER OF THE PRÆTORIAN GUARD.
A. D. 192–245.

During nearly a century after the death of Commodus, son of Aurelius, and last of the Antonines, the empire was in the hands of the army, which would brook no commander save at their own pleasure.

The army consisted of thirty legions, enlisted from every part of the empire—Italians, Greeks, of Egypt, Asia, and Greece; Kelts, of Spain, Gaul, and Britain; Arabs; and even Germans, who came to acquire pay, plunder, and training, in the ranks of the Romans, and then returned home to use their lessons against their former masters. This force was dispersed wherever it was needed: guarding the wall raised by Adrian between his British dominions and the wild Scots; waging war with the Germans along the banks of the Rhone, Rhine, and Danube; struggling with the Parthians and Persians on the Euphrates; and garrisoning the towns on the shores of the Mediterranean. Roman camps and Roman roads still exist through all the vast region thus bounded; coins of the different Emperors, weapons, ornaments, and beautiful tesselated pavements, are continually discovered, witnessing to the extent both of their power and civilization. Each principal town had a garrison, and as the soldiers owned no authority save that of their military superiors, and the inhabitants of the country were completely under them, the whole dominion was in the hands of the army.

The Emperor was guarded by a band called the Prætorian, because before the time of Augustus it had been attached to the service of the Prætors. The men were chosen from the bravest of the legions, and having the person of the Emperor always in their hands, had full power over his life, so that it was in them that the whole overgrown influence of the army was concentrated.

They raised Emperors, and killed them at their pleasure, and were the real masters of Rome. The names of the persons whom they thus elevated are, for the most part, not worth recording. Severus was the ablest of them. He was raised to the Empire in 194, gained several victories over the Germans, went to Britain, and penetrated further into Scotland than any Roman had yet ventured; after which he built a second wall across the island, and was returning southwards, when he was taken ill, and died at York. The soldiers allowed the succession to remain in his family; but Caracalla, his son, proved cruel and wicked. Heliogabalus, his grandson, went beyond all the rest of the emperors in the wildness of his profligacy; and though Alexander Severus, the last of the family, was a youth of promise, the avarice of his mother, Julia Sæmias, so irritated the soldiers, that they killed them both, and then sold the empire to the highest bidder.

All this time the persecution of the Church was more or less severe, according to the disposition of the ruling power. There was hardly a Bishop of Rome that was not martyred; but let the heathen do their worst, they could only shed the blood of the martyrs, which is the seed of the Church, and so the Church grew and flourished in spite of their utmost efforts.

And persecuting Rome was feeling the approach of the hour of vengeance. The iron of her temper was passing away, and leaving clay in its stead, and her enemies began to close in upon her. The Goths, a powerful tribe of the great Teutonic race, broke into the Thracian provinces, where the Emperor Decius, a great persecutor, was killed in battle with them. At the same time, the Franks, another Teutonic tribe, began to ravage Gaul, and on the eastern frontier the ancient Persian monarchy of Cyrus, and the old fire-worshipping religion, were restored by Ardisheer, the founder of what is called the Sassanid dynasty, because he claimed to be descended from Sassan, son of Xerxes.

Shahpoor, or Sapor, son of Ardisheer, conquered Armenia, and in the plains of Mesopotamia, met the Roman forces under the Emperor Valerian, routed his army, made him prisoner, and carried him off to Persia. Here Valerian suffered the utmost indignities, of which the most degrading was, that he was forced to crouch on his hands and knees, that his back might serve as a step for Shahpoor, whenever he mounted his elephant; and when he died, worn out with sufferings, the savage conqueror caused his skin to be taken off, and spread upon his throne.

The first check in his course of conquest that Shahpoor experienced, was from Zenobia, the brave Arab Queen of Palmyra, a beautiful city built by Solomon on an oasis in the Syrian desert. It was a colony in Trajan's time, but it seems that some Arabs had since been allowed to establish a sort of kingdom there, and Odenatus, the husband of Zenobia, was acknowledged as a friend and ally by the Emperor. On his death, Zenobia reigned in the name of her sons. She was very beautiful, and learned in Greek literature; and her chief counsellor, Longinus, was a celebrated philosopher; the city was embellished with splendid works of art, and she extended her power on all sides, until she thought herself able to be independent of Rome, and assumed the title of Queen of the East.

The Emperor Aurelianus marched against her, overcame her forces, forced the town to surrender, and carried her and her children to Rome, where they were led in his triumphal procession in chains of gold, the last royal captives who were made to suffer that humiliation. After her fall, Palmyra was soon deserted, but the white marble columns which still remain among the palms on the oasis, witness to the beauty of the City of Palms, and the splendour of the Queen of the East.

PART III.   THE LAST PERSECUTION.   A. D. 284–311.

In 284 the soldiers raised to the imperial power Diocletian, the son of a Dalmatian peasant, a man of great ability, who immediately proceeded to place his authority on a more secure footing. He abolished the Prætorian guard, and wishing to be considered as a monarch, instead of only a general like the former emperors, he assumed the diadem instead of the laurel wreath, wore royal robes of cloth of gold, and purple silk buskins worked with golden eagles.

Thinking the empire too large to be ruled by one man, he chose Maximian, a fellow soldier, to reign jointly with him, and share with him the title of Augustus; and still further to strengthen themselves they each of them chose a successor, to whom they gave the name of Cæsar. The Cæsar chosen by Diocletian was his son-in-law, Galerius; while Maximian made choice of Flavius Constantius Chlorus, Governor of Britain, Gaul, and Spain.

For some time past the enmity of heathenism to Christianity had seemed to be silent; believers professed their faith without danger, kept their holy days openly, and had built churches, where the Liturgy was used in the face of day. Helena, a British princess and the wife of the Cæsar Constantius, was a Christian the wife and daughter of Diocletian were inclined t the same belief, and Christians were to be found in great numbers in the houses of both emperors.

The last and worst storm, however, was now to come; and darkness made its most violent attack upon light. The emperors sent forth express orders that the edicts against Christianity should be enforced with the utmost rigour, and provinces which had hitherto escaped began to suffer. Although Constantius would gladly have protected the Christians, he thought himself at first obliged to let the law take its course; and it was not till after the death of St. Alban, the British martyr, that he interfered to check the persecution in the three provinces subject to him.

Elsewhere the fury of the heathen raged unrestrained. Diocletian required his household to sacrifice to Jupiter, beginning with his wife and daughter, who yielded, but many refused, and bore with patience the most dreadful torments. One of the servants was scourged till the flesh parted from his bones, and his wounds were then rubbed with salt and vinegar. Others were stretched on the rack till their bones were dislocated, they were hung up by the hands with heavy weights fastened to their feet, their flesh was torn with iron hooks; but in every extremity of torture the faith of the Christians endured to the end. Of them it might be said, as of their predecessors of the Jewish Church, in the very words, which were doubtless their consolation and example, "They were tortured, not accepting deliverance; they had trial of cruel mockings and scourgings; yea, moreover, of bonds and imprisonment; they were stoned, were tempted, were slain with the sword, were destitute, afflicted, tormented: of whom the world was not worthy."

A town in Phrygia was hemmed in by soldiers, and burnt, with all the inhabitants, because the greater part were Christians; so many were torn by wild beasts, that it was hard to find animals enough to devour them, and every kind of new torture was invented. Agapius of Cæsarea was torn by a bear, left with his wounds bleeding all day, and then thrown into the sea, with weights fastened to his feet. St. Lawrence, a young deacon at Rome, was roasted to death on bars of iron over a fire. Children were not spared, but showed their constancy; and many were the young virgins whose names have ever since been honoured by the Church for the purity of their lives, and the glory of their deaths. St. Barbara was killed by her own father at Rome; there, too, died by the sword, St. Agnes, at twelve years old; and the next night she appeared in a dream to her sorrowing parents, a spotless lamb by her side. St. Margaret of Antioch was but fifteen when she was thrown into prison, and there a vision of treading down the dragon encouraged her the next day to meet the sword of the executioner. St. Katherine, a rich, noble, and learned maiden of Alexandria, who had devoted herself to Christ, as a bride to her spouse, was sentenced to be broken upon a wheel armed with sharp teeth; but while she was being bound to it, the machine was suddenly broken to pieces, and she was afterwards slain with the sword.

In 305, Diocletian and Maximian resigned the empire to Galerius and Constantius; the latter of whom instantly put a stop to the persecution in the West, but under Galerius and his newly appointed Cæsar

Maximus, it raged as fiercely as ever in the East. At last Galerius was seized with a lingering, loathsome, and horrible disease, under which he suffered frightful agonies, not unlike those under which Antiochus Epiphanes, the persecutor of the Jews, had died. Galerius sent for physicians from every quarter, and finding them all unable to afford him any relief, he ordered one after another to be put to death. At last one of them told him that his sufferings were sent by the God whom he had offended, and were beyond the art of man; Galerius felt the truth of his words, commanded the persecution to cease, and sent orders to the Christians to rebuild their churches and pray for his recovery; and having been thus brought to own the Power he had defied, he died in the year 311.

PART IV. CONVERSION OF CONSTANTINE. A.D. 311–323.

CONSTANTIUS CHLORUS had died in 307, leaving his portion of the empire to his son Constantinus; and on the death of Galerius, a period of great confusion ensued. The old Emperor Maximian tried to persuade his former colleague, Diocletian, who was living a retired life in Dalmatia, to come forward and resume the power they had given up; but Diocletian was so happy in his retirement, that all the answer he would make was, "Come and see the cabbages I have planted."

Maximian then gave his daughter Fausta in marriage to Constantine, and invited him from his government to come and dethrone his wicked son Maxentius, who, in the general confusion, was exercising a cruel tyranny upon Rome and Italy. He was treated with great respect by Constantine, but soon grew jealous of him, and tried to persuade his daughter to murder him;

then, on being detected, strangled himself to avoid punishment. This took place at Marseilles, whence Constantine set forward with great doubts of success, since the power of Maxentius was great, and he had already repelled an attack of the Eastern Emperor Maximinus. The mind of Constantine was at this time wavering between the religion of his mother, Helena, and that of his forefathers; he still was inclined to the old sacrifices and superstitions, but at the same time he admired the purity of life enjoined by the Divine law, and had kept himself clear from the cruelties and grosser sins of his time.

He was marching at the head of his troops towards the Alps, doubting to what Divine Power he should address himself for aid in his dangerous enterprise, when at mid-day he and his whole army suddenly beheld in the eastern quarter of the sky a luminous Cross, surrounded by these words, "*In hoc signo vinces*"—In this sign thou shalt conquer. He accepted the token, and from that time forth was a believer, though he did not receive Holy Baptism for a long time after. Adopting the Cross as his ensign, he caused it to be raised upon a pole, or above a circle, in which were the letters in Greek, the two first of the name of Christ, and below it was a purple silk banner covered with embroidery. This standard was called the Labarum, and was carried at the head of the legions instead of the Eagle, hitherto the standard of the Romans; and according to the promise it brought victory to Constantine.

Three times did he defeat the forces of Maxentius; and at length pursuing him into Rome, caused him to be put to death, and was joyfully received by the people as their deliverer. About the same time Maximin was overthrown in the East by a usurper named Licinius, who murdered him with his whole family. For eight years Constantine and Licinius reigned in the west and east, but in 323 a quarrel arose between them, Licinius was defeated at Adrianople, and the whole empire acknowledged Constantine as its lord.

CHAPTER XV.

FALL OF THE WESTERN EMPIRE. A.D. 323–476.

PART I. CONSTANTINE THE GREAT. A.D. 323–337.

WITH the victory of Constantine began the dominion of the Church, and the fulfilment of the prophecy that the kingdoms of this world should be the kingdoms of the Lord.

The Empress Helena, mother of Constantine, though seventy-nine years old, set out for Jerusalem to seek for traces of the great events that had there taken place. She was the first to lead the way in the path of pilgrimage, in which so many have since followed. Since the ruin of Jerusalem, two centuries and a half before, a new city, called Elia Capitolina, had been built on Mount Zion by the Emperor Adrian, and a Temple of Venus had been erected on Mount Calvary in contempt of the Christians; but both city and temple had fast gone to decay, and the fair hill of Zion lay waste and desolate, with only a few huts around it, inhabited by a small remnant of Jews and Christians.

Helena inquired of them respecting the sacred spots, and caused the heaps of ruin to be cleared away, and the ground to be dug, until at length she had the joy of discovering the Holy Sepulchre, and at no great distance from it, three crosses, with the nails by which the crucified had been fastened to them. One of these was believed to be the actual Instrument of our Redemption, and St. Helena, full of joy and thankfulness, built a church to receive it, large enough to contain not only the Holy Sepulchre, but the spot where the Crucifixion had taken place, making the tomb itself into a beautiful inner shrine, encrusted with gold and marble, and lighted with silver lamps. She raised another church over the cave of the Nativity at Bethlehem, and another on Mount Carmel, and then returned to her son, bringing the precious nails with her, and followed by the blessings of the inhabitants of the countries through which she passed, on whom she bestowed great alms.

Constantine seems to have felt that it was difficult to obtain the observance of Christianity in a city so full of heathen memorials connected with national pride as Rome; he likewise wished to be nearer the centre of his empire, and resolved to build a new capital. The spot which he chose was that where Europe and Asia almost meet, under the most delicious climate in the world, on the banks of the beautiful Bosphorus, where stood the old Greek city of Byzantium. This was the site of the new capital, which he made the seat of government, and after greatly enlarging and embellishing the town, called it after his own name, Constantinople and New Rome. He built a splendid church, with a dome encrusted with Mosaic work and gold, and it was dedicated to the Wisdom of God—in Greek, Sophia—

and the ignorance of after ages has converted this title into St. Sophia, as if it were the name of some Saint. Many of the Basilica, or royal halls of justice, at Rome and elsewhere, were at the same time converted into churches, the heathen temples were deserted, victims were no longer offered to the ancient gods, or demons, as they were now called, and the Church seemed everywhere flourishing.

Yet, now that the dangers and sufferings of the persecuting days were at an end, many of the more earnest Christians could not bear to live in ease and prosperity, but desired to prove their sincerity as followers of the Cross by seeking out the mortifications for themselves which no longer came from without. The chief of these was St. Antony, an Egyptian, who sold his lands, gave the money to the poor, and retired to the rocks in the Egyptian desert, where he lived on food of the coarsest kind, and barely sufficient to support life, slept on the ground, and spent his time in praying. For twenty years he was not seen, only his voice was heard when he sung psalms; but at length he was sought out by other persons, who were struck with his example, and persuaded him to be their guide in the same way of life. From that time the caves of the hilly portion of Egypt were full of hermits, spending their lives in prayer, hard labour, and self-denial of the strictest kind; and the same custom of retiring from the world began to spread through the whole Church. Both men and women had, from very early times, been in the habit of binding themselves by a vow to lead a virgin life; and these began, instead of living in their families as before, to seclude themselves in monasteries, where they might give themselves up with greater regularity to a life of strict devotion and labour.

The combat with heathenism was no sooner at an end, than foes arose to the Church from within her own household. Arius, a priest at Alexandria, began to preach a blasphemous heresy, denying the Godhead of our Lord, and saying that he had been created like angels and men. Great numbers were led away by this false doctrine, and it spread like a plague-spot through Egypt and the East, and at last it was resolved to call together the representatives of the whole Church to confute it. The place of meeting was the town of Nicea, in Asia Minor, whither came three hundred and eighteen bishops, some of them still bearing the marks of the persecutions they had undergone, and many others, who could not attend in person, sent priests as their deputies. This was the first General or Œcumenical Council of the Church, and was held in the year 325; the Emperor was there in person, and the faith that the Church had held from the first was set forth by many of the bishops, and in especial by St. Athanasius, a deacon. The confession of faith called the Nicene Creed was drawn up, and all the bishops, except eighteen, set their hand and seal to it, declaring it was the truth which they had received to hand down to the Church. Arius was put out of the communion of the Church, and his doctrine publicly condemned. The right faith now began to be called Catholic, or universal, and orthodox, or straight and true teaching.

In all this Constantine had taken the right side, but he was of a vain and hasty temper; he had not yet been baptized, and dark clouds obscured his greatness in his latter years. He listened to a wicked accusation of his wife, Fausta, against Crispus, the son of his first wife, and in a fit of passion caused his head to be cut off. Then followed bitter remorse; when he discovered the innocence of the victim, he spent forty days in tears, unable to attend to anything else, and overwhelmed with grief. His first care was to raise a silver statue in honour of Crispus, bearing the inscription, "My son whom I condemned unjustly;" and he soon after, on discovering further crimes of Fausta, caused her to be suffocated in a stove.

He began to interfere in the affairs of the Church in a manner unsuitable to his position; he let himself be deceived by the partizans of Arius, and sent orders to St. Athanasius, who was now Bishop of Alexandria, to receive him back to communion, saying that the best way of maintaining peace was to exclude nobody. Athanasius, the noble guardian of the faith, well knowing that seeming peace may not be purchased at the expense of corruption, firmly refused, upon which his enemies slandered him to the Emperor, and though all the crimes laid to his charge were disproved, Constantine, displeased at his resistance, banished him to Trèves, in Gaul.

Arius now expected to be received to Communion again, and went to Constantinople, where he deceived the Emperor by a vague profession of faith, and, it is said, by swearing to the truth of what he held in his hands, displaying as he did so, the Symbol of Nicea, as it was called, while he concealed beneath it a statement of his own heresy.

"Go," said Constantine; "if your faith agree with your oath, you are blameless; if not, God be your judge." And he gave orders that he should be received to Communion the next day, which was Sunday. The Catholic Bishops retired to their Churches, weeping and praying with one voice that heresy might not be admitted into the Church, and that the enemy might not prevail over the truth. Arius, meanwhile, triumphant in his perjury and deception, was parading the town with his friends, but in the very midst of his exultation he was suddenly taken ill, and died in the course of a few moments.

The faithful thought that the Hand of God was plainly seen in this judgment, and it seemed to cure the Emperor of any leaning to the heresy, but he still listened to the slanderers of Athanasius, and refused to allow him to return to Alexandria.

Just after Easter, in the year 337, Constantine, who was 64 years old, was taken ill, and feeling his death approach, received from the bishops the Sacraments which he had so long deferred. He wore white garments from that hour, and never again touched the imperial purple, and thanking God for the promise of eternal life, he died on Whit-Sunday of the same year, leaving the empire to be divided between his three sons, Constantine, Constantius, and Constans.

PART II. JULIAN THE APOSTATE. A. D. 337–363.

GREAT troubles to the Church ensued upon the death of Constantine. His eldest and youngest sons, Constantine and Constans, held the Catholic faith, and restored St. Athanasius to his See, but they died early, and their brother Constantius was an Arian. He sent a heretic bishop to Alexandria, with a body of troops to support him, so that Athanasius was forced to escape into the desert, where he was sheltered by the hermits. The Emperor did all in his power to favour the Arians and depress the Catholics, but though the Eastern Church was deeply infected by the heresy, the Western held fast to the true faith.

St. James, the Catholic Bishop of Nisibis, in Syria,

rendered a great service to the Empire. Shahpoor II. King of Persia, was fast extending his conquests, and totally routed Constantius in Mesopotamia, after which he advanced without opposition until he reached Nisibis, where the bishop exhorted his flock to resist, calling on them to serve as the bulwark of their country, and promising them the aid of Heaven. For four months did this gallant city hold out without a hope of relief, and so wonderfully were all Shahpoor's attacks disconcerted, that even he became persuaded that angels protected it, and he was forced to give up the siege, and retreat into Persia.

Constantius was fond of pomp and luxury, and adopted the customs of the eastern princes, once despised by the Romans. His dress was loaded with jewels, and his servants waited upon him as if he were completely helpless; his palace was filled with useless extravagant servants, and his personal attendants each had many more slaves, and lived in a far more rich and stately manner than the noblest patricians in days gone by.

He had no children, and looked with jealousy on his heir, Julianus, the son of a brother of Constantine the Great. Julian had been baptized in his infancy, educated by Christian teachers, and, in early youth, sent to study at Athens, where young men were educated in the philosophy and literature of ancient Greece. Such studies, rightly used, served to enlarge and increase the powers of the mind, and to further polish and sharpen the weapons of the champions of the Church; and thus were these lessons used by Basil and Gregory, two scholars in the groves of Athens at the same time as Julian, and afterwards two of the great Fathers of the Church. Far different was it with Julian, who turned from the truth to embrace the religion which flattered his pride of intellect, delighted in the profane old legends of Greece, and returned to the idolatry of the dark ages past.

At present he did not profess his unbelief, and Constantius, who disliked him, and wished to keep him at a distance, gave him the title of Cæsar, and sent him to command in Gaul against the Franks. Here he remained, conducting the war with great skill until 361, when a quarrel arose between him and Constantius, and the soldiers, who were much attached to him, proclaimed him Emperor. He set out from Gaul, and on the way met the tidings that his cousin Constantius had died of a fever, and he was undisputed lord of the empire. On this, he openly declared his apostasy, and professed that though no one should henceforth suffer for his religion, he hoped to see his subjects return to the faith of their forefathers.

Few enemies to the Church could be more perilous, for Julian was by nature amiable and generous, and besides, he wanted to show that the Stoic philosophy could make men as virtuous as the Divine grace, so that in his conduct heathenism did not show itself in as hateful a light as in most other cases. He was, outwardly, much like such a Greek as Cleomenes, or such a Roman as Cato, with this great difference, that whereas they lived by the law within themselves, he rejected the revealed will of Heaven; they were in darkness, but not wilfully, and he turned his back upon the light. He was frank, open-hearted, and forgiving, and imitated them in their severe strictness of life, going far beyond them in his hatred of show and pomp, which was perhaps increased by his comtempt for the effeminate Constantius.

He lived plainly, thinking it befitted the character both of a soldier and philosopher; his food was coarse and scanty; he allowed his beard to grow, and his imperial purple was never the cleanest garment in the camp; his bed was a lion's skin laid upon the ground, and he allowed few observances to be paid to his rank, gratifying his vanity as much by this affectation of simplicity as Constantius could ever have done by his parade.

With all his desire to do so, Julian could not persuade himself that his baptism was nothing, and as a seal of his apostasy, he bathed in the blood of animals, in the vain hope of washing away the sacred sign, and being as the heathen. He abased his powerful mind to believe all the wildest and most foolish superstitions of the heathen, and was swayed by every absurd omen or lying answer of the almost forgotten oracles. At the same time, to show his contempt for Christian prophecy, he attempted to rebuild the Temple of Jerusalem; but the Power he defied asserted itself, and an earthquake, with flames bursting from the ground, prevented even the foundation from being laid.

Notwithstanding his promise of toleration, it was soon evident that he meant indirectly to persecute the Christians. St. Athanasius was a third time obliged to fly: the Christians could obtain no redress when illtreated or pillaged by the heathen, whilst any fault which they committed was punished with the utmost rigour. He tried to cheat some of his soldiers into forsaking their religion, by causing them to march past his throne, and ordering each man as he went by to throw a morsel of incense into a fire which was burning before it. The men obeyed as they would any other command, but great was their dismay when they were told that the fire was on an altar of Jupiter, whom, by this ceremony, they had adored. They rushed back with one accord to the Emperor, and begged to die, as an expiation for their fault. He at first sentenced them all, but afterwards relented, and reprieved them just as the sword was lifted over the head of the first.

He succeeded no better with the officers, when he required them either to renounce their faith or his service. The captain of his guards, the brave and honest young Jovian, was the first to offer to give up his sword; and Julian found that by insisting, he should lose all the most trustworthy men in his army.

Though some showed such constancy, there were many others but too willing to gain the Emperor's favour by imitating his apostasy, and as their number increased, and his hatred to the truth grew ever more violent, the Church seemed in great danger; but happily his time was not long.

His flattering oracles and heathen priests well knowing the bent of his mind, encouraged him to set out on a rash expedition into Persia, where he involved his army in a barren and dangerous country, and at last, in a skirmish with the Persians on the banks of the Tigris, was pierced in the side by a javelin. He fell, and after trying in vain to rise and remount his horse, was carried on his shield to his tent. It is said, that when he was told that his wound was mortal, he caught some of his blood in his hand, and throwing it towards Heaven, cried, "Galilean, Thou hast conquered." He died the same evening, A. D. 362, after a reign of less than two years, at the age of thirty-two; just in time to prevent the execution of orders for the persecution of the Catholics in Alexandria, which had actually been sent from his camp a few days before his death.

PART III. VALENTINIAN. A. D. 362–383.

The army which Julian left at his death, beset with dangers from which he himself could scarcely have led them with honour, proceeded to choose as Emperor the person whom they thought best fitted to command them in this emergency. This was the captain of the guards, Jovian, who had lately so nobly proved his constancy to the faith; but his talents do not seem to have been equal to his virtues, and he soon found himself obliged to purchase from Shahpoor permission to retreat by yielding up five provinces of Armenia, and the brave frontier town of Nisibis. He set out on his return to Constantinople, but died suddenly in Syria, after having enjoyed the imperial power only eight months.

An officer named Valentinian was chosen in his place, and he again divided the empire, keeping Rome for himself, and giving Constantinople to his brother Valens. Valentinian was a Catholic, Valens an Arian, and the latter did much harm in the East by promoting the spread of this heresy. About this time St. Athanasius died at Alexandria, leaving the Church that Creed which is called by his name, and which, if not actually drawn up by himself, contains the doctrine of which he was the great confessor and champion.

St. Jerome was at this time leading a monastic life in Palestine, and being greatly noted for his learning in the Greek and Hebrew tongues, was desired by Damasus, the Bishop or Pope of Rome, to make a translation of the Scriptures into Latin. He examined into the authenticity of the Books of the New Testament, and translated the Old Testament from the

Septuagint, corrected by Hebrew manuscripts; and this translation, called the Vulgate, has ever since been used in the Western Church.

A translation of the Bible into the Teutonic tongue was about the same time made by Ulphilas, the Arian Bishop of the Goths, on the banks of the Danube; and a beautiful copy of this work, written on purple parchment, with silver letters, is preserved at Upsal, in Sweden. It is uncertain when the Goths had received Christianity, but it was by Arians that they were taught, and the heresy had taken deep root among them. Their neighbourhood to the Empire had caused them to take several steps towards civilization, and their brave King Hermanric was considered at Constantinople as a friend and ally.

Valentinian was a skilful warrior, and gained several great victories over the different barbarous tribes surrounding the empire; but he was of a merciless temper, and some of his cruelties were dreadful. It was said that he kept two tame bears, which he fed upon the flesh of such persons as offended him. In 375 he burst a blood-vessel in a fit of passion, and died, leaving two sons, Gratian, about seventeen, and Valentinian, a child of two years old, the son of his second wife Justina.

A new and formidable race of enemies began to make themselves known in Europe—the Huns, a Tartar tribe, of ferocious temper and predatory habits. They were excellent horsemen, but could not move fast on foot; and they had small eyes, low foreheads, and diminutive forms, such as are now to be seen in the Tartars in Asia. They scarred the faces of their infants with hot irons, which added to their savage appearance, and so frightful was their aspect, that the

Romans and Greeks almost believed them the offspring of evil spirits.

They broke into the settlements of the Goths, on the northern bank of the Danube, and cruelly ravaged them. The Goths begged for a refuge in the Empire, and had it not been for the misconduct of the Greek officers, would have made common cause with Valens against the Huns. But Valens allowed his officers to treat the fugitives with such insolence and rapacity, that they were roused to revenge, took up arms, attacked the Eastern Empire, and in 378 Valens was killed in a battle with them at Adrianople. They advanced to Constantinople, but the widowed Empress, Dominica, encouraged the citizens to resist, and the Goths, who had no means of taking a fortified city, retired into Illyria.

Young Gratian, feeling his inability to encounter all the dangers that beset the empire, made a wise and excellent choice of a colleague in his authority, an officer named Theodosius, of tried worth and bravery, and sincerely attached to the Catholic faith. Theodosius hastened to the East, and there, by his well-known uprightness and good faith, succeeded in calming the passions excited by the injuries the Goths had recieved, concluded a peace with them, obtained the friendship of their King Athanaric, and took many of them into his army, where they served him far more bravely than the degenerate Greeks and Romans.

Gratian, though an amiable and virtuous youth, could not make his power equally respected in the West; and a soldier, named Maximus, at this time greatly weakened the Empire in the Keltic provinces. His mother was a relation of the British princess Helena, mother of Constantine, and he took advantage of this connection with the Imperial line, to set himself up as Emperor in Gaul, Britain, and Spain.

He was a cruel and ambitious man, although he held the Catholic faith, and highly esteemed the great Bishop of Tours, St. Martin. Martin had been a soldier in his youth, and was even then so charitable that he cut his cloak in two and shared it with a beggar. He completed the conversion of the Gauls, many of whom in the more remote provinces had still remained attached to the Druidical worship, and he was always held in high honour at the court of Maximus, although he did not obtain this favour by any flattery of the pride of the usurper, for at table he would pass the drinking-cup to his attendant priests before giving it to Maximus, in order to show that the minister of God is greater than the crowned prince.

Gratian marched against Maximus, but was defeated, made prisoner, and murdered at Lyons in 383, calling with his last breath upon the name of Ambrose, the Bishop of Milan.

PART IV. THEODOSIUS THE GREAT. A.D. 383–395.

VALENTINIAN II. the son of the Emperor Valentinian, was brought up by his mother Justina, in the Arian heresy, and wished to secure its predominance. They usually lived at Milan, and here the great Archbishop, St. Ambrose, had a long and severe struggle to maintain the faith against them. He would not permit their corrupt worship to be celebrated in any one of his churches, and remained night and day with his faithful flock, to guard one which the empress had threatened to take by force. No weapons were used save prayers by these defenders, and the soldiers sent by Justina did not dare to offer them any injury, until at length she was obliged to give up the attempt.

Yet St. Ambrose, though so firm in supporting the right, would not permit the persons of heretics to be injured. Maximus, now called Emperor of Gaul, had, by the advice of certain bishops, put to death a heretical teacher, and five of his followers, and both St. Ambrose and St. Martin refused to communicate with these bishops until they had given proofs of repentance.

In 387 Maximus crossed the Alps, and suddenly attacking Italy, put to flight Justina and her son ; but the great Theodosius came to their assistance, defeated Maximus, drove him to the banks of the Save, and there caused him to be beheaded. He then reinstated Valentinian, giving him Britain and Gaul ; but these countries never again completely returned under the authority of the Emperor, and were continually setting up usurpers, who much weakened the power of Rome.

Theodosius imposed a tax upon his dominions in the East, which was considered at Antioch as so oppressive, that the people rose in tumult, overthrew the statues of the Emperor, and dragged them through the mire. This was so great an insult to his authority that the severest punishments were apprehended, and as soon as the people of Antioch had recovered from their blind fury, their terror was extreme. The aged patriarch hastened to implore the clemency of the Emperor, and the people, during his absence, strove themselves to avert the wrath of Heaven, while St. John, called, from his eloquence, Chrysostom, or the golden-mouthed, preached to them a series of sermons, calling on them to repent of the sins to which they were most addicted. After twenty-four days they were relieved by letters bringing an assurance of the pardon of Theodosius, upon which they showed the greatest joy and thankfulness.

Theodosius was naturally hasty and violent, and another sedition, three years after, so enraged him, that he forgot all the dictates of mercy. The people of Thessalonica, enraged that Botheric, the commander of the forces in Illyria, had imprisoned a favourite performer in the games in the circus, attacked the general with stones, and killed him, together with several other magistrates. Theodosius, in his first hasty indignation, commanded that the unhappy citizens should be punished by a general massacre; and his orders were but too promptly executed, so that the messengers, whom he had sent to countermand the slaughter when his anger began to cool, found the streets strewn with corpses and the town on fire.

The Emperor was at this time at Milan, and St. Ambrose thought it his duty to bring him to a sense of his sin by refusing to admit him to the Holy Eucharist. Theodosius in vain presented himself as a suppliant at the gate of the church; Ambrose met him, and turned him back, bidding him not to add sacrilege to murder. Theodosius pleaded that David had sinned more deeply. "If you have sinned like him," said the Archbishop, "repent like him;" and the Emperor submitted, and went back weeping to his palace. The usual time for reconciling penitents to the Church was Easter; but when the feast of Christmas approached, Theodosius hoped to persuade the Archbishop to admit him at that time. Still Ambrose was firm, and again met the Emperor at the entrance, reproaching him with attempting to break through the dicipline of the Church. "No," said Theodosius, "I am not come to break the laws, but to entreat you to imitate the mercy of God whom we serve, who opens the gates of his mercy to contrite sinners."

After this St. Ambrose allowed him to enter the Church, though he was not received to the Holy Communion again for some time, during which his penance was strict, and he abstained from wearing his imperial robes. He made a law, by the advice of St. Ambrose, that no sentence of death should be executed for thirty days, so as to give time for reflection, and he ever after curbed in his stern and hasty temper.

Soon after his return to Constantinople, he was again recalled to Italy, by the murder of the young Valentinian, who was killed by one of his Gothic officer. Theodosius overcame the murderer, put him to death, and assumed the government of the whole empire; but he did not long retain it, dying at Milan in his fiftieth year, in 395.

During the reign of Theodosius was held the Council of Constantinople, where, in order to refute certain heresies which had of late arisen, the latter portion was added to the Nicene Creed, so that it might assert the Divinity of the Holy Ghost as clearly as that of the other Persons of the Holy Trinity.

It was in this reign that the Ambrosian Hymn, or Te Deum, one of the Church's highest notes of praise, was composed. It is said to have been written by St. Ambrose, to be sung at the baptism of Augustin, who, after a youth of doubt and dissipation, was at length brought by the prayers and tears of his pious mother, Monica, to embrace the truth. He afterwards became Bishop of Hippo, in Africa, and is revered as one of the greatest of the Fathers of the Church.

PART V. ALARIC THE GOTH. A. D. 395-410.

THEODOSIUS the Great was the last who deserved even the name of a Roman Emperor. He left two sons, Arcadius and Honorius, both weak and timid in mind and body, but of whom Honorius, who had received the western half of the empire, was the most imbecile.

The state of the Roman power was such that it could hardly have been saved by the most vigorous Emperor. The Goths had, as has already been shown, obtained a settlement south of the Danube, where they had lived on friendly terms with the Romans, until Alaric, a young man of their royal tribe, received some affront from the officers of Arcadius, upon which he took up arms against the Emperors. He overran Greece, Thessaly, and Macedon, and after training his soldiers in the Roman dicipline, passed the Julian Alps and entered Italy.

Honorius had at this time never even heard the name of this formidable enemy. He spent his whole time in attending to some favourite poultry, which would come at his call and sit on his shoulder, while the government was left to Stilicho, the last Roman general. Stilicho called in the legions from the more remote parts of the empire to defend the capital, entirely giving up Britain, and leaving Gaul and Spain undefended, and with these troops he gained a great victory at Verona, and forced Alaric to retreat.

In honour of this victory Honorius enjoyed a triumph, the last which ever proceeded along the streets of Rome. After it there was a show of gladiators, and this also was the last, for in the midst of the shameful scene, a hermit named Telemachus, who had come from Syria, with the very purpose of putting a stop to these cruel exhibitions, sprung from his seat into the midst of the arena, and holding up a cross, threw himself between the victorious gladiator and his victim. The people in a rage at the interruption of their sport, overwhelmed him with a shower of stones, and he was crushed to death; but he had won the victory, and the shame of having thus murdered him prevented any return to these atrocious sports, the disgrace of the Roman name.

Stilicho's victory had gained Rome but a short respite; Alaric again advanced, and Honorius fled to Ravenna on the Adriatic, which was so well protected by marshes, that he thought himself and his chicken quite secure, and left Rome to its fate. He listened to wicked flatterers, and by their persuasions, on a false accusation, sentenced to death Stilicho, the only man capable of defending the empire. After his execution Alaric met with nothing to oppose him through all the north of Italy, and arrived before the walls of Rome, which had not seen an hostile army since the time of Hannibal.

For that time Rome was spared by the generosity and forbearance of Alaric, but the falsehood and self-will of Honorius again provoked him, and he advanced again; but even then he would not enter Rome, wishing to spare it from his wild soldiers. A third time he offered peace, but was insultingly refused, and marching to Rome, the gates were opened by his friends within the walls, and on the 24th of August, 410, the Goths entered the great city.

Alaric saved the lives of the Romans, though he allowed their property to be plundered: he protected the churches and their gold and silver, and, at the end of six days, put a stop to the pillage by leading his army into Campania.

So little did Honorius concern himself about this event, that it is said that when he was told that Rome was lost, he answered, "That cannot be, for I fed her out of my hand a moment ago," meaning a hen which he had named Rome.

The great Alaric did not live long after the taking of Rome. He was preparing for the invasion of Sicily, when he was taken suddenly ill at Cosenza, and died in 410, leaving his crown to his brave brother-in-law, Ataulf. As it was the custom among the Teutonic nations to conceal the graves of their illustrious men, the Goths turned the stream of the Bisenzio, caused their slaves to dig a grave in the bed of the river, and after burying him there with all his treasures, they turned back the waters into their course, and slew all the slaves who had been employed in the work.

The name of the Roman Empire subsisted a little longer, though it was only owned in the walled cities, which could not easily be taken by the barbarians. Honorius and his son Valentinian reigned at Ravenna. Rome was under the care of the bishop, who was usually called Pope, a word signifying father or patriarch, and the other towns were governed by their own councils.

PART VI.   ATTILA THE HUN.   A. D. 395–457.

THE Eastern Empire had prospered better than the Western. Arcadius was far less imbecile than his brother Honorius, and his government was tolerably successful; but he allowed himself to be persuaded by his wife Eudoxia into a shameful persecution of St.

John Chrysostom, who had been made Patriarch of Constantinople, who had rebuked her sternly for her pride and her love of amusement unfit for Christians.

By her persuasion Arcadius caused St. Chrysostom to be deposed from his see and driven into exile; but as the people of Constantinople still continued to manifest the utmost affection and respect for him, Eudoxia insisted on his being sent to a greater distance, to Armenia; and the persons who conducted him used him so ill on the journey, that his health gave way under his sufferings. and he died at Comana, in Pontus, exclaiming, "Glory be to God in all things."

Arcadius died in 408, leaving an infant son, Theodosius II., under the care of his daughter Pulcheria, who ruled so wisely, that on the death of her brother, the Greeks promised to obey as Emperor whomsoever she would choose as a husband. Her choice fell on Marcian, an old senator, who reigned till 457, when Leo became Emperor. He is noted as the first Christian prince who was crowned and anointed by a bishop, after the example of the monarchs of Israel.

In the meantime fresh troubles had befallen the West. It may be remembered that in the time of Valens, the Goths had been driven into Illyria by the Huns, a tribe of the Tartar or Sclavonic race. These Huns, early in the fifth century, fell under the dominion of an able, enterprising, and ferocious chieftain, named Attila, who gave himself the title of the Scourge of God, one which he well deserved. His power was acknowledged from the borders of China to the White Sea, and multitudes of Tartar hordes followed what was at once his idol and his standard, a sword raised upon a pole. In 451, after ravaging the Thracian provinces, he turned to the west, and invaded Gaul, but his savage followers were as hateful to the Teutonic nations as to the Romans, and Goths and Franks joined with the Romans and Gauls, under the command of Aëtius, and at the battle of Chalons forced Attila to retreat.

He then laid waste the north of Italy, but spared Rome at the intercession of the Pope, Leo the Great, who, at the peril of his life, sought the savage in his camp, and so impressed him with his calm dignity, that he consented to allow the city to be ransomed.

Many of the people of northern ▓▓▓▓ flying from the cruelty of the Huns, took refuge in the little isles among the salt marshes at the mouths of the rivers Po and Adige. The numerous shallows and channels of water rendered these a secure retreat from the enemy; the fugitives became unwilling to leave it; they built huts, collected such property as they had been able to save, and thus founded the city of Venice.

Attila quitted Italy, and soon after died in a fit of drunkenness in Hungary. His warriors tore their cheeks with their daggers, saying the tears with which he should be mourned should be tears of blood; they buried him with all his riches, and then most of them returned to their wandering life in the north-east, one tribe, however, still remaining in the country which bears their name.

Romulus Augustus, the last Roman Emperor, was deposed in 476 by Odoacer, Gothic King of Italy, who sent the purple robes and diadem to Constantinople, saying that one Emperor was enough.

It was in the end of this century that St. Patrick converted the Irish to Christianity, while, at the same period, St. Germain was opposing the heresy of

Pelagius, who disputed the doctrine of original sin. Another heresy, which has perverted many of the Churches of the East, where it unhappily still prevails, was that of Nestorius, who denied the true faith respecting the Incarnation of our Blessed Lord.

About this time was born St. Benedict, who afterwards became Abbot of Monte Casino, in Italy, and there established the rule of monastic dicipline which is called by his name. Those persons who dedicated themselves to the service of Heaven, now no longer dwelt only in hermitages, but were gathered together in brotherhoods, or sisterhoods, under the name of monks, or nuns, taking vows of chastity, obedience, and poverty, and labouring hard in works of charity and devotion. In these houses were preserved the last remnants of the learning of ancient times, as well as the writings of the Fathers of the Church, and it was to them that the gradual civilization of the rude conquerors of Europe was chiefly owing. It was St. Benedict who devised the best rule for the government of these abbeys that was ever framed, and it prevailed in almost every monastic establishment of the Western Church.

A plain dark robe, with a hood, a shaven head, and bare feet, distinguished the monk or nun; their food was as plain as possible, their fasts frequent, their bed hard; they were to labour hard through the day, only interrupting their work to observe the hours of prayer; in short, everything was done to cut off occasions of sin, and to lead them on through a life of strict obedience, devotion, and self-denial, to the rest above, for which they hoped to be thus prepared.

CHAPTER XVI.

THE PARTITION OF THE EMPIRE. A.D. 450-628.

PART I. THE TEUTONIC NATIONS. A.D. 504-522.

From the middle of the fifth century, when the Roman empire was destroyed, history is principally concerned with the Teutonic nations who had spread themselves over Europe.

It seems as if the north of Europe had been like a great hive, from which these swarms all proceeded, since they all came from that direction, and differed but little in language, habits, dress, or religion. They had a tradition that Odin, whom they worshiped as a god, and from whom all their royal lines traced their descent, had led them from warmer climates in the east to their dwellings in Norway and Sweden; and this is not improbable, since, from the first time they are mentioned, they seem to have come in a stream from east to west.

First came the Teutones, from whom the name of the language, Deutch, is derived, who, after asking a settlement in Italy, were destroyed by Marius in Gaul. Next the Allemans, or Germans, with whom Drusus Germanicus had so many battles, and whose name still remains as a general appellation for the lands of their descendants.—The Schwaben, or Suevi, were one of their lesser tribes, who have left their name to Swabia. The third great wave was of Goths, whose name, with that of their royal tribe, the Balti, is still remaining in the north. They settled in Illyria, and afterwards, under Alaric, conquered Rome and Italy.

At the same time three other great general divisions of the same stock were effecting their conquests—the Vandals in Gaul, Spain, and Africa; the Franks in northern Gaul; and the Saxons in Britain.

The Saxons had at first inhabited Jutland, and the neighbouring country, now called the Duchy of Holstein, and usually made their conquering expeditions by sea. Henghist, head of the Jutish tribe, first settled in Kent, and was soon followed by many other chieftains, who at length, after almost a century of hard fighting with the Romanized Britons, subdued all the south-eastern portion of the island, and set up their seven kingdoms there.

The Vandals, under Genseric, conquered Africa in 429, the year of the death of St. Augustin, Bishop of Hippo; and they likewise desolated Spain, but without long retaining it, for Ataulf, the Goth, brother-in-law of Alaric, followed them thither, overcame them, and established a monarchy, which may be regarded as the origin of the present kingdom of Spain. The name of the province of Andalusia remains to remind us of the Vandal conquest.

These Spanish Goths were called the Visigoths, or Western Goths, while those who remained in Italy were known as the Austro, or Eastern Goths. The Goths were much more civilized than any of the other Teutonic tribes, and Theodorik, King of Italy, from 508 to 522, was a truly great man. He had recieved a good education at Constantinople, and was very highly esteemed for his wisdom and justice. "Our design," said he, in the preface to his laws, "is not to conquer, but to render our subjects happy." And he favoured alike both Romans and Goths, so that Italy began, under his government, to recover from her sufferings. Like all the other Goths, he was bred up an Arian, but he showed great respect to the Pope; and when one of his officers, in hopes of gaining his favour, renounced the Catholic faith, he put him to death, saying that one who was faithless to his God, could never be faithful to his king.

The Vandals in the south-east of France and Switzerland were Catholics, and were fast learning civilization of the Romanized Gauls, with whom they lived on friendly terms. From living in towns or burghs, these civilized Vandals acquired the name of Burgundians.

PART II. THE FRANKS. A.D. 448–539.

THE Franks were the wildest and most untamed of all. Their name signified free, which, in their ideas, meant ferocious, or untamed. They allowed their hair to grow, tying it together at the top of their head in a knot, from which it flowed down on all sides; they shaved their faces closely, only leaving a long pair of moustaches; they wore a close-fitting dress of cloth, and used as weapons a sword, a battle-axe, and a short pike covered with barbs and hooks of iron, with a rope fastened to it, so that they might throw it at their enemy, and, keeping hold of the rope, draw him up to them, and kill or plunder him. Their royal tribe was called the Salic, from Saliland, the country near the Yssel. The kings and their sons wore their hair still longer than the other Franks, never having it clipped from their birth; and to cut short these flowing locks was considered to degrade a prince from his rank, and render him incapable of ever reigning.

Merowig was the first Salic king whose name has been preserved, and from him the appellation of Merovingians has been given to the whole race, who are also sometimes called the Long-haired Kings. Clodowig, whom the Latin authors call Clovis, was the first chieftain of this line who succeeded in effecting a permanent conquest on the western side of the Rhine, where his predecessors had only made passing inroads. In 494 Clodowig took up his abode at Soissons, quartering his Franks in the houses of the Gallo-Romans, whom they treated with great insolence and cruelty. Clodowig asked and obtained in marriage Clotilda, a Burgundian princess, who was a Catholic Christian, and set herself earnestly to effect his conversion.

For some time her persuasions were fruitless, and the death of her first child, who had been baptized, seems to have made her husband still more averse to her religion. At length, while Clodowig was engaged in a battle with the Germans on the banks of the Moselle, seeing the day going against him, he called for aid on "Clotilda's God." At that moment the tide of battle turned, the German chief was slain, and his followers submitted to Clodowig.

On his return to Soissons, the king desired to become a catechumen, and on Christmas-day, 496, he was baptized by St. Remigius, Archbishop of Rheims, in the cathedral of that city. As there was at that time no other Catholic prince, the Greek Emperor, Zeno, having fallen into heresy, Clodowig received the title of Eldest Son of the Church, which descended to all his susccessors, the Kings of France.

He was a powerful and successful prince; he built churches and monasteries, and spared those of his newly-conquered territories; but it was long before the

Christian religion tamed the fierce nature of the Franks, and there is scarcely one of the sons and grandsons of Clodowig who was not stained by horrible cruelties. On his death his sons divided his possessions, but it must not be supposed that this was a partition of territory. These Frankish kings were not governors or rulers, but were themselves subject to the Salic law, which prescribed the sum to be paid in conpensation for any injury done to another, even for murder, setting a far higher price on the death of a Frank than on that of a Roman or Gaul. What they sought were slaves, cattle, gold, and silver; warriors to follow them to battle, cities to pay them tribute, a country to plunder, estates, where their slaves worked for them, and they feasted and drank in their great farm-houses.

The Frank settlements were north of the Loire, divided into the kingdoms of Oster-rik, Austria, the eastern kingdom, and Ne-oster-rik, Neustria, the not-eastern or western kingdom. Here lived the long-haired princes, in palaces, or rather on farms, at no great distance from each other, the Frank warriors divided between them the towns paying them tribute, and all the unhappy country to the south, as far as the Pyrenees and Mediterranean, partitioned into plundering grounds, so to speak, where the kings made expeditions in the summer, burnt and devastated without mercy carried off treasures and slaves, and returned to feast with their rude followers.

Disputes perpetually broke out among these kings, and battles and murders among kindred were frequent. One instance will suffice to show the cruelty of this race. Theudebert, eldest son of Clodowig, died early, leaving three young sons. His two brothers divided his wealth between them, but hearing that their mother,

16 *a*

Clotilda, was much attached to the poor boys, they feared that she would put forward their claims to their father's inheritance, and therefore contrived by a stratagem to get them into their power. They then sent her a sword and a pair of shears, bidding her choose between them, meaning that the children must either be killed or have their hair cut, so as to render them incapable of reigning. Clotilda exclaimed that she had rather they were dead than degraded, upon which the uncles seized them, dragged them into a room apart, and there killed the eldest, who was about ten years old. The second clung about their knees, and begged to be spared, but they shook him off, and slew him likewise. Clodoald, the third, was, however, rescued, for the cries of his brothers attracted a party of Franks, who broke in, and carried him off, in spite of the two kings. He was obliged to cut his hair and enter a monastery, where he lived a far better and happier life than could have been his as a Frankish king at that time, and when he died was honoured by the Church under the name of St. Cloud.

PART III. JUSTINIAN. A.D. 527–565.

THE Vandal kingdom in Africa was of no long duration; the state was weakened by the dissensions of the royal family, and there was at this time such reviving vigour at Constantinople, that the Greek empire seemed likely to recover all that the Roman had lost.

Justinian, who became Emperor in 527, was not a great man himself, but knew how to choose his ministers and generals, and thus rendered his reign one of the most illustrious in history. He is remembered as the second founder of the church of St. Sophia, which had been consumed by fire early in his reign, and which he rebuilt with such magnificence, and regarded with so much vanity, that the first time he entered it after its completion, he exclaimed, "Solomon, I have surpassed thee!" He likewise collected the whole body of ancient Roman laws, adapted them to Christianity, and formed them into an excellent code, called the Pandects of Justinian, which have been the basis of almost every table of laws that has since been drawn up.

The greatest and ablest subject of Justinian was his general, Belisarius, a man of high talent and noble spirit, who gained for him all his chief triumphs. Gelimer, the last Vandal King of Africa, gained the throne by the murder of his kinsman, an ally of Justinian, and thus gave cause for the Greek Empire to commence a war. Belisarius had the command, and in four years reduced the Vandals, and returned in triumph to Constantinople, bringing Gelimer with him as a prisoner. He likewise brought back the treasures of the Temple of Jerusalem, which the barbarians had carried off from Rome to Carthage. Justinian proposed to present them to the church of St. Sophia, but his bishops represented that disaster had followed their arrival both at Rome and Carthage, and advised him to send them to their proper home, the Cathedral of Jerusalem, which he accordingly did, and their subsequent fate is not known.

The Gothic kingdom of Italy had likewise fallen into decay; Amalosontha, the daughter of Theodorik the Great, was stifled in a bath by the husband whom she had chosen to share her throne; he was soon after put to death, and Vitiges, a brave warrior, had seized the throne. Justinian undertook to avenge her death, and in 537 Belisarius led an army into Italy. He entered it from the south, took Naples by introducing his men through an old forgotten aqueduct, which opened into the court of an old woman's house, and marched towards Rome. Here he was admitted into the city, and was besieged by the Goths, till such famine reigned within the city, that the Romans, little used to privation, were only prevented by his constant vigilance from betraying him to the enemy. At last ships entered the Tiber, bringing fresh supplies, and Vitiges was forced to retreat. Belisarius followed him, drove him from one stronghold to another, and finally, in 539, made him prisoner in the city of Ravenna, and a second time returned to Constantinople the conqueror of a kingdom, and with a captive monarch in his train.

His next war was in the East. Nushirvan, or Khoosrou, the same name as Cyrus, but which the Greeks were now pleased to turn into Chosroes, was one of the most warlike of the Persian kings, and entering Justinian's dominions, overran all the eastern part of Syria, and carried off a great quantity of spoil and many captives from Antioch. Belisarius marched against him, and had gained several important successes, when he was suddenly recalled to Constantinople, and Narses, also an able officer, though far from being his equal in any of his good qualities, was sent to reap the fruits of his victories.

It appears that a report of Justinian's death had reached the army, upon which Belisarius had declared that his voice should be in favour of Justin, the Emperor's nephew, as his successor, instead of the Empress Theodora, a violent and profligate woman, who had far too much influence over her husband; and this being reported to her, occasioned his recall.

The Empress could not deprive him of all his honours, and he remained at Constantinople as the master of the horse, *comes stabuli*, or count of the stable, a high office in the imperial household, until his presence was again required in Italy.

Totila, nephew of Vitiges, having persuaded the Goths to revolt, at their head had repulsed the Greeks, and recovered all the cities they had taken, even Rome itself. Belisarius was sent to the rescue of his own conquests, but with so few men that he could effect nothing, and the jealousy of Theodora prevailed so as to prevent any effectual succour being sent him. He returned to Constantinople, and Narses, who had made himself a favourite at court, again took his place, and was properly supported. Totila was defeated and slain at Gualdo, on the Apennines; Rome was taken; the other towns of Italy surrendered, and the Ostrogoth kingdom was finally destroyed. A governor, appointed by the Greek Emperor, received the title of Exarch of Ravenna, and the whole of Italy was once more subject to the Emperors.

Belisarius was treated in his old age with the utmost ingratitude by the master whom he had so bravely served; falsely accused of rebellion; deprived of his servants, his guards, and his wealth, and his eyes put out. It is even said that he was reduced to stand begging before the door of a church, holding out a wooden dish, and saying, "Give a penny to Belisarius the General." The shame was more to the Emperor than to him, and Justinian perhaps so felt it, for he gave orders that he should be brought back to his own house, and part of his wealth restored to him. This noble, valiant, and loyal man died in 564, a year before the death of his jealous and ungrateful master.

PART IV. FREDEGONDA. A.D. 561–613.

The latter part of the sixth century was a time of almost equal confusion and bloodshed with that period which had just passed. Two Vandal tribes, the Lombards, or more properly, the Long-beards, and the Gepidæ, had hitherto inhabited the district between Italy and Thrace. Alboin, the Lombard King, killed Kunimund, the chief of the Gepidæ, married his beautiful daughter Rosamond, and at the head of both tribes entered Italy, and overran the whole country.

Pavia was the only town of any great importance which he was able to take, and he rendered it the capital of the new kingdom, which received the name of Lombardy. Rome, Ravenna, and Venice, were, however, never subdued by the Lombards, and, together with Sicily, and southern Italy, continued to adhere to the eastern empire. Alboin had caused the skull of his enemy, Kunimund, to be made into a drinking-cup, and one day in a fit of intoxication at one of his savage banquets, he actually sent this horrible goblet full of wine to his wife Rosamond, Kunimund's daughter, desiring her to pledge him in it. This outrage awoke her desire for vengeance, and she caused two of Alboin's guards to murder him in 583. Another king was elected to succeed him, raised on the bucklers of his warriors, and crowned with the iron crown of Lombardy.

Among the Franks, the grandsons of Clodowig were even worse, if possible, than his sons. There were four of them, sons of Chloter I. Hilperik and Sigebert, the two youngest, were the most noted, **chiefly in** consequence of the mortal hatred of their wives. Hilperik and Sigebert married two sisters, Gothic princesses of Spain, but Hilperik soon murdered his wife in order to marry Fredegonda, a slave. Brynhilda, Sigebert's wife, stirred up her husband to revenge her sister's death, until Fredegonda sent men armed with poisoned daggers, who killed him, leaving a son, Hildebert, who afterwards reigned in Neustria. It was at this time that a good bishop, looking up to Hilperik's palace, exclaimed, "I see the sword of the wrath of God hanging over this house!" and so indeed it proved.

Fredegonda's hatred pursued to the death all the sons of her husband by his first wife, whom she had supplanted; her own two sons died of an infectious disorder; and soon after the birth of her youngest child, Chloter, Hilperik was murdered by some unknown assassin. It would be needless to go through the whole course of treacheries, deceits, and murders, on the part of Fredegonda; to describe her poisoned daggers, her intoxicating beverages, her newly invented tortures, and her revolting hypocrisy; or, on the other hand, to dwell upon the proud, cruel, unforgiving temper of her rival, Brynhilda. The close of their history is, that Fredegonda died in triumphant wickedness at Paris, in 597, and that, twenty-one years after, her son Chloter took prisoner the aged Brynhilda, with her infant great-grandsons. He dashed the heads of the children against the ground, and caused Brynhilda to be tied by one foot and one arm to the tail of a wild horse, which was then let loose, so that the unhappy woman was torn to pieces in its career.

It is remarkable that during this time of horrible wickedness in France, two Frank princesses were the means of spreading the knowledge of the truth into the adjoining countries. Ingunda, daughter of Brynhilda, was married to Hermanigild, eldest son of Leovigild, Visigoth king of Spain. Leovigild's wife, Goiswintha, was resolved to make her embrace the Arian heresy, and on her refusal treated her cruelly, and at last threw her into a pond of water in the gardens of the palace.

The constancy of the young wife had such an effect on her husband, that he became a Catholic. His father persecuted him till he fled and raised a rebellion, but was defeated, made prisoner, and shut up in the tower at Tarragona. Arian bishops were sent to him, and his life was promised him on condition he would renounce the Catholic faith; but he remained firm, and at length was martyred by order of his father, Leovigild.

His example had not been lost upon his brother Recared, who, on succeeding his father in 583, professed himself a Catholic. Many of his subjects followed his example, but the Arians who still remained, were continually plotting against his life, with the old queen Goiswintha, his step-mother. He behaved with admirable forbearance and patience, and forgave their wicked attempts repeatedly, until at last Goiswintha died of grief and rage at the detection of one of her conspiracies, and her guilty associates were, for the most part, exiled. Recared was a great and glorious king, and made himself highly respected. He was an excellent warrior, though too just to be a conqueror, and his reign was the most prosperous period of the Gothic kingdom in Spain.

Another Frank princess, Bertha, daughter of Brynhilda's son Hildebert, married Ethelbert, King of Kent, and introduced to her husband, St. Augustin, who had been sent by Pope Gregory the Great to preach the Gospel to the Saxons.

PART V. THE GREEK EMPIRE. 582–6??

St. Gregory was one of the greatest and best of all the Popes, most pious and self-denying, and a firm champion of the truth. He wrote many works on religious subjects, and was especially remarkable for the controversy of the Greek Church. When the emperor wished to subject the See of Rome to that of Constantinople, St. Gregory demonstrated that one patriarch ought not to interfere in the jurisdiction of another, and used arguments which tell strongly against the dominion claimed in after ages by his own successors.

The Greek Emperor, Maurice, who came to the throne in 582, was an excellent warrior and a sincerely religious man. He gained several great successes over the Persians, and repressed the incursions of the savage Tartar tribes who had settled on the banks of the Danube, and were known by the general name of Bulgarians; but he fell into one great crime, which he expiated by a fearful punishment.

There was one division in his army so mutinous and ferocious, that the whole country was in dread of them, and it seemed impossible to disarm or overcome them. These men were sent by Maurice to the Bulgarian frontier, and being there left unsupported they were made prisoners. The ransom required for them was refused, and they were all massacred. Whether Maurice had actually intended thus to rid himself of these unhappy men is uncertain, but from that time he was given up to the most acute grief, regarding their death as a murder for which he must give an account. He scarcely slept, never had a moment's peace, performed constant penances, and wrote to all the bishops, abbots, and hermits, entreating that prayers might be offered, that his punishment might be in this world, and not in the next.

The prayer was granted. A wicked centurion, named Phocas, took advantage of some discontent of the soldiers respecting their pay, to excite them to revenge the death of their comrades. They named him emperor, and marched upon Constantinople, where the people daily deserted to him. The broken-hearted Maurice tried to escape by sea into Asia, but he was driven back by a tempest, and made prisoner at Chalcedon, with his six sons. Soon, orders came from the usurper that all should be put to death; Maurice saw in this the answer to his prayer, and gave thanks that his sin was visited upon his children while they were yet innocent. The nurse of the youngest devoted her own child to save the little prince, by placing it in his cradle; but Maurice, who discovered the expedient, informed the executioners, saying, "I should be guilty of murder did I suffer another person's infant to perish, in order to save my own from the decree of Providence against my family." The children were all beheaded before his eyes, and as each fell he repeated, "Righteous art Thou, O God, and just is Thy judgment," and then calmly himself recieved the stroke.

This was in the year 603. Phocas reigned for seven years of bloodshed, intemperance, and disgrace, and at last, in 610, was deposed and put to death by Heraclius.

The Persian kings had taken advantage of the late misfortunes of the empire to overrun Syria, and this time with more success. In 614 Khoosroo III. took Jerusalem, pillaged the churches, carried away the true Cross, which had been inclosed in a golden case and buried under ground, massacred 90,000 Christians, and obliged a multitude of others, among whom was the patriarch, to follow him back as prisoners to Persia. He likewise conquered Egypt, invaded Asia Minor, and even advanced as far as the Thracian Bosphorus, in sight of Constantinople.

All this time Heraclius had been lost in luxury and indolence; and on this near approach of the enemy he would have fled, had not the patriarch of Constantinople upbraided him with his cowardice, and at last forced him to swear on the altar to defend his religion and his country.

He took the command of the army, and to the surprise of all, showed that when once roused he possessed vigour, activity, and talent, such as had long been wanting on the imperial throne. Instead of attacking the Persian army on the Bosphorus, he sailed to Cilicia, burst into Syria, recovered the lost towns, and advancing into Persia burnt all the chief cities there, and after penetrating further than any European since the time of Alexander, he came back in triumph, bringing with him the Cross.

A treaty was at length concluded with the Persians in the year 628, by which the empire was restored to its former extent, and the Euphrates was once more its boundary. But at this very time the enemy was arising whose power was destined to be in the end the overthrow of both these mighty empires.

CHAPTER XVII.

THE MAHOMETAN CONQUESTS. A.D. 609-732.

PART I. MAHOMET. A.D. 569-632.

During the first four thousand and a half years of the world, the great Asiatic peninsular of Arabia was scarcely mentioned in history. The sons of Ishmael "wandered with their flocks and herds, from one spring of water to another," and were better protected from invasion by their desert sands than by the strongest fortifications. Their most peaceful occupation was the carrying the merchandise of India to the borders of Syria, or escorting such travellers as desired to traverse their wastes; their dwellings were tents, and only two towns in the whole country, Mecca and Medina, had attained any size or importance.

The consideration which Mecca enjoyed was derived from a black stone named the Kaaba, to which the Arabs paid great reverence, and came in great numbers to offer some sort of adoration. How it was connected with their religion is not known, nor have we much idea of their religion itself. It certainly condemned idolatry, and had perhaps retained some glimmerings of the truth handed down from Abraham, more especially as the rite of circumcision was still observed. They had no regular government, but were divided into tribes, each conducted by the Sheik, that is, the elder, or head of the family, who managed the affairs of his kindred, directed their wanderings, and made peace or war with the other tribes.

Mohammed, or as he is universally called in Europe, Mahomet, was born at Mecca about the year 569, of the tribe to which the guardianship of the Kaaba was committed. He became the servant of a rich widow named Kadijeh, conducted her caravans, and served her so well that she married him, and raised him to much wealth. He became possessed with ideas of rendering himself for ever famous as the founder of a new religion, and began to weave a tissue of blasphemy, which he spread abroad as a new revelation. He was subject to epileptic fits, and in these he pretended the angel Gabriel spoke to him, and informed him that he was a greater prophet than had ever yet appeared. To the Arabs, Mahomet announced himself as come to restore the faith of Abraham to its purity; to the Jews he called himself the Prophet like unto Moses; to the Christians, the Comforter promised by our Lord; and in confirmation of his pretensions he produced at different times a number of writings, partly taken from the Scriptures, partly from wild Jewish legends and spurious Gospels, and partly the work of his own imagination. These were called in the Arabic tongue Al Koran, the book, and the first sentence was the whole Mahometan Creed, the watchword repeated by his followers on every occasion—"There is no God but one God, and Mahomet is his prophet."

This confession was intended as a contradiction of the Christian doctrine of the Holy Trinity, and of the Divine nature of our Lord. Mahomet gave himself out as superior to Him in the same degree as He was greater than Moses. All adoration, and even the making of any sort of image, was forbidden by the Koran; no wine was to be touched, and regular times for prayer, fasting, and ablutions, were enjoined, almsgiving was also made a duty, and every Mahometan was bound, if required, to spread his religion by the sword. All this faithfully observed, the Mahometan was secure, the prophet's hand would aid him to cross the bridge, consisting of a single hair, which led to eternal life, and such happiness as the coarse-minded Arab thought most alluring, where a host of beautiful maidens would wait upon him, and supply him with the most delicious fruits.

These houris of Paradise were not to be the women of earth. What was to be their fate Mahomet never declared, for he thought them beneath his attention. A Mahometan might have as many as four wives, and their faces were never to be seen by any man but their husbands—this indeed having been for a long time past customary in the east.

Such is the outline of the hard, cold system, spread by this impostor over the greater part of Asia, where it prevailed by flattering the worst passions of the eastern nations, and promising them salvation to be bought by fixed outward observances, instead of any inward love or devotion. It was the judgment long before denounced by St. John on the Churches whose candlestick was to be removed.

Mahomet began his preaching in 609. His wife Kadijeh, and Abubeker, a citizen of Mecca, were his first followers; and he then proceeded to unfold his new teaching to the pilgrims of the Kaaba. After he had converted a number of Arabs to what he called Islam, the faith, the other tribes grew indignant at his alteration of their old religion, and resolved to put him to death. In 622 he was obliged to escape to Medina, and this flight, called in Arabic, Hejira, is the era from which the Mahometans reckon their dates.

His disciples followed him, and Mahomet, whose anger was excited by the persecution, produced a chapter of the Koran, declaring that the mission of the true believer was to spread his religion by the sword, and pursue the infidel to the ends of the earth. "A drop of blood shed in the cause of Allah," said he, "is reckoned as worth two months of fasting and prayer—all the sins of him who falls in battle are forgiven." He then began attacking and pillaging the caravans as they crossed the desert, and thus rendered his cause attractive to all the robber tribes, who, joining him, soon rendered his army strong enough to take Mecca, and four years after to subdue the whole of Arabia.

He called himself Kalif, or Vicegerent of Allah upon earth, and ruled as a king and conqueror for ten years, at the end of which time he died, in the year 632, keeping up to the last his imposture, which, perhaps, he believed himself, since we know that the punishment often sent upon such men is, that "God sendeth upon them a strong delusion that they should believe a lie."

PART II.   CONQUESTS OF THE ARABS.   A. D. 632–732.

ABUBEKER, whose daughter Ayesha was the favourite among Mahomet's fifteen wives, became Kalif in his place, and as the prophet had made conquest a part of his religion, the Arabs, or Saracens, as they began to be called, from the name of one of their chief tribes, fast extended their dominions.

Their victories were rapid; the Greek army was defeated near Damascus, and that city was taken;

Jerusalem itself was obliged to yield in the year 636 to the Mahometan power, from which it has never since been free, except for one short interval. The Saracens spared the lives of the Christians, and left them in possession of their churches; but Omar, who was at that time Kalif, erected a magnificent mosque on the site of the Jewish Temple, which has ever since been an object of great veneration to the Mahometans.

All Syria soon after fell into their hands, and the year 637 beheld the overthrow of the ancient line of Sassanid kings of Persia. Yezdigird, the last king of that country, was defeated near Bagdad, and fled into the mountains, where he was murdered, and the whole monarchy became part of the new empire. The capital of the Mahometan dominions was established at Damascus, and the Arabs began to live in cities, and to cultivate peaceful arts. As yet their ignorance was so great, that after pillaging the Persian camp, one of them was heard seeking for someone "to change all this yellow, for a little white metal."

In 641 Egypt was betrayed by the heretics to Amrou, an officer of Omar, and Alexandria fell into his hands. Amrou sent word to the Kalif that the city contained four thousand palaces, four thousand baths, four hundred theatres, twelve thousand shops for the sale of vegetables, and forty thousand tributary Jews; and it is said, desired to know what he was to do with the great library which had first been commenced by Ptolemy Philadelphus. The answer of Omar was, "If these books contain the same doctrine as the Koran they are useless; if they are contrary to it, they are mischievous." The Arabs accordingly devoted them all to destruction, and for six months the public baths of Alexandria were heated with these choicest works of the learning of ancient Greece.

After Omar's death the Kalifate was disputed between Ali, the son-in-law of Mahomet, and Moavieh, who had been a favourite of Omar. There was a civil war, and at last, after much bloodshed, the Mahometans were split into two sects—that of Ali, called the Fatimites, from Fatima, the daughter of Mahomet, being acknowledged in Persia : while another line of Kalifs continued to reign in Damascus, and afterwards removed thier seat of government to Bagdad, which thus became the centre of an immense empire, where science and art were cultivated to a high degree.

Nearly half Asia Minor was conquered by Moavieh, and Constantinople became the bulwark of Christendom on that side. Akbar, an officer of the Kalifs, in the year 689, subdued the north of Africa, as far as Morocco, and galloping into the sea on the western coast, cried out, " Why do these waves stop my course? I would announce to unknown realms in the west that there is but one Allah, and Mahomet is his prophet."

The Gothic kingdom of Spain was the next object of the desires of the Saracens, but without the crimes and treacheries of its Christian inhabitants they could never have obtained a footing there. The Goths of Spain had early laid aside their barbarous habits, and adopted the language and customs of their Roman subjects, but in so doing they had learnt to give themselves up to indolence and luxury, to which, indeed, they were invited by the delicious climate of southern Spain. They were self-indulgent, unwarlike, and yet of violent passions, and these faults led to their ruin.

Don Rodrigo, King of Spain, carried off the beautiful

Florinda, daughter of Count Julian, a powerful noble, who was governor of Ceuta, and her father, in his desire of vengeance, sent to Musa, the Arab governor of Africa, to invite him to Spain. The Arabs and Moors (who had become Mahometans) came in great multitudes, under the command of a brave chieftain named Tarik; a number of traitorous Spaniards joined them, and they proceeded to overrun the country.

On the 26th of July, 710, Rodrigo met them at the head of his army at Xeres, on the Guadalete. The battle lasted eight days, the Goths fighting gallantly; but on the evening of the last day they found their ranks cruelly thined, and their king was lost. His horse Orelia, his bow, and his helmet with long golden horns, were found, but he was never seen again. Some believed he was drowned in trying to cross the river, but in after times a belief arose that Rodrigo, the last of the Goths, had escaped the carnage, retired to the mountains, and there lived a hermit's life, in deep repentance for the crime which had brought desolation on his Church and country.

Before the end of 713 Spain was entirely in the possession of the Saracens, excepting the small mountainous district of the Asturias. There all who had higher and more warlike spirits, or any desire to prove themselves constant to the true cause, drew together, careless of the privations they endured among those rugged hills, sloping northwards to the stormy Bay of Biscay; they raised on their bucklers and proclaimed as king, the noble Count Pelayo, and defended themselves so bravely that the Mahometans were never able to overcome their resistance.

Constantinople and the Asturias were thus the barriers of the Christians of Europe against victorious

Islamism, and it soon proved that Catholic France was likewise enabled to check the tide of conquest. Abderrahman, an Arab chief, crossed the Pyrennees in 732, and overran the south of Gaul, where several nobles willingly submitted to him; but at Tours the Franks met him under the command of Charles Martel, and a battle was fought, in which Abderrahman was killed, his men dispersed, and the Churches of Europe saved from the subjugation of the Mahometan.

THE END.

CHRONOLOGICAL

Egyptians.	Hebrews.		2247 Dispersion at Babel. Assyrians.	
			2234 Nimrod.	
			Nineveh.	Babylon
	1996 Abraham			
1899 Dynasty of the Pharaohs	1896 Isaac			
	1836 Jacob			
1706 Joseph governor of Egypt				
1491 Moses leads out the Israelites				
	1451 Joshua wins the land			
1327 Mœris	Deborah			
	Gideon			
1308 Sesostris	Jephtha			
	Samson—Eli			1300 Semira
	Samuel			
1082 Cheops	1096 Saul chosen king			
	1056 K David			
	1016 K Solomon			
	976 K Rehoboam			
		Israel.		
	Kingdom of Judah.	976 K Jeroboam		
		955 K Nadab		
		953 Baasha		
972 Shishak	959 K Abijah	931 K Elah		
	956 K Asa	930 K Zimri		
		930 K Omri		
	915 K Jehoshaphat	919 K Ahab		
	891 K Joram	896 K Ahaziah		
	885 K Ahaziah	895 K Joram		
	883 K Athaliah	883 K Jehu		
	877 K Joash	855 K Jehoahaz		
	837 K Amaziah	839 K Jehoash	821 K Pul	K Nabon
		823 K Jeroboam II		
	808 K Uzziah	770 K Zachariah		
		K Manahem		
	756 K Jotham	759 K Pekaiah	747 K Tiglath Pilesar	
	741 K Ahaz	738 K Pekah		
		730 K Hoshea	729 K Shalmanesar	
	726 K Hezekiah			721 K Mero
	697 K Manasseh	721 Israel carried away captive		Bal
	642 K Amon	714 K Sennacherib		
616 Pharaoh Necho	640 K Josiah	711 K Esarhaddon		
	609 K Jehoahaz	650 K Sardanapalus		
	609 K Jehoiakim	606 Nineveh destroyed.		
	598 K Zedekiah			604 Nebuchadnezzar
595 Pharaoh Hophra				
	587 Jerusalem destroyed			
570 Egypt overrun by the Assyrians				
		Period of Assyrian Empire.		
		561 Belshazzar		
		538 Babylon taken by the Persians		

Persian Empire.

529 K Cambyses

529 Overruns Egypt

521 K Darius Hystaspes

                                                                         Marathon

485 K Xerxes

                                                                     480 Thermopylæ

465 K Artaxerxes I

425 K Xerxes II

405 K Artaxerxes II

                                      401 Battle of Cunaxa, and retreat of 10,000 Greek

349 K Artaxerxes III Ochus

336 K Darius Codomanus

TABLES.

Persians and Medes.	Greeks.			Romans.
	Athens.	*Sparta.*	*Other States.*	
	1313 Cadmus			
	1183 Siege of Troy			1170 Ascanius founds Alba Longa
	1045 Codrus			
		817 Lycurgus		
	776 Olympiads			
				753 K Romulus founds Rome
				716 K Numa Pompilius
Deioces, 1st King of Medes				679 K Tullus Hostilius
				640 K Ancus Martius
K Phraortes				618 K Tarquinius Priscus
	621 Draco			
K Cyaxares				578 K Servius Tullius
K Astyages	594 Solon			534 K Tarquinius Superbus
				509 Expulsion of Tarquinius
	560 Pisistratus			509 Brutus and Collatinus Consuls
Cyrus the Persian	527 Hippias and Hipparchus			491 Coriolanus
	510 Expulsion of Pisistratides			
	Miltiades			479 Slaughter of the Fabii
	Aristides			451 Cincinnatus
	Themistocles	Leonidas		
		Pausanias		447 End of Decemvirate
	Pericles			
	Socrates			
	Alcibiades	Lysander		445 Camillus
	Xenophon		Pelopidas	
		Agesilaus	Epaminondas	390 Rome sacked by Brennus
		359 K Philip of Macedon		
	Demosthenes	334 Alexander		

CHRONOLOGICAL

323 Alexander's death at Babylon

Egypt.

323	Ptolemy Lagus
283	Ptolemy Philadelphus
247	Ptolemy Euergetes
221	Ptolemy Philopater
205	Ptolemy Epiphanes
181	Ptolemy Philometer
146	Ptolemy Euergetes II
117	Ptolemy Soter
81	Cleopatra

Syria.

321	Seleucus I. Nicator
280	Antiochus I. Soter
260	Antiochus II. Theos
246	Seleucus II
226	Seleucus III
223	Antiochus III. Great
187	Seleucus IV
175	Antiochus Epiphanes
153	Alexander Bala
111	Syria subdued by the Romans

Jews.

167	Maccabeus Mattathias
166	Judas Maccabeus
161	Jonathan
135	Simon
130	John Hyrcanus
107	K Aristobulus
106	K Alexander Jannæus
98	K Jannæus
70	K Aristobulus
48	K Antipater
38	K Herod the Great reigns subject to the Romans

B. C. 30 Battle of Actium, death of Cleopatra

A. D. 4 Herod Antipas

37 Herod Agrippa

49 Agrippa

70 Jerusalem destroyed

TABLES.

:edonian Empire.			Samnite Wars.
Thrace.	*Macedon.*		
323 Lysimachus killed 280	302 Cassander		321 Caudine Forks
		275 Pyrrhus invades Italy	272 Tarentum taken
239 Demetrius K of Macedon 229 Antigonus Doson 222 Philip			264 1st Punic war
	Sparta Agis Cleomenes	*Achæan League* Aratus Philopæmon	218 2nd Punic war
			Hannibal invades Italy 210 Scipio
			212 Syracuse taken
179 Perseus			
			146 Carthage taken
	145 Macedon subdued by Rome		
			133 Gracchi
			100 Marius
			82 Sylla
	63 Death of Mithridates		
			60 Triumvirate
	Pompey—Julius Cæsar		
			54 Gaul subdued
	B. C. 30 Augustus Cæsar Emperor		
	A. D. 14 Tiberius		
	37 Caligula		
	41 Claudius		
			Britain subdued
	54 Nero		
	69 Galba		
	67 Otho	Vespasian	
	79 Titus		
	81 Domitian		

INDEX.

INTRODUCTION.

		Page
PART I.	The Antediluvians	i
II.	The Dispersion of the Nations	v
III.	Sources of History	xvi

CHAPTER I.

PART I.	The Patriarchs	1
II.	Egypt	3
III.	The Phœnicians	5
IV.	The Kingdom of Israel	7

CHAPTER II.
THE ASSYRIAN EMPIRE.

PART I.	Nineveh	9
II.	Babylon	12

CHAPTER III.
THE PERSIAN EMPIRE.

PART I.	The Fall of Crœsus	15
II.	The Fall of Babylon	18
III.	Successors of Cyrus	20

CHAPTER IV.
GREECE.

PART I.	Greek Mythology	23
II.	Siege of Troy	26
III.	Greek Manners	28
IV.	Sparta	31
V.	Athens	34
VI.	Other Greek States and Colonies	37

CHAPTER V.

PERSIAN INVASION OF GREECE

		Page
PART I.	Marathon	39
II.	Thermopylæ	42
III.	Defeat of Xerxes	45

CHAPTER VI.

THE GREEK STATES.

PART I.	The Peloponnesian War	48
II.	Socrates and Greek Philosophy	53
III.	Retreat of the Ten Thousand	55
IV.	Theban Supremacy	58

CHAPTER VII.

THE MACEDONIAN EMPIRE.

PART I.	Philip of Macedon	61
II.	Alexander in Asia Minor	63
III.	Conquest of Palestine and Egypt	67
IV.	Conquest of Persia	69
V.	Indian Expedition and Death of Alexander	71

CHAPTER VIII.

THE FOUR HORNS.

PART I.	Partition of the Empire	75
II.	The Kingdom of Egypt	79
III.	The Kingdom of Syria	80
IV.	The Achæan League	82

CHAPTER IX.
ROMAN CONQUEST OF ITALY.

		Page
Part i.	Roman Mythology	85
ii.	Founding of Rome	88
iii.	The Tarquins	91
iv.	The Republic	94
v.	Early Wars of Rome	98
vi.	The Gauls in Italy	101
vii.	Invasion of Pyrrhus	105

CHAPTER X.
PERIOD OF THE PUNIC WARS.

Part i.	Carthage and Syracuse	110
ii.	First Punic War	112
iii.	Hannibal in Italy	115
iv.	Conclusion of the Second Punic War	118

CHAPTER XI.
GROWTH OF THE ROMAN POWER.

Part i.	Manners of the later Commonwealth	121
ii.	War with Macedon	126
iii.	Persecution of the Jews	129
iv.	Final Conquest of Greece	133
v.	Third Punic War	135

CHAPTER XII.
FACTIONS OF ROME.

Part i.	The Gracchi	138
ii.	Marius	140
iii.	Sylla	144
iv.	Pompey	146
v.	The First Triumvirate	149
vi.	Julius Cæsar	153
vii.	The Second Triumvirate	156
viii.	Antony and Cleopatra	158

CHAPTER XIII.
THE TWELVE CÆSARS.

		Page
PART I.	Augustus	163
II.	The Teutones	166
III.	Tiberius	168
IV.	Caligula, Claudius, and Nero	170
V.	Destruction of Jerusalem	174

CHAPTER XIV.
THE GREAT PERSECUTIONS.

PART I.	The Primitive Church	178
II.	Power of the Prætorian Guard	182
III.	The Last Persecution	185
IV.	Conversion of Constantine	188

CHAPTER XV.
FALL OF THE WESTERN EMPIRE.

PART I.	Constantine the Great	190
II.	Julian the Apostate	195
III.	Valentinian	200
IV.	Theodosius the Great	203
V.	Alaric the Goth	207
VI.	Attila the Hun	209

CHAPTER XVI.
THE PARTITION OF THE EMPIRE.

PART I.	The Teutonic Nations	213
II.	The Franks	215
III.	Justinian	218
IV.	Fredegonda	222
V.	The Greek Empire	225

CHAPTER XVII.
THE MAHOMETAN CONQUESTS.

PART I.	Mahomet	228
II.	Conquests of the Arabs	231

www.ingramcontent.com/pod-product-compliance
Lightning Source LLC
Chambersburg PA
CBHW032007230426
43672CB00010B/2283